Caves, Huts, and Monasteries

Caves, Huts, and Monasteries

Finding the deeper self along the footpaths of Asia

Mark S. Kacik

TURNING
STONE
PRESS

Copyright © 2015
by Mark S. Kacik
All rights reserved, including the right to reproduce this
work in any form whatsoever, without permission
in writing from the publisher, except for brief passages
in connection with a review.

Cover design by Paul Tamulewicz
Cover art by Jyoti Prakash Tsapa
Interior design by Jane Hagaman
Map of Asia courtesy of the Central Intelligence Agency
All photos (except where noted) by Mark S. Kacik
Photos of Kopan Monastery (pages 50, 53, and 56) by Artis Rams

Turning Stone Press
8301 Broadway St. Ste. 422
San Antonio TX, 78209
www.turningstonepress.com

Library of Congress Cataloging-in-Publication Data available upon request.

ISBN 978-1-61852-100-2

10 9 8 7 6 5 4 3 2 1

Printed in the United States of America

To all seekers

May the whispered teachings of the sages
lead you to a clear comprehension of truth.

Contents

Foreword ix
Preface xi
Map xiv

Part One—India

Chapter 1 3
    Compelled to Seek—Delhi, India

Chapter 2 7
    Desert Distress—Jodhpur, India

Chapter 3 17
    A Bad Break—Jodhpur, India

Chapter 4 25
    Serendipity Starts—Jodhpur, India

Part Two—Nepal

Chapter 5 43
    Building a Foundation—Boudhnath, Kathmandu, Nepal

Chapter 6 61
    A Date with Death—Pashupatinath, Kathmandu, Nepal

Chapter 7 71
    Climbing High and Away—Nepal, Himalaya near Mt. Everest

Chapter 8 89
    A Cave in the Clouds—Nepal, Himalaya near Mt. Everest

Chapter 9 111
    Diving Deep—Lumbini, Nepal

Chapter 10 125
   Inner Explorer—Lumbini, Nepal

Chapter 11 137
   A Humble Monk—Lumbini, Nepal

Chapter 12 153
   A Back Door Exit—Lumbini, Nepal

Part Three- Vietnam

Chapter 13 171
   The Gift—Ho Chi Minh City, Vietnam

Chapter 14 187
   A Hidden Hut—Vietnam

Chapter 15 195
   Communist Entanglement—Vietnam

Chapter 16 205
   No Pain, No Gain—Vietnam

Chapter 17 219
   Cool Zen—Dalat, Vietnam

Part Four—Korea

Chapter 18 241
   West in the East—Daejeon, South Korea

Chapter 19 257
   A Fitting Finale—Seoul, South Korea

Part Five—Home

Epilogue—Cleveland, Ohio 277
Acknowledgments 281

Foreword

Nowadays there are many sincere seekers on the spiritual path both in the East and the West. Living as I do in India, I am constantly approached by sincere aspirants for guidance in finding a teacher. So many potential practitioners, although willing to dedicate themselves wholeheartedly to practice, still have a problem in finding anyone willing to guide and counsel them. One cannot walk the path of inner cultivation through books and internet downloads alone. Even after having renounced their professions and often their relationships, still, many westerners experience great difficulty in being taken seriously in their spiritual aspirations.

Therefore when **Mark Kacik** headed off to find authentic meditation instruction in Asia he was following a well-beaten trail that has often ended in disillusionment for so many. In his favour were past practice in Zen meditation for many years and a genuine willingness to put whatever teachings he received into immediate effect along with a spirit of courageous determination.

Therefore it seems the gods (and good karma) smiled kindly on his efforts. His book ***Caves, Huts, and Monasteries*** combines the best of travelogue with a spiritual odyssey. Mark Kacik set out on his Asian pilgrimage with the intention of finding qualified masters and an ideal environment for practice. His journey takes him to India, Nepal, Vietnam, and Korea where he serendipitously meets with meditation masters willing (often eager) to teach and guide him. As a result throughout this fascinating book are sprinkled jewels of helpful advice on practice, together with Mark's candid account of both his struggles and triumphs.

This is both an interesting and inspiring account of a spiritual journey together with the honest dilemma of how to integrate the realisations and inner changes brought about by his experiences with the kind of lifestyle required in the West. Clearly this requires a blending of kindness and mindful clarity: an opening of the heart towards compassionate awareness under all circumstances. This is no easy task and the inner journey continues.

—Jetsunma Tenzin Palmo
Dongyu Gatsal Ling Nunnery
Himichal Pradesh, India

Preface

Within each of us, at times, arises an inexplicable message or calling that we simply cannot ignore. If we follow it, we'll be lead somewhere important. We just don't know the path or destination.

Such a calling led me to a journey that changed my life. It was an outward journey away from my hectic and complex, but comfortable American lifestyle into simple, even primitive, caves, huts, and monasteries in remote Asian territories. Some were excruciatingly cold, others blistering hot.

I was propelled on this journey by an inner wailing to break the shackles of my achievement-driven lifestyle which often left me mentally dizzy and physically exhausted. I wanted to pull myself away from the tug of materialistic success and instead move toward a deepened consciousness. Within me was a deep yearning to explore my soul and my mind, to know myself. I aspired to face myself squarely and directly through intensive meditation practice. Blessed with the support of my wife and family, I resolved not to return from Asia until my heart told me so.

Through this journey I realized an essence of *self* that I'd never known and I came away with a diminished interest in materialism.

For much of my life, I've searched the depths of religions for answers to my questions about life. I've studied world religions, explored numerous churches, and belonged to various congregations. I've joined lay religious communities and been close to people whose spirituality is practiced through touch, nature, and healing.

Eastern spirituality grabbed a firm hold of me and wouldn't let go. Caught, I dove deeply into Hinduism, Taoism, and finally, Buddhism. Ultimately, I was attracted to Buddhism because it's a logical, scientific, and experience-based means to develop my mind with payoffs in this very lifetime. Its open-minded approach to seeking truth is something I can trust and believe in.

I traversed the Asian continent to investigate alternative approaches to Japanese Zen, the form of Buddhism I had practiced for years. I encountered monks, nuns, lay practitioners, and highly accomplished teachers, some in quite removed and hidden places, from whom I learned a great deal. I observed and participated in religious aspects of Buddhism with its richly symbolic rituals, traditions, and deities. I also practiced philosophical-based Buddhism that focused on deep exploration of the mind—both simple and complex; it's this latter aspect of Buddhism that most appealed to me.

I experienced a diverse array of sects within the Buddhist tradition, and I want to share a sampling of that panorama. One of my core goals was to better understand and comprehend Buddhism. Even after this journey, I remain humbly aware that there is so much more to Buddhism that I have not yet experienced. Yet, the common message of each tradition speaks to me: "True peace can only be realized through intimate contact with our minds obscure inner purity present in each of us."

There's a marvelous beauty in the Asian people and in their culture that I wish to share. In the West, we often claim to have the "highest standard of living" in the world, but after spending many months in Asia, I suggest a rephrasing to the "highest standard of comfort." Amidst the poorest of the poor with whom I lived, I observed a spiritual devotion and happiness that I can only hope for—the kind of "high standard of living" I want. To be sure, there are tradeoffs between the comfortable, complex western lifestyle and that of a simple, uncluttered, less comfortable way. But those tradeoffs seem a bargain weighed against the deeper gains of self-discovery. I chose Asia because the study of the mind has been practiced and perfected there for more than twenty-five hundred years.

One expects traveling and living in such dramatically different cultures to be challenging. I encountered a number of adventurous—sometimes precarious and frightening—situations. Through the arid deserts of India, the snow-painted peaks of the Himalayas, the sweltering jungles of Vietnam, and the culturally rich Korean mountains, the struggles of traveling, communicating, and negotiating cultures proved significant learning experiences.

I don't intend this book to be read as a "how to" guide for the aspirant; a wealth of resources from the great Masters over more than twenty-five hundred years of Buddhism are readily available. Perhaps, though, I can whet someone's appetite to know himself or herself in a deeper way by weaving precious Buddhist teachings into enchanting travel experiences along the back roads of Asia.

Although this journey and its story are true, I've taken some liberties in expressing my experiences. I've changed the names of some people, places, and even things to protect the privacy of friendships I've made. Conversations are sometimes condensed and what was said in multiple encounters is sometimes combined into one. I intend only unembellished accuracy.

I learned much from this journey. May others benefit.

With deepest respect,
Mark S. Kacik

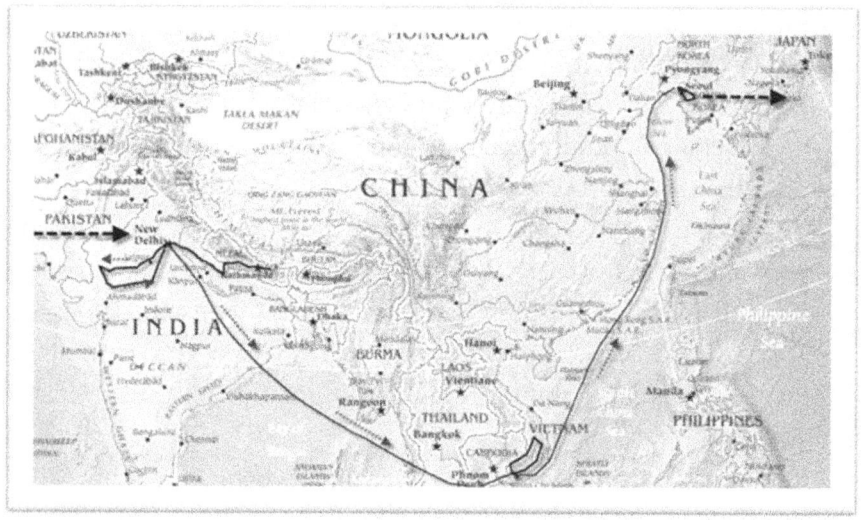

Author's Route Across Asia

— PART ONE —

India

Chapter 1

Compelled to Seek
Delhi, India

> **All journeys have secret destinations of which the traveler is unaware.**
> —Martin Buber

The undersized minivan in which I'm a passenger screeches to a stop when a motorcycle jumps through a narrow opening directly into our path. I glance at my thirty-something male Indian driver, expecting him to spit out a vulgar word or yell. Instead, he simply stares into the traffic as if nothing happened.

I'm in Delhi, India, one of the most densely populated cities in the world. My plane landed an hour ago, and I prearranged with the guesthouse for its minivan to pick me up.

I chose Delhi as the starting point of a long journey because of its proximity to Nepal—one of my destinations—and because I want to immerse myself in the highly devotional Indian culture as I acclimate to the weather, food, and lifestyle changes. I carry only a backpack stuffed with basic needs for up to a year of travel. It's 11:00 PM here but morning at my Ohio home. I've been traveling for more than twenty hours.

In two days my twenty-four-year old daughter, Maria, will arrive and we'll tour the culturally rich desert region of Rajasthan in northwest

India. Our aim is to taste the culture, meet the people, experience a different lifestyle, see an exotic land, and spend some time together.

For me, this will be a time to let the 'feel' of this ancient holy land sink in. I hope my mind will settle into a calmer state so that I can more easily peer inward when my time of retreat and isolation comes. That's in three weeks when Maria returns home and I move to Nepal to start my core journey, which is more an inward one than outward.

This is much more than a vacation. And despite what some of my friends think, it's much deeper than a midlife crisis. You see, I've hit the spiritual reset button, and done so in no subtle manner. After spending a lifetime holding a traditional Western materialistic value system while pursuing spiritual development in the background, the latter has finally overridden the former. I can no longer continue a materialistic lifestyle and need an extended separation from a culture that drives me to always pursue 'more' and incessantly engage my mind in 'striving'.

To enable travel, I've resigned my lucrative corporate engineering job. Committed to a simpler lifestyle, I sold most of my belongings including my car, moved out of my house, and rented it. I bid family and friends a temporary farewell but promised I'd return . . . someday.

My itinerary is sketchy, but my aim is to visit Buddhist monasteries, meet teachers of differing Buddhist traditions, and seize every opportunity to meditate and explore the inner workings of my mind. So I think of this time with Maria as an important preparatory segment of my journey

Large and colorfully ornate trucks, their beds overflowing with produce, mingle on the narrow congested road with subcompact cars, motorcycles, bicycles, and a wood-framed cart pulled by a tired looking ox. A noisy, motorized rickshaw squeezes just inches from my elbow, which rests across my open window. Several wandering cows blend with the mass of vehicles and four men cling to a ladder backside the bus in front of us, swaying sideways with each turn. The whole scene feels chaotic and surreal.

As we sit in traffic, my mind wanders to my Japanese Zen practice back home. Zen has helped me immensely. My weekly meditation practice leaves my mind refreshed and calm. But it's easy to get caught up in the hustle and bustle of life in the West and anxiety can quickly move back in. My casual Zen practice hasn't undone my addiction to materialism either, to accumulating possessions.

As a mechanical engineer, I've worked for many years in the corporate world amidst an endless list of tasks and deadlines. My schedule was crammed with plans, commitments, and unfinished projects—which, although fun and challenging, were also dizzying and straining. I've been running for years at a sprinter's pace to keep up, and the ongoing marathon has brought on bouts of mental and physical exhaustion.

Although relatively successful as a design engineer, I sometimes struggle to find meaning in creating products that often seem extravagant. Yet it was difficult to say goodbye to the brilliant people I worked with and to the intellectual challenge of being an engineer. Perhaps this time away will allow me to sort out a direction for my career as well.

The only way I could keep up with the long list of projects around the house was to work hard and use every moment efficiently. While I waited in the grocery line, I made a phone call. In the car, I planned a work project. While shaving, I solved a family problem. "Once I catch up," I've often told myself, "then I can relax." But I never caught up.

"Slow down," my wife, Jayne, has often said. "You drive yourself so hard, and then it catches up with you."

But who else is going to fix the broken window or repair the car's exhaust system? And will I finish those house projects before I leave town on a business trip? I admit I was driven.

I remarried several years ago, and Jayne and I have a stepfamily of four children. Our blended family struggled for years from internal drama and continual crises. Recently Jayne and I decided, as a last resort, to separate, and she moved out and bought a house. Remarkably though, as I prepared for this trip, we reconciled and rejoined. We found that by separating our finances and, more significantly, our stepfamilies, we solved many of the problems that had pulled us apart. We rediscovered our deep love for each other. This trip will give us valuable time apart to let the dust settle so we can start afresh.

Jayne has been fully supportive of my journey. She's not religious and she isn't a Buddhist. Yet she has a practical spirituality and she recognizes and understands how I aspire to quiet my mind.

"You must take this trip," she's told me more than once. "But I worry that you will find something greater and not return."

Her fears aren't unfounded. Given the life-changing nature of this journey, I too wonder what risk it places on our relationship. Jayne is a spirited life force, with a broad social network that stems from her stage acting at community theaters. She's often bluntly honest, a quality that has helped me confront my own ego. I wish not to lose this woman again.

So here I am in India, ready for inner discoveries. I'm fifty-three years old, unemployed but financially stable, with grown children who are self-sufficient. A window of time has been opened to me. I accept it as gift.

Chapter 2

Desert Distress
Jodhpur, India

> **Silence is a source of great strength.**
> —Lao Tzu

My daughter, Maria, and I have just arrived in Jodhpur, a quant village in the Rajasthan region of India, surrounded by desert. We've spent the last few days travelling here by train car, and finally rickshaw.

We've been touring over a week now, exploring back alleys, probing temples, mingling with the common folk, and tasting the Indian way of life. Everywhere we go Maria draws attention. She's a tall and slender woman with short blond hair, blazing green eyes, high energy, and, a spirited way about her that sets her apart in streets packed with shorter black-haired people.

This time with her is more important than she realizes. Before I left home, her boyfriend invited me to dinner and asked my permission to marry her. His respect for tradition was appreciated. I gave my blessing. Now I know—while Maria does not—that on her return home—he'll propose to her. I treasure this last trip with my daughter as a single person.

Seemingly barricaded from civilization by surrounding desert, Jodhpur is a collage of iconic Indian desert living. Its remote location has preserved ancient Indian culture. Six-story concrete structures, most painted powder blue, form an almost unnavigable maze. Children play in the streets, rolling old bicycle tires down the passages barely wide enough for a small car. Bike riders weave between women in colorful saris. Dogs and cows roam everywhere, blending with camels and their staff-wielding herders. An ancient fort and a temple grandly tower on the edge of cliffs over the hilly city. Absent is western restaurants and hotels; it's all family businesses here.

Yogi's Guesthouse is situated in the city center. Terracotta clay pots with fresh magenta flowers floating in water—a traditional symbol of welcome—rest either side of the entrance. In the lobby, a sign reads, "Come as friends—Leave as family." At this point, walking in, Maria and I could never have guessed how that sign would prove true for us. Vases with freshly picked flowers rest on every tabletop. Behind the counter is a tiny altar with a sculpture of Ganesh, a Hindu deity. Aside the statue is a silver chalice of fresh oranges and a small urn with unlit incense sticks.

As we register with Viki, the attendant, I watch his brother, Bundy, as he works at a nearby desk. Pausing from his bookkeeping, Bundy rises, approaches the altar, and faces it standing perfectly still for a full minute. Slowly and deliberately, he reaches out and lifts small handbells with his right hand and gently rings them for several minutes. He puts down the bells and lights an incense stick. Then he stands a short time in prayerful contemplation before returning to his desk to resume his work.

I feel privileged to witness his worship ritual and I admire his devotion. It's impressive how he incorporates ritual into his workday. How do I integrate mindfulness and devotion smack into the middle of my daily activities? I can't imagine myself bringing a cushion to work and taking pause to meditate during the day. Yet, Bundy's devotion moves—and challenges—me. This is one reason why I'm here: to learn how to integrate spirituality into my daily western life and make it less chaotic.

Viki, Bundy, and Raj, the hotel driver, are friendly to us and we extend our stay to spend a few days with a desert-dwelling family. Raj shuttles us several-hours to the desert's edge where our host, Danta Ram, waits at the side of a dusty road with two camels and a tethered cart.

"Danta Ram is good man," Raj says. "Very kind. Will take good care of you. Camels take you six miles in desert. Small hut for you. You live with desert family for three days. Then I meet you again."

"What about food and water, Raj?" Maria asks.

"You eat melons, beans, and berries from desert. Water come from well with bucket. You drink goat milk too. No problem."

"I wasn't expecting wells and goats in a desert," I say. "I was expecting sand dunes without vegetation."

"It's desert. You see," Raj says, smiling. How right he was.

As Danta Ram shows us his cart, Maria and I stroke the camel's neck. Two hand-carved wooden poles link the camel to the cart, which has a single axle and wide tires to roll atop sand. Sitting on the cart's crude wooden platform, our feet dangling over the edge, Danta Ram prods the camel with a stick and our cart lurches forward. Danta Ram turns around. "You okay?" he asks.

"Yes, I like," Maria says, grinning.

Rolling sand dunes are speckled with patches of dried grass, bushes and occasional small trees. After the first sand dune, the road ends and we're engulfed in pure silence—the unfamiliar sound of nothing. It's as if I stuffed cotton in my ears.

"Listen Maria, do you hear that?"

She pauses and listens.

"Hear what?"

"Exactly. When's the last time you heard that?"

"Cool." We both take in the silence.

For ninety minutes we crawl up and over dunes as the heat toasts us. Finally, we peak a crest that overlooks two huts down between dunes. "My family. My house," Danta Ram says with a broad smile. "Four children have. New baby. Soon see."

Danta Ram introduces us to Samu, his wife, who wears a full-length green and peach sari with a matching peach head veil that covers all but her eyes. His three children are ages three- to eight-years-old. Danta Ram shows us our hut.

The huts are only four-feet high with red baked-mud walls and straw

Maria and author in the desert
Rajasthan, India

roofs. They are linked by a small courtyard. The smooth floors are sun-baked from dirt, cow dung, and straw and are comfortable to walk on. Our hut is swept clean. Inside are two stick cots with blankets stacked on top.

A short distance from the hut is a dome-shaped pile of sticks, hollow on the inside. I find it is the toilet. It's only three-feet high—and completely see-through. Danta Ram removes a couple of sticks to open it for me. There's barely enough room to crouch in.

"You WC this side," he says. Then he points left. "Woman there. Use stick cover with sand. Okay?" He looks doubtful that I'll think this is okay.

"Okay!" I say. "No problem!"

I chuckle to myself. I've encountered many types of WCs in my travels but this is the first time I've used a see-through kitty litter box.

Samu fixes a spicy vegetarian meal: we're all famished.

"Now take you camel ride, "Danta Ram says afterward. "Long ride. Watch sun."

Three camels are tethered to a tree behind the hut; one is young, half the size of the other two.

"Baby camel," says Danta Ram, pointing to the young one. "Very difficult," he says shaking his head.

He gives the tallest camel a strange command that sounds like "Brahhhh," the camel folds its legs and rests its belly in the sand. He straps a woolen blanket on his back and motions me to sit between the humps. With the same command the camel stands. Feeling unsteady I struggle to stabilize myself atop the blanket that seems loosely secured. Maria chuckles at my clumsiness.

Both saddled, Danta Ram guides our camels while his son struggles to ride baby camel. Baby camel blurts bugling sounds and swings its neck wildly from side to side looking oddly similar to an ostrich.

Danta Ram points to a distant sand dune that rises elegantly above the rest. "We climb. Go top. Very beautiful."

We reach the top just in time watch the magenta ball of flame settle behind a sand dune. Maria has fallen in love with her camel and lies next to it, her head cuddled on the animal's neck as if it were her pet dog. Her face is full of delight; it makes me happy to see her happy.

We lie in the warm sand for fifteen minutes letting the tranquil scene penetrate our souls. Our moods transform with the setting—from the energy and excitement of the day to a serene, introspective calm. The air starts to cool.

Danta Ram breaks the silence. "Must go now. Dark fast. Find way back," he says.

I realize Danta Ram has no flashlight, nor do I. *This should be interesting.*

At first, we walk next to our camels, giving the beasts a break, but eventually Danta Ram tells us to mount them. "No step on bush," he explains. "No trip."

Darkness is upon us and each sand dune looks like any other. Without the sun to orient me, I'm hopelessly lost. But Danta Ram seems confident, so I relax.

As the last trickle of sunlight disappears, a brilliant array of stars emerges like salt speckled across a black table cloth. The dense frosted streak of the Milky Way galaxy shows its beauty. There is only silence,

Author's daughter Maria, Danta Ram and his son during an evening camel trek
—Rajasthan, India

except for the whoosh of camel breath and the occasional crunch when it steps on a small bush. Danta Ram is in the lead; his son still lags behind on baby camel.

Then I hear voices, not far away. I can barely see Danta Ram just in front of me through the blackness. He stops dead in his tracks and holds up his hand to signal a stop.

"Shhhhhh," he whispers, staring intently ahead.

He seems concerned, but I don't know why. My fatherly instincts kick in and I become keenly aware. Our camels stand perfectly still while we wait. The voices stop. I hear nothing more and Danta Ram cautiously resumes. He's keenly alert though, like a bow hunter tracking a bear. We drop into a valley between dunes where the air is quite chilly. I wonder how he's navigating. A rustling noise comes from some bushes out of sight. Again Danta Ram freezes and the camels stop at his hand gesture. He looks concerned and again we freeze in silence.

What's the threat? I wonder. Does he perceive a wildlife or human threat? Now's not the time to question. Danta Ram begins again. During the next half hour, we are quiet and watchful. Danta Ram seems more relaxed, but my imagination is at a heightened pitch and my fearful thoughts won't quit; the snap of a twig jumps out of the silence. What or who is there? Do I hear a voice?

Safely back at Danta Ram's home we find his family asleep. I breathe a sigh of relief. I ask him about his concerns in the desert, but communication falls short. "Night is problem," is the best explanation I can get.

Maria and I grab our cots and drag them under the starlit spectacle. The thick blankets are plenty warm but both the cot and blankets are Indian-sized and leave my feet overhanging the edge.

We lay in pristine silence for a long time, counting falling stars. I feel groggy but the silence and darkness are so impressive that I force myself awake. I don't want to miss this magic.

An hour later I hear voices. People are approaching on the sand path that passes our hut. Why would anyone walk through the desert chatting at this late hour?

The male voices get closer and I worry that they'll be startled to find us lying outdoors. As the voice gets close, emerging from the blackness is a man wearing a white robe and a turban, riding a camel with a smaller camel in tow. He's alone—and he's talking on a cell phone!

Unbelievable! I'm in a remote part of the world, in the silence of a wild desert—and I see this?—a man using a camel for transportation and a cell phone for communication? Cell phone waves reach this unspoiled spot? I have a moment of disappointment.

The person passes without noticing us. I lie back again, relax, and admire the universe, imagining it wrapped around me like a second blanket and let sleep overcome me.

The first sign of trouble begins the next morning. At breakfast Maria tells me her stomach feels queasy. Ever the trooper, she's determined to take our days' journey by camel-cart to higher sand dunes and climb them. Shaded under an umbrella we take in the desert scene for the hour-and-a-half journey as the temperature skyrockets in the already intense sun. A half-hour into our trek, Maria lies on the platform, not feeling well. Her color is reddening but she insists we continue. At our destination, Danta Ram and I hike the ridge and return fifteen minutes later to find Maria looking even worse.

"We should go now, Dad," she says.

"You don't look well. What are you feeling?"

"A really queasy stomach. Let's go—Now!" she says.

I turn to our host. "Danta Ram, Maria sick. Very sick. We must go back quickly please."

Danta Ram looks at Maria; now he's concerned. We board the cart and head back while I hold the umbrella over Maria. But she begins to experience bouts of explosive vomiting and violent diarrhea. Every few minutes she has an urgent need to get off the cart and find a small bush to give her a minimum of privacy. At one such stop near a family hut, a group of young children run over to gawk at the blond woman.

"Get them out of here, Dad! Tell them to go away!" she cries in agony and embarrassment. I yell and wave for them to leave but they just move to another spot. Danta Ram shouts a Hindi command at them, but they don't respond.

The violent episodes continue and Danta Ram pushes the camels on as quickly as he can, but the sluggish animals refuse to rush. Maria's face is now pink and flushed. The air, very hot and dry, is getting hotter by the minute. I touch her forehead; she's clammy. I plan to treat her when we arrive at our hut, but I realize that in an effort to lighten my load, I left my medical kit at the guest house. *What an idiot!* I desperately need a thermometer. From my limited wilderness medical training I suspect she has a stomach infection but it could be heatstroke as well.

The combination of dry heat, sun exposure, fever, vomiting, and diarrhea pose a serious and potentially deadly risk of dehydration. She's lost a lot of fluids, and the well water she's drinking goes in and out of her within minutes. We need to leave quickly for an air-conditioned room in the city.

At Danta Ram's home, Maria wobbles into our shaded hut. Her condition is not improving. Neighboring children again gather to stare at her so I prop my cot sideways in the doorway to give her some privacy.

I remember then that soda pop provides electrolytes essential to offset depleted fluids. "Danta Ram! Do you have any soda pop?"

He looks confused but then his eyebrows lift. "Have some. Have Fanta. I get." Visibly nervous, he runs to a distant neighbor's hut and returns a few minutes later.

Desert Distress

Maria drinks the warm Fanta and momentarily looks better—but just minutes later her body rejects it. Her red face is now hot to the touch. I wish I knew her temperature. I'm unequipped to deal with the situation.

We need to evacuate immediately. But how? It'll take hours to get to the city by camel cart—all the while exposing her to the sun. Then I remember I have Yogi's phone number at the guest house. But I don't have my cell phone; I assumed we wouldn't have reception in the desert.

"Danta Ram, I need a cell phone now. Can you find one?"

"Friend nearby. Friend phone have. I go get." Again he darts off, this time over a dune and out of sight. Ten minutes later, he comes running over a dune waving a phone in his hand.

I call Viki, the attendant at Yogi's guest house. I'm relieved to speak English. Viki has a plan.

Cresting over the dune thirty minutes later is a white, 4-wheel-drive Jeep with large traction tires. It backs up to the hut for easy loading. The driver, from some neighboring city, is kind and concerned. He brought cold soda pop for Maria. She quickly drinks a can—again she's better for a moment before her body rejects it.

We quickly load the jeep with Maria slumped in the back seat, shaded by the canvas top.

I express our gratitude to Danta Ram and Samu and slip them a large tip for their special attention. They treated us like family. Despite having few material possessions, their hearts are full of compassion, contentment, and selflessness.

As the jeep heads into the desert, the driver maneuvers around a steep grade and gets stuck in the sand. I hop out, grip the rear bumper, and help the driver rock the vehicle. We struggle for several minutes until, with a forceful spray of sand all over me, the jeep breaks free. We push forward but it isn't long before we get stuck again. Finally, we reach the desert's edge.

Raj is waiting in his air-conditioned car! A few hours later we're in an air-conditioned room at Yogi's Guesthouse and Maria's condition is stabilizing. Raj, Viki, and Bundy spend the next day and a half caring for Maria, offering medicines, food, and drink. Almost like family.

Relieved that Maria will mend soon, I'm nevertheless disappointed that we had to leave the simple and pristine desert where I felt more connected with myself. Everything in the desert is unhurried—from the camels to our host to the endless sand dunes—a contrast to the frazzled commotion of Delhi and Jaipur. In the desert I realized how little I need to live happily.

Chapter 3

A Bad Break

Jodhpur, India

Out of suffering have emerged the strongest of souls; the most massive characters are seared with scars.
—Khalil Gibran

Maria bounces back in a day-and-a-half. I'm relieved. The problem is over. Then I'm overcome with the same—but much less severe—intestinal affliction. It's my turn to take to bed.

I keep remembering why I've come to Asia—to clear my mind, to become aware and more conscious. But I've had little time to meditate and now that I'm sick and bed-bound I'm unable to expose myself to the spiritual richness of the Indian culture—the temples, the calls to prayer, the open practices. I'm thirsting to begin my inner journey in full earnest.

Outside my window, Diwali, a five-day Indian festival—also known as the "Festival of Lights,"—is due to peak tonight with massive displays of lighting and prolific use of fireworks. The tempo of the celebration builds by the hour. I glance out the window as everyone—even five-year-old children—light firecrackers and toss them haphazardly into the jam-packed streets. It looks and sounds like a war zone with small rockets zipping about and loud explosives going off in the crowds.

Maria's been mingling with the younger backpacking crowd at the guesthouse. She returns to our room, excited.

"Dad, Viki's invited me and an Italian couple to join him and his parents at their house tonight. We'll hang out on the rooftop to watch the fireworks. Viki has some fireworks too!" She watches my face for reaction. "You don't mind, do you?"

"No dear. Go ahead. I'm going to rest. I still don't have any energy. Have fun."

"Thanks Dad. It's really exciting, the streets are buzzing with people and things going on."

"Just be careful, please," I say. "Be aware of your surroundings and look all around. Please."

"I'll be careful."

As I lie listening to the festivities, I begin to feel better. Just as I generate enough energy to sit up in bed, a knock on my door startles me. It's 11:00PM. It's the young Italian couple who were joining Maria. They look worried. My heart drops as I wait for an explanation.

"Sir, your daughter, she downstairs. She falls and feels very hurt. Maybe you come see her."

Downstairs Maria is on a couch, leaning to one side, her right arm resting on her lap. I gasp at the sight of her shoulder, which is swollen huge; she looks like she's wearing a football shoulder pad underneath her clothes. I can tell she's in severe pain.

She struggles not to cry. "I slipped on the stairway. It was concrete. It was dark. I feel so stupid. It hurts really bad, Dad."

"Can you walk?"

"Kinda, but I can't move my shoulder or my arm."

Her arm is obviously broken, but how bad? Back home we'd simply drive to the emergency room. Things are different here. This is the peak of Diwali and the streets are jam-packed with people celebrating. It's nothing short of mayhem everywhere. Pushing through the crowds to get her to a hospital will be difficult but once there, we'll be competing with the firework injuries. Staffing shortages are likely on this biggest holiday in India.

"Can you wait until morning, Maria? We can get you much better medical attention after this festival ends."

"Okay, I'll try," she says.

I help her struggle to our air-conditioned room, but she can't find a comfortable position. With great difficulty, she lies down but she can't roll over or move without pain. I give her a painkiller I carried in my medical kit, but it's inadequate. For hours she tries to sleep but can only squirm in pain. Halfway through the night she tries to use the bathroom. She calls me for help as she comes out and faints as I catch her. She's cold and clammy, and I worry about shock. I lay her down and cover her with a blanket.

I'm wishing for the medical facilities back home. Toward morning, Maria begins to stabilize and we find ourselves in the quiet of the morning with the sun rising. The riot-like activities outside have stopped and our reliable friend, Raj, helps me get Maria into his car and to the hospital.

"We go to best hospital in town," Raj says. "Very good. She'll have good care."

The streets are empty like Christmas morning back home but covered with shredded paper from exploded fireworks. Raj drives slowly but each time he rolls over a bump, Maria grimaces in pain.

India is still a developing nation. Windows in the hospital are open and flies buzz around. A cow lies in the street just outside one of the open windows. The rooms are crammed full of patients and the hallway floors are lined with people sitting, waiting for attention.

Maria is quickly taken into an examination room. She lies on a rolling hospital bed as she waits to be examined. She doesn't notice that on the bed next to her is a blanketed dead body.

We are taken around the corner to an antiquated X-ray machine. I have to prompt the assistants to manipulate Maria's arm with care while they position her for the x-rays.

Ten minutes later a doctor enters, looks at the x-ray, frowns, shakes his head, and mumbles something out loud in Hindi. He turns to us. "A bad break. Very bad. Must call surgeon. Must wait," he tells us and steps away. He comes back with a hand scribbled piece of paper and hands it to me. "Outside, around corner. You get pain medicine. Bring back," he says before abruptly walking away.

Sure enough, down the street is a shop that, like most Indian shops, has no front wall, simply an open counter facing the sidewalk. Customers crowd three layers deep waiting their turn. Three men behind the counter busily tend to orders, pulling packets of medicine from rows of unnumbered, cluttered, and dirty wooden shelves. Anxious customers in back stretch their arms toward the front struggling to be served next. The three men behind the counter climb over each other in the narrow space.

Slowly I squeeze my way to the counter. Finally a worker looks at my prescription, grabs a packet of syringes, needles, and a bottle of liquid medicine, stuffs it into a brown paper bag and slips me a scribbled note listing the rupees equivalent of US$1.50.

Meds in hand, I rush to the hospital and hand them to a woman whose blue headdress and cleaner street clothes identify her as head nurse. She prepares to administer the pain shot to Maria. I ask that she first wash her hands and disinfect Maria's arm. She objects. I insist, so she obliges. When the dose is administered, she casually tosses the used syringe into an open desk drawer.

Soon, we find ourselves talking to Dr. Das, an articulate man in his fifties who trained as a surgeon in Austria, the United States, and Venezuela. He speaks fluent English.

"Maria's fracture very bad," he says. "Her humerus is broken at the shoulder joint. The good news is it doesn't need to be set. However, it must be reinforced with screws and requires surgery. I can do this," he explains. "Only very small incision is needed and I have equipment that provides display while I'm working. This is what I recommend. Other option is a plaster cast and send her home for surgery in the US."

Maria and I exchange glances and she turns to Dr. Das. "Can we discuss this and get back to you?

"Of course, Maria," he says. "We have time. Meanwhile I'll order you an air-conditioned room".

The doctor seems very capable, but the facilities worry me. Cleanliness is inadequate. I noticed one central desk in the hallway with a single glass jar filled with a disinfectant in which all the prongs, tweezers, and knives are universally placed for disinfecting and then pulled out and reused on the next patient.

"On the other hand Maria, we're a long way from home," I say. "You know how hard it was to travel to this remote town. If Dr. Das were to cast that monster shoulder, it would be extremely difficult and painful to get home like that. Forget about the packed trains or buses! Hiring a taxi means two days of swerving in a car as the driver avoids the jarring potholes, cows, and chaotic traffic. From Delhi you have at least a day-and-a-half travel on a cramped airplane. Neither option is desirable."

I sit in a chair near her bed. "Let's talk to the doctor about the cleanliness thing," I say. "Let's see what he says."

Dr. Das does not dispute our concern. "I'll make sure she's the first person on the table in the morning," was his best offer. "Sir, I understand your fatherly concern," Dr. Das says. "I am also a father and have a daughter slightly younger than Maria. Let me be your representative. Let me use my hands as yours. I'll treat her like my own daughter. This is the decision I'd make for my own daughter."

He seems sincere and capable and other people I've asked have said he's very good. We elect for surgery.

Maria's prepared for surgery early the next morning and wheeled outside the operating room. I try to be upbeat and confident as I kiss her. Shaking hands with the doctor I repeat my request for special care. She's then wheeled away behind the surgery room doors. I claim the single wooden chair in the hallway and second-guess our decision. It's better to simply relax and wait. Worrying does no good and I'll need that energy later.

The need for energy comes all too quickly. Five minutes later the door swings open and an elderly woman, dressed more like a housekeeper than a nurse, steps out holding a piece of paper with a scribbled list. She waves it at me, and says, "You get!"

"Me get? Me get what?"

"You get," she repeats waving the paper.

I know what this is, but I don't want to believe it. There must be twenty or thirty items listed in Hindi—the supplies they need to do the surgery. The surgeon, nurse, anesthesiologist, and Maria are in the operating room waiting for me to run down the street and buy surgical supplies.

I rush across the hall, dart down the stairs, and sprint across the sidewalk to the large mob collected at the pharmacy counter. I've never been one to cut in line but I find a new level of assertiveness. Forcefully I shoulder my way through the crowd to the front of the counter, wave down an attendant, and give him the paper. "Quickly please! Quickly," I beg.

He frowns as he studies the paper with lazy interest. "Thirty minutes, I bring to you, you go."

"No! No, I wait here. You give to me please."

"Go, go hospital. I bring to you."

I don't believe him. I'm certain my order will get lost in this crowd. If I walk away someone else will immediately get priority.

"Sir, please, I need now," I try again. "I must have now. Please."

He looks stern. "I bring to you."

If I upset him then I risk an inaccurate filling of the order. I back down, walk back to the hospital entrance, glance at my watch, and wait. Two minutes go by, then three, five, seven minutes. I can't wait any longer. I go back to find him filling another order and my paper unmoved on the countertop. Damn! I knew it!

I grab the paper and flag down another attendant who's more interested and studies it carefully. "Yes, wait a few minutes. I get." He then scurries about stuffing surgeon gloves, face masks, scalpel, needles and thread, antibiotics, IV bag, and other medicines into a large paper shopping bag.

"All here," he says holding the bag out to me. The bill comes to "five thousand one hundred twenty-one rupee," just over US$100. I don't have that amount of cash and don't have the time to find an ATM.

"Okay, I come back and pay you in just a few minutes. Okay?"

"Okay, you see me."

Amazed that he lets me leave without paying, I swiftly get the supplies to the woman at the operating room. She seems put out that it took so long. I head to the pharmacy to pay the bill, I return to that single chair and try to regain my composure. Once again I've an opportunity alone, and although the thought of closing my eyes to meditate and calm myself enters my mind, it's all I can do to let my mind run its course through various scenarios of tragedy.

An hour later, the doors swing open and Dr. Das comes with a smile. "Maria will be well now," he announces. "I put two screws into her bone. She'll wake up in one hour and stay in an air-conditioned room for two days."

Within an hour Maria awakens with her ardent smile. She feels the ordeal is over, but I don't—not until the risk of infection is past.

Viki, Raj, Bundy, and even Viki's parents visit several times over the next two days. She's entertained and showered with gifts of nice fabric, flowers, and food. The news of her incident has spread within the community. As I walk the street near the guesthouse, Indian men I don't recognize occasionally yell from their shops, "How you daughter?" or "Blonde girl, how blonde girl?"

The contrast between the care Maria received and that given to average Indians makes me feel both grateful and guilty. Why should Maria, a foreigner, have the only air-conditioned room in the hospital while the locals are in hot and buggy rooms without windows? Some locals don't have the option even to lie down—they can only sit. I don't feel good that my wealth allows Maria to "be first on the table in the morning," to prevent infection. And what happens to those who cannot afford the medicines? I suspect the average Indian with Maria's injury would be crippled for life.

I'm part of the caste system; Maria and I have been treated with elite status. I've often pondered why I was born with wealth and fortune, but here, in this remote place, the contrast of fortunes cannot be ignored. I'm indebted. I hope someday to pay it back in some way.

Two days later we leave the hospital with Maria carrying a remanufactured shoulder. I carry a crumpled brown bag of antibiotics and painkillers.

I was terrified in the desert when Maria became ill and now I'm shaken from her injury and surgical ordeal. I didn't come here to be confronted with challenges. I came to study my mind—to find inner peace and tranquility. Exasperation was not in my plan.

But this is life, isn't it? The sages teach us not to run from problems but to face them head-on in a detached, aware manner. What good is inner peace if it crumbles into panic when things don't go right? Perhaps these challenges are what I need as a first-step in this journey. Maybe I need to adjust my expectations. I now see that whatever spiritual learnings I take home with me, they need the durability to hold up through the struggles of daily life.

Shortly before Maria leaves for home, we lunch on a rooftop restaurant. I look down over the railing to watch monkeys scramble across window sills. Two floors below on a flat and open apartment rooftop stands a small altar with fruit, incense, and a deity. Leading up to the altar on the concrete roof is a two-foot-wide by twenty-foot-long carpet of fresh red rose petals, hundreds of them, meticulously arranged. On either side of the red petals is a one-foot-wide layer of orange rose petals. Each delicate petal has been painstakingly plucked, placed, and perfectly positioned. This personal offering took hours of devotional care. It's mere coincidence to stumble upon it. It's not a tourist display. Someone took hours without economic benefit or even recognition. I feel privileged to witness it.

Everywhere I turn, I see similar demonstrations of devotion and faith. I'm here in part because a nearly endless list of yogis, gurus, and swamis have arisen from this land, including Mahatma Gandhi and the Dalai Lama, who is currently living in the Indian Himalayas in exile. It's exactly for this reason that I view these first few touring weeks as an important segue to my now imminent internal sojourn. The spirit of these people inspires me to continue walking my path. I feel in my heart I'm in the right land for spiritual development.

I escort Maria to the airport. I give her a tender hug with a lump in my throat knowing that her soon-to-be fiancé will be waiting for her at the other end of her flight with a ring in his hand. I wave to her, then turn ready—so ready—to begin the inward journey I came here to experience. I'm ready for Nepal.

Chapter 4

Serendipity Starts

Between India and Nepal

We can never obtain peace in the outer world until we make peace with ourselves.

—Dalai Lama

At this moment, Maria is soaring over the Atlantic. I now begin a new phase of this journey, an earnest search within. I'll study my mind, my focus now shifting from outward tourist to inward explorer.

I'm in the Delhi train station, running late for my trip to the Nepali border. I make my train with seven minutes to spare.

Cramped in the upper bunk of a crowded car, with an elderly man wearing an orange robe and turban staring at me, the rocking train and track clatter relax my mind, so I close my eyes and try to clear my thoughts—an attempt at an informal sort of meditation. Initially, my mind is quiet, but the sensory overload from three weeks of exotic sights, flamboyant colors, the sounds and smells of the streets, and Maria's illness and injury leave my mind garbled. My efforts to concentrate fail. I'm mentally agitated and my thoughts skip uncontrollably between the past and the future.

I notice that I'm once again nervously picking at my fingers, a life-long habit I've often tried to overcome. How can I control my mind if

I can't control my actions? This is only one of several nervous habits. I also absent mindedly chew the inside of my cheek and lips, which leaves a telltale rawness inside my mouth—another indication of how madly active and unaware my mind is. I blame these nervous habits on my fast-paced lifestyle.

I hope my efforts to deepen my meditation practice—beginning now on this train—will help me overcome these obstinate habits. But here and now, my attempt isn't making a dent. Thoughts keep kicking in: I hope Maria's flight goes well. Then I worry: What if she missed a connection? What if her surgery incision became infected? What if . . .

"STOP!" I tell myself, interrupting the thinking. I breathe in, breathe out. No thinking allowed. It doesn't last. Shall I travel by rickshaw or bus tomorrow? What if I get lost? What if I end up in the wrong city? I continue in this way for at least ten minutes until I find myself hiking in a Vietnamese jungle.

This is a typical meditation experience for me. My mind begins an independent journey through a chain of weakly linked subjects that ends up who knows where. This mind is wild and uncontrollable, like a runaway stallion charging in whatever direction it chooses, kicking about every which way while I—the wrangler—try to harness it. It resists my efforts and gallops away. It's odd, but meditation has shown me two independent entities within: my mind and my self—and they often oppose each other. When I consciously place full attention on a given task—like quieting my mind—it isn't long before my mind breaks off in a direction of its own.

I aim to lasso this wild stallion that is my mind, to haul it into the corral, and to train it to follow my directions. I'll take every opportunity I can to do this. It's guaranteed that my mind will vehemently resist, but with patience, persistence, and guidance from masters I hope to meet, my mission can be accomplished. Someday, as I ride bareback, my mind and self will be as one through the busiest of streets with calmness, direction, and purpose. This I seek.

Over the next ten days, I'll find my way up the mountains into a monastery in Kathmandu for a month-long course in Tibetan Buddhism.

On the way, I'll stop briefly in Lumbini, the birthplace of the Buddha, to arrange a retreat at a meditation center there later in this trip.

By mid-afternoon, the train rolls into the Gorakhpur station. Outside the train station, I'm enveloped by a crowd of barefoot taxi and rickshaw drivers, all wanting to take me to the Nepali border, about two hours away. It's easy to become overwhelmed with so many frantic, pleading people. I detach, follow my intuition, and end up in a dilapidated 4-wheel-drive Jeep with bald rear tires and a deflated spare mounted on the back. I'm seated with a Nepali businessman and a pretty Asian woman who's dressed too daintily for the rather dirty environment.

After an hour, the driver stops at a roadside stand where cooks tend charcoal-fired woks brimming with delicious-looking potato, bean, and chicken meals. The aromas are nearly irresistible but the collection of flies on each dish ruins my appetite, so I elect not to eat. Several small buses also pull over, and I glance at one bus just as a young mother, still inside, holds her year-old son up to the window as he urinates onto the dusty parking area. A ten-year-old girl hurrying by inadvertently walks into the yellow stream. She screams in shock, and then dashes off embarrassed as people eating lunch chuckle.

After another hour our jeep stops and unloads. I find myself in a sandy turnoff littered with plastic bags and cups. This small Indian town borders Nepal. The driver points up a crowded street toward the border.

I strap on my backpack and walk past a backup of trucks, buses, cars, and stalled rickshaws to the black and white checkpoint gate.

As I near the gate, a man in the street points to a storefront insisting, "Here, here." I'm suspicious that he's another vendor wanting to sell me something. A couple of young backpackers are filling out forms on a dirty plastic table with cracked plastic chairs. A small handwritten paper is taped to the table: "India Immigration." The dirty street stand looks incredibly unofficial but I judge it authentic.

The immigration officer, dressed in street clothes but wearing a tarnished badge, peruses my passport, stamps me out of the country, and points to a black and white gate. "Walk Nepal," he says.

I walk past two guards through a tattered wooden gate into Nepal. Just past the gate is Nepal customs, an open garage where a mix of bus and truck drivers blend with a few backpackers. Scattered across a wooden desk are eighty or so passports in disarray. I don't like it. How do I prevent my passport mixing with this mess?

I chat with a man in tidy clothes and single him out as an official. I must've smiled just right because he carries my passport through the system and, with a kind smile, hands it to me, approved. I clasp my hands, bow, and say "Namaste."

I'm in Sunnouli, a very small Nepalese town, I wander up the street and book a room at a clean guesthouse. It's a plain room, only a handmade wood-frame bed with a sliver-thin mattress and a tiny single-drawer dresser. I lie on the bed and smile as I take in the plain room. Simple. Ahhhh yes! It's taken much of my life to fully appreciate the significance of simplicity. I fondly remember my first apartment, void of all but a few naked pieces of furniture, plastic place settings for two, enough cookware to warm canned soup, and a few drawers stuffed with jeans and tattered tee shirts.

As an adult hiking alone in a wilderness, I carried only necessities on my back and a clear mind. Simplicity has always elevated my experience of the present moment. No luxury-filled house can compete with an empty room with only a pillow and a blanket on the floor.

"Why does it bother you to have a few piles of things here and there?" Jayne often asks, trying to understand my need to eliminate clutter. The best I could come up with was that the absence of clutter keeps me relaxed and undistracted. In truth, the explanation goes deeper. Being surrounded by things is being surrounded by tasks. Possessions send messages: that woodwork needs to be washed; those tools need to be put away; the crooked picture needs to be straightened; that borrowed book must be returned. Things create worry, too. I must be careful not to knock that expensive glass figure off the shelf, lose the car title amidst a stack of papers, or drop my expensive phone.

Worry becomes diluted amidst simplicity. Maybe that's why I enjoy business travel. Hotel rooms are usually uncluttered and simple. They hold none of the "should-do" tasks that torment me at home.

Having too many things also drove me to take this journey. "Enough is enough," I told myself as I sifted through my belongings. I was on a mission to purge the unnecessary. I sold my car and most of my furniture. I rented my house, gave away much of my clothing, and placed my remaining belongings in storage. I interrogated every item based on *need* versus *want*. Every item was scrutinized; nothing was exempt. Well, almost nothing. I gave tools a pardon—garden tools, repair tools, automotive tools, computer, and the phone. Anything that allows me to create, build, or work received amnesty.

Jayne and I easily negotiated an understanding; she respects my need to release most of my belongings, and I put no expectations on her to do the same.

Purging felt great! It was a stride toward freeing my mind and an advance out of the imprisonment of things. I had no regrets.

But clearing out was only the first step. This journey is a second clearing—a clearing of mind. One-by-one, I'll bring my values and beliefs to the surface and question my deepest self about them. I'll toss out the unnecessary beliefs and replace them with healthier ones. At journey's end, I intend to return with a refined vision of how to live life with rich meaning and calm presence.

The next morning, I ask the guesthouse owner for directions to Lumbini.

"No bus to Lumbini. No, sir," the owner tells me. "There's Bandh today. Maybe no Bandh tomorrow. Don't know."

"Bandh" is a form of political protest here in Nepal. Opposition groups call for a Bandh to express disapproval of government policies. It's a mandatory transportation strike. Anyone who violates the Bandh is at risk of attack.

"Why Bandh?" I ask him. "What are they protesting?"

"Not know sir. Not know how long either. Only way get to Lumbini is rickshaw to next town, Bhairawa. One hour rickshaw. There catch bus to Lumbini. Two hours bus."

Outside the guesthouse, I negotiate a price with a needy-looking older bicycle rickshaw driver. It's the dry season. The parched farm fields are brown and the hot breeze sucks humidity out of everybody and everything. The dirt on the road is a thick powder, much like a layer of wheat flour, which puffs a cloud with each step. It may be pleasant weather for my travels but it certainly poses difficulties for this elderly man peddling me cross country.

In Bhairawa, the bus station is empty. The Bandh affects buses here too, so I hire a young taxi driver to take me to Lumbini. The trip turns into a nail-biter as he swerves around potholes and darts wildly across center to pass most every vehicle, narrowly missing oncoming trucks. I'd gotten used to the mad driving in India, but this man is in a class by himself.

He stops at a large gateway that has a pair of crumbling stone pillars on either side of a rusty steel gate. "Lumbini entrance here," he says. I'm relieved to be out of his taxi.

This is a simple village with no neon lights or billboards. It feels even more remote than India. I like it. I arrange to stay at a small guesthouse, then buy some bananas from a woman sitting road-side with a gold ring in her nose. I head into the Lumbini preserve.

At the gate, my heart sinks at the sight of a mother with a naked boy, about five-years old, who has the revealingly swollen abdomen of a malnourished child. The mother looks at me without a word. I motion her to follow me to a street vendor as a group of begging children tag along. I hand the vendor money for a hearty dinner for the mother and her son. I also buy five small bags of potato chips for the other children, who respond with delight.

I've encountered poverty every day since arriving on this continent, and it's been difficult to cope with. I've learned to avoid handing out money—especially to children. I realize my gesture today to this mother and child is insufficient; it's no more than a temporary remedy. That realization will not fade easily.

Lumbini is a designated United Nations (UNESCO) world heritage site in which three-square-miles of dedicated, fenced-in flatlands surround an ancient shrine known throughout the millennia to be Buddha's birthplace. The Nepali government allocated this land, situated at the base of the Himalayas, for the construction of Buddhist temples that represent the architecture and culture of various nations that practice Buddhism, including Nepal, Korea, China, France, Germany—sixteen in all.

The immense swath of property is crisscrossed with dirt roads riddled with potholes that link the temples, which are interspersed between stretching fields of high grasses. As the sun beats down, sweat tacks my shirt to my body. An elderly bicycle rickshaw driver slips out of the shade of trees and approaches.

"Very big here. Much walking. Six kilometers. Very hot," his sales pitch begins. "I give you ride, show all temples."

I prefer to hoof it but I'll be here only one day. We negotiate a price and I jump in.

"What's your name?" I ask.

"My name Samuella," he replies.

Samuella knows just enough English to give simple explanations and answer questions.

"I grandfather," he beams when asked about his family. "Four children have; two boy, two girl. Five grandchild. Must work for family," he says looking at me with deep brown eyes.

"How old are you?" I venture.

"Me fivety fives," he says, showing his fingers to count.

He's older than I. This grandfather spends his days pedaling a heavy, three-wheeled bicycle with adult passengers through difficult dirt trails in the blazing sun. His firm and muscular calves tell the story. For the next several hours, he shuttles me from temple to temple. Each is an exquisite masterpiece. Even without printed explanations of the architecture and symbolic imagery, I still gain a sense of each Buddhist tradition.

Seeing these temples makes me reflect again on my mission here. I know there's more to be gained from meditation practice than achieving a peaceful state of mind. Accomplished meditation masters have consistently affirmed that one can gain an understanding of the nature of the self and of our existence beyond the limitations of our normal perspectives. These masters teach that once we achieve such deep levels of insight, a boundless compassion for all living beings arises within us. It is not forced, it just happens.

I believe that if I learn techniques, practices, and wisdom from Buddhist masters in a setting remote from the incessant demands back home, like this land where Buddhism originated, that my practice will lead to a more meaningful life. Perhaps by sampling Buddhist traditions other than Japanese Zen—Tibetan, Vipassana, Vietnamese, Korean—I'll establish a broader perspective on which I can base the changes I want to make in my life. This is yet another goal for this journey, to investigate other traditions of Buddhism.

As a philosophy, I find Buddhism intellectually challenging and compelling. My deepest hope is that by immersing myself in the practice of Buddhism, I'll develop an unwavering focus on what I consider the foundation for a meaningful life: a still and focused mind, equanimity, non-attachment, peace.

The huge, unfinished, four-story Korean Temple is a prominent sight with its magnificent tiled roof sweeping outward and upward at the corners. I'm planning to later visit South Korea, so I stop to inquire. The resident monk isn't available, however, so we head to the Vietnamese Temple where I find a side entrance and yell through the locked gates, "Hello, anyone there? Hello?" I call for five minutes without an answer.

An inner nudge has been directing me to Vietnam. I'm not sure why but I want to follow that intuition. I've almost no itinerary for that trip segment, so it'd help to talk with someone here. There's no response, so I decide to stay in Lumbini another day and try again tomorrow.

Our last stop on Samuella's tour of the preserve is Panditarama, the Burmese Vipassana meditation center. I had emailed the center from back home. At the end of a gravel footpath and nearly concealed by tropical brush and palm trees is an inconspicuous, metal gate. With a cackle, a bright green bird flushes out of a bush startling me. There's no attendant and I don't want to disturb the silence so I reach through the gate, unlatch it, and enter. The buildings are unobtrusive, single-story brick structures, simple and unadorned—dramatically different from the other temples. It's silent and still as I walk through a corridor that leads to an open-air lobby with a canopied circular path for walking meditation. On a bulletin board the meditation schedule is posted:

4:00 a.m.	Wake up
4:30 to 5:00 a.m.	Walking meditation
5:00 to 6:00 a.m.	Sitting meditation
6:00 to 7:00 a.m.	Breakfast
7:00 to 8:00 a.m.	Sitting meditation
8:00 to 9:00 a.m.	Walking meditation
9:00 to 10:00 a.m.	Sitting meditation
10:00 to 11:00 a.m.	Walking meditation
11:00 a.m. to 12:00	Lunch
12:00 to 12:30 p.m.	Rest
12:30 to 1:00 p.m.	Walking meditation
1:00 to 2:00 p.m.	Sitting meditation
2:00 to 3:00 p.m.	Walking meditation
3:00 to 4:30 p.m.	Sitting meditation
4:30 to 5:30 p.m.	Walking meditation
5:30 to 7:00 p.m.	Dharma talk
7:00 to 8:00 p.m.	Juice break/ walking meditation
8:00 to 9:00 p.m.	Sitting meditation
9:00 to 10:00 p.m.	Walking meditation.

That's intimidating! I count twelve-and-one-half hours of meditation every day! I shudder. I've never sat longer than one half-hour after which my knees and back usually screamed for relief. And look at the hour they awaken! I can't imagine myself crawling onto a meditation cushion and focusing my mind at 4:30AM, still sleepy and groggy. Yuck!

Still, I didn't come here for a sleep-in, cozy vacation.

Halfway around the looped walkway, I find a screened door and a plaque reading "meditation room." I take a peek. It's a triangular-shaped room, clean and organized, with white concrete walls, a thinly carpeted floor, and sitting mats with cushions evenly spaced about. A simple table altar is at the apex with a small but elegant statue of Buddha. It's the only sculpture in the room and there's no other artwork and no smell of incense. Cylindrical mosquito nets envelope each cushion and about twenty practitioners—women on the left and men on the right—sit motionless within the netted cocoons. The scene strikes me as a bit surreal.

The quiet environment is perfect for meditation. It's simple with no distractions. Despite the intimidating schedule, I feel compelled to practice here. Certainly, focusing the mind inward for nearly thirteen hours a day has to affect one's understanding of self! I feel poised at the starting line, ready for the gun to pop. I must return here.

A monk steps out of a nearby room, notices me, and strides over. His head is cleanly shaven and he wears burnt amber robes that cover only one shoulder leaving bare his other shoulder, one arm, and the calf of one leg. A maroon shawl is draped over his robed shoulder. He looks to be in his late forties and of European decent. He walks energetically yet mindfully. He looks at me with green eyes that are piercing but peaceful.

"I am Vivekananda. May I help you?" he says in a whisper.

I'm relieved that he speaks English. I clasp my hands and give a slight bow. "I'm Mark. I sent an e-mail requesting to meditate here," I say quietly. "I didn't receive a response."

"I'm sorry, Mark. I really don't recall," Vivekananda says. "Communications are not good here though. Power is often disrupted and phone lines are even less reliable since people climb the poles and snip the wires for fun." He motions me out of the way so we can converse away from the meditators.

"My e-mail said that I would like to practice here for several weeks, probably starting in late January. I'm really interested. Do you have openings?"

"I need to ask a few questions first, if I may," he says.

His questions gauge my commitment and ability to handle the rigorous schedule. He asks about my prior practice, my objectives, and the traditions with which I'm familiar. He also assesses my physical ability with questions about medications and overall health.

I share my ten-year history in Japanese Zen and my commitment to simplifying my life. I describe my frustration with concentration.

"I'll keep a spot open for you, Mark," Vivekananda says. "We're busy with a retreat at that time but you can practice here. Please let me know as soon as you have a firm date."

He steps into a room and comes out with a book in hand. "This book is very detailed on the Vipassana meditation," Vivekananda says. "It'll guide you through the type of practice we do here. Please read it and bring it back with you. It will help you get a quicker start."

As I walk through the sandy yard, I watch someone practicing walking meditation and I picture myself here. It's quiet, far from traffic noise, and situated in a huge grassland nature preserve. I'll receive daily instruction and Dharma talks, and become part of the group of practitioners, called the sangha, which practices together and silently learns from one another. The nonreligious nature of the practice appeals to my logic-inclined mind. It seems perfect.

Samuella is patiently waiting and I ask him to pedal me back to the village. He's really struggled in carrying me around in the intense heat and he did it without a complaint. He seems kind and humble. I wonder how he supports children and grandchildren with his meager pay. How can he afford healthcare and education for his family? I notice he doesn't wear that heavy, worried look, I've so often seen—even on myself—from the stress and burdens of life. Samuella may not have wealth in his pocket, but he carries a certain wealth in his poise. I tip him well.

That night, I awaken at 4:00AM to the distant striking of a gong. For minutes, I lie awake absorbing the mystical sound slicing through the silence. I want to awaken and meditate but feel too groggy. I know that gong is calling others to do so though. I'd meditated before retiring last night, but realize I must develop more stamina if I'm going to adhere to Panditarama's schedule. *Later. Much later.* I roll over and go back to sleep.

The next morning, I rent a rickety bicycle and pedal back to the Korean and Vietnamese temples. An attendant at the Korean Temple recognizes me from yesterday's visit. With a smile, he says, "Monk here now, I get for you."

The middle-aged Korean monk speaks little English but understands my questions.

"Many temple you can visit in Korea. Many temple let you stay and practice. I have map. I give you."

He retrieves a full-color map of Korea showing the location of over thirty temples. "You call temple when in Korea. You ask to stay. Explain you are Buddhist. Daily cost reasonable."

I want to chat longer but our communication is bumpy, and he seems pressed for time. I bow and move on.

Again there's no attendant at the front gate of the Vietnamese Temple but I call out for assistance. A short, bare-foot Nepali man approaches with an energetic stride and a bright smile.

"Temple closed, sir!" he says. "Under construction. So sorry."

"I'd like to speak with a monk. I have question about Vietnam travel."

"Okay, I get monk." He opens the gate and lets me in. "Wait here."

A few minutes later, a short and slender Vietnamese monk in dark brown robes approaches. He looks to be in his late fifties, has a clean-shaven head and wears large, rectangular wire-framed glasses. He has an unusually peaceful and collected air about him.

"Hello, I Thay Minh Do. How I help?" he says softly, with a strong accent and reasonably clear English.

I introduce myself. "Please, what is the proper way to address you?" I ask.

"Minh Do. It okay you call me Minh Do. Thay, it mean monk. Thay Minh Do mean monk Minh Do. Either way good."

I tell him my intention to visit Vietnam. "Do you know of any temples or monasteries that I may visit and practice at?"

"Maybe I help. We talk. You join for tea, OK?"

I'm excited that he's taking the time to talk. We walk through a courtyard along a brick-lined gravel path and across a beautiful tropical garden. Two small lakes are bordered with bamboo groves and rocks. Traditional arched bridges cross the lakes, shaded by lush banana trees. In the middle of one lake, a small temple is perched atop a single thick pillar that's raised above the lake. The glass-windowed temple has a narrow, second-story balcony that wraps around it and a red-tiled roof with flared-out corners. It's beautiful and Thay Minh Do notices my interest.

"Yes," he begins with a smile, nodding to the temple. "This is One Pillar Pagoda," he says. "Very special. Similar to Hanoi Temple made by Emperor over one thousand years ago. Emperor build for wife. Had dream Buddha would give him son. Dream come true so Emperor build One Pillar Pagoda."

As he speaks I notice, with reverence, his deeply peaceful presence. His attention seems uncluttered and focused. He's unhurried and he walks with intention. His eyes sparkle.

The complex is large with several buildings nestled among tropical trees and gardens. At the center of the complex is a huge marble temple standing high above the trees. A one-hundred-step staircase with white dragon-shaped railings leads to the door.

I follow Thay Minh Do to a large, three-story residential building where we sit in the lobby on bamboo furniture.

"What you seek, Mark?" he asks pouring a cup of green tea.

"I seek to understand my mind," I tell him. I summarize my story, stopping to clarify when I speak too fast.

"I think you wait a minute please," Minh Do says. "I get master. He reading upstairs. I think master want talk to you."

Ten minutes later Thay Minh Do returns with his master. "My Master Thay Huyen Dieu," he says gesturing to the slight man wearing a deep amber, waist-length robe and matching slacks. His hair is cut close to his scalp and he wears wire-framed glasses with oval, tinted lenses. He has a distinguished and intellectual way about him.

"Hello, how may I help you?"

I explain my story and mission. He's absorbed and attentive. When I finish, he addresses Thay Minh Do in Vietnamese.

Thay Minh Do turns to me. "Master say you have good intention. Master have no recommendation for temple in Vietnam but want to help. He say you can stay here if you want. He say I teach you meditation if you stay here." He pauses for my reply.

"I'd be privileged to stay here," I say, smiling at them both. "I could help around the temple to repay you. I'm an engineer, maybe I can help with your construction."

"Not necessary," Thay Huyen Dieu says quickly. "We have hired help for construction. It more important that you focus on practice."

With that, the Master rises and excuses himself. Thay Minh Do and I stand, clasp our hands, and bow as he exits.

"Master very special," says Minh Do focusing his deep brown eyes on me. "He very great man. Come to Lumbini when no temples here. Only have ruins where Buddha born. Garbage everywhere. Master very sad that Buddha birthplace not kept well. He make commitment to improve. Master work very hard to convince Nepali government to preserve Lumbini. He talk government official and explain importance. Not listen at first but finally they convinced. Government create Lumbini preserve and give land to Thay Huyen Dieu for first temple in Lumbini. This Vietnamese Temple was constructed under Thay Huyen Dieu direction."

Minh Do is fervent. "He have very little money, only sixty dollar. At first nowhere to sleep. Many poisonous snakes so he sleep in tree. Then build small hut in swampy area. He get donation from European students. Temple start to build."

Minh Do leans forward and lowers his voice "Some people no want Buddhist Temple. Men sneak at night with knife and gun. Want kill Thay Huyen Dieu but he hide. No can find. Try several times kill Thay Huyen Dieu. Each time hide. Very, very dangerous." He leans back in his chair. "After that, master build temple with diligence. Almost finish now. Now, I take you up to temple. Teach meditation."

How fortunate to be invited to this tropical paradise, Buddha's birthplace, surrounded by temples, to practice with this special monk and his master. How could I be so lucky?

The temple is beside a lake where six-foot Sarus cranes wade in search of unlucky fish; it's surrounded by a flowery garden. Minh Do leads me up the staircase into the temple, grabs a couple of mats and places them at the foot of an altar. The room is constructed almost entirely of marble. With a two-story-high ceiling, our words echo endlessly. Two side altars hold fierce-looking deities that protect the three statues of Buddha on the main altar. Candles are lit and incense is burning.

As we sit on our meditation cushions, Minh Do first instructs me on posture. Then, here—towering over the land where Buddha was born and in a temple with an almost magical ambience—Minh Do counsels me on how to enter the mind.

"Mark, mind is like monkey if you let. Monkey mind swings through trees and grabs whatever catches attention. See banana, grab banana. See fruit, grab fruit. Feel itch, pick bug off fur. Monkey mind goes wherever wants." As he sits in full lotus position, he speaks passionately. "Must not monkey mind. Must first aware of mind. Aware of mind jumping. Then begin control mind. First like buffalo. Buffalo go where want to. You have rope, put rope on buffalo neck and can guide. Later, like horse. You train mind obey and do as you want. You in control. But you must aware of monkey mind."

I chuckle inwardly. He calls it monkey mind and I've been calling it a wild stallion on the loose.

"You walk down street must be aware of your mind. Watch mind, it follow everything interesting. See colors, jump to colors. Smell food, mind jump to food. Hear sound, mind jump on sound. Must watch this monkey mind, Mark. Turn into buffalo. Then turn into horse."

"Now we sit," Minh Do says. "Clear thoughts. No thinking. If thought comes, okay, no problem, just let go away. Now sit and focus on breath," he says as he closes his eyes and inhales deeply through his nostrils. We sit for several minutes. Then he exhales, "yessss."

"Now," Minh Do continues, "before inhale, tell yourself 'now I inhale.' Before exhale, tell self 'now I exhale.' Not speak, not use words, just command before do breath."

I'd never heard of this technique.

"This good for hold attention. No breathe without conscious of breathing," he says. "Prevents mind from wander. Helps train the mind be intentional. We try. You command breath before breathing. We sit for a while."

For twenty minutes I work his technique in the cool shadows of the temple as the cackle of tropical birds shoots through the doors and reverberates off the marble walls. My monkey mind grabs at these sounds. I catch myself. *Now I inhale, now I exhale. Now I inhale, now I exhale. I wonder how long we'll sit. I'll bet a long time. What time will I get back? What should I eat for supper?*

But then my breath runs short and I catch my mind wandering. *Now I inhale.* By breathing with intention, the mind can only wander until I become short of breath. The urge for breath pulls my attention back to the moment. Interesting!

With three successive deep breaths Minh Do signals a stop. We clasp our hands and bow to each other in respect. In silence, we replace our mats and pillows and quietly go down the stairway. He walks me to the gate.

"You come back here practice?" he asks.

"Yes, Thay Minh Do, I'll definitely return."

We face each other. There's a special connection between us, some inherent mutual respect. We bow again and I walk away.

PART TWO

Nepal

Chapter 5

Building a Foundation

Boudhanath, Kathmandu, Nepal

We are Buddhist scientists doing inner exploration and discovery.

Ven. Dondrub
Kopan Monastery

Our ten-passenger minibus strains over the rugged road taking us from the tropical lowlands of Lumbini into the mile-high Kathmandu valley. The Himalayan terrain is breathtakingly beautiful. Huge metal truss bridges span wide, dry riverbeds that become raging torrents during monsoon season. Flatlands become foothills and then mountains as we follow a whitewater river up a lush green valley. Everywhere, terraced rice paddies are carved into the steep slopes. In them, families harvest rice stalks and dry them on the sunny concrete rooftops. Men and women carry bundles of bagged rice atop their heads, hauling them to the market in town. From now on, I'll think twice whenever I grab a bag of rice off the supermarket shelf.

I'm heading to Boudhanath, a spiritual and cultural focal point for Tibetan Buddhists in a district of Kathmandu. The 1959 Chinese invasion and oppression of Tibet sent refugees into Boudhanath and a community of Tibetan Buddhists continues to this day. Boudhanath, some argue, has preserved more of the Tibetan culture than has Tibet. In a few days, I'll start a month-long course on Tibetan Buddhism at Kopan Monastery on a rural hilltop at the edge of Boudhanath. Kopan is known for making Tibetan Buddhism accessible to western seekers. The month-long course in English aligns with my goal to understand various traditions so I can refine my practice back home. But will I make it there in one piece?

Nepal's government cannot afford to build better roads. Heavily loaded trucks frequently break down on the steep inclines. Only a single vehicle in each direction can squeeze onto the narrow roads. A crippled truck causes long traffic jams. Looking out the minibus window, I see large engine parts spread on the road in front of a disabled truck and the mechanic's feet project from underneath. Further on, a recent landslide has covered the road and vehicles are creeping over and through the mess. Without a bulldozer, it's all they can do.

As we near the Kathmandu Valley, the road becomes steeper, and I cringe as our wheels roll just inches from the precipitous edge. We finally reach the summit, which has a stunning view of the Kathmandu Valley. At 4600-feet altitude, Kathmandu is surrounded by 8,000-foot peaks. But the mammoth peaks—starting at 14,000 feet and rising to Mount Everest's commanding 29,029-foot height—are hidden on the other side these 'baby' mountains.

Boudhanath is a dense cluster of three-story apartments, guesthouses, family restaurants, and monasteries stitched together by narrow alleys. In the center of the city is an ancient stupa, a circular monument with a spherical dome, and a massive golden spire. Painted on the spire is a distinct pair of eyes that symbolize the Buddha in meditation. Colorful Tibetan prayer flags flutter in the wind; they're believed to send goodwill to humanity. Devotees place fruit and money at the stupa and sit in meditation. Grey clouds of fragrant incense hover everywhere. Most striking, though, is the continuous flow of Tibetans who devotedly walk clockwise around the stupa, fingering prayer beads while singing or chanting. On the periphery, vendors sell religious artwork and handmade artifacts.

I'm fortunate to have a few days here before the course begins. I'm sitting in a rooftop café sipping tea and admiring the stupa when someone says, "It's an awesome sight, isn't it?"

At the next table sits a tall, slender Caucasian man, about sixty-years-old, with white hair, wire-framed glasses, and a neatly trimmed beard. Sam is from England; he lived in Boudhanath as a hippie decades ago. He's returned to study Tibetan Buddhism.

"Many people spend their life savings to come out of the mountain villages on pilgrimage to the stupa," Sam says. "People the world over travel here to worship." He points to a woman of about sixty who is doing prostrations around the stupa. "She'll do one hundred thousand prostrations to achieve the merit she seeks," he says.

The woman kneels, places her hands on the ground, slides her hands forward against the ground, then lies face down for ten seconds, her arms fully outstretched. Then she stands, takes three steps forward, and repeats the prostration.

"That's remarkable devotion," I admit.

"The march around the stupa is called 'Kora,'" Sam continues. "Walking clockwise, chanting a mantra, spinning the prayer wheels, and burning incense all gain merit that cancels negative karma people have accumulated from past lives."

An elderly man with a cane limps forward, slowly spins a wooden prayer wheel as two children, possibly his grandchildren, walk patiently behind, following his example.

Sam tells me I'm lucky to be here on a night when the moon is full. "More merit is gained with the full moon," he says. "That's why there are more people tonight than usual."

Sam's been a practicing Buddhist for thirty years. He and his wife started a small retreat center in England; they host traveling lamas as they pass through the UK. But, like me, he's been caught up in working, raising a family, and acquiring material possessions. Now he's quit his job to study for several months. In fact, he's thinking of living here six months every year to practice meditation.

Six months every year? I'm intrigued. "What about your family?" I ask.

"My family understands my spiritual drive," Sam says. "We can work that out."

I'm beginning to miss home. At the same time, I'm excited to start the core part of my journey. I call Jayne, Maria, and my son, Matt on a cell phone. It feels good to get caught up. Jayne is fine and excited to hear about Boudhanath, yet I sense tension in her voice because she knows that when I start the course at Kopan, I won't be able to call her. The monastery asks participants to use the course as a quiet time, like a retreat, and to communicate with no one.

The full moon brings extra merit to those who circumambulate the Boudnath Stupa
Boudhnath, Kathmandu, Nepal

Maria's now with her fiancé and happily engaged. An infection in her shoulder is better now; a screw was improperly placed requiring surgical removal. It's a low risk operation that she'll have soon. My son's happily involved with work and college classes. Knowing all's well at home frees me to concentrate on my purpose here.

Nighttime in Boudhanath is magical. A single floodlight beams on the stupa's white dome at night as the stream of believers continues its circular flow lit by an amber glow from tables of yak butter candles. Tibetan monks, in full length, maroon robes, sit on the cobblestone walkways cross-legged chanting from Tibetan texts.

By 9:00PM, a thick layer of darkness settles. The dirt alleys become vacant and silence as delicate as a silk scarf falls gently across the community. This culture is 'early to bed, early to rise.' At 4:00AM, I'm awakened by the deep rumble of horns and the beating of a base drum. I smile. I somehow feel at home with the musical ritual, but I'm not ready to sacrifice my precious sleep to rise and meditate. I listen and fall back to sleep.

Later, a rooster's crow wakes me, and I yank off the cozy woolen blanket exposing my body to the morning chill. Having no warm water, I take a quick sponge bath. Out my window and two stories below, locals line up at a pair of open air showers, which are no more than open pipes spouting a stream of gurgling water. They quickly wash in the frigid water, wearing only underwear.

For the next two days, I do nothing more than sit listening to and watching the people encircle the stupa. It's a spiritually charged environment. There's no flat-screen TVs, neon lights, billboards, or clever marketing ploys. No cars or other vehicles are permitted here. I feel a reprieve from commercialism, which enables me to shift my focus inward.

On the bench next to me, an aging woman uses her wooden cane to scratch the back of a small cow lying at her feet. The cow's eyes are closed in delight. I have an urge to hug this woman.

The alley at my guesthouse is home to a few beggars. I face the reality of poverty . . . and decide to act. A woman pleads with me to buy milk for her baby as a passerby shakes his head indicating—I think—that the woman is a farce. But I'd rather be deceived by someone not in need than ignore someone who's truly needy, so I buy infant formula from a nearby shop and hand it to her. The mother seems grateful and invites me to visit her house for tea. My intuition tells me *no*, so I refuse, but she's insistent. I politely refuse and walk away.

"No you good. No good!" she yells as I leave. I'm saddened. Was this a cultural misunderstanding?

The next day I come upon two nine-year-old boys, with pleading eyes and extended hands. I'm not about to hand money to children, but I have an idea.

"Okay. You want money?"

"Yes, yes!" they exclaim with delight, hands open and ready.

"You work. I give you money. Come with me." I lead the way to an alley littered with trash. "You pick up garbage. Make clean. I come back one hour. If clean, I give thirty rupees each." I assign one boy to each side.

They're disappointed that there's no free handout, but seem motivated to earn the cash. As I leave, I look back to see them busy working.

An hour later I find the alley much cleaner.

"Good. Very good, I like," I say. They smile with pride as I pay them, adding a tip. They clasp their palms and bow. "Namaste," they say, and run off in glee.

Two days slip by as if I were immersed in a great movie. Sam and I share a few meals. I ask about the mantra I often hear recited around the stupa.

"You mean '*Om Mani Padme Hum*?" he asks.

"What does it mean?"

"It's an ancient mantra that originated from Chenrezig, the bodhisattva of compassion," Sam says. "To some it describes virtues; to others it implies states of purification. Some people think it communicates truth about different realms of existence. Many believe that the effects of reciting the mantra lie in the sound and extend beyond meaning and interpretation. You'll hear '*Om Mani Padme Hum*' everywhere," Sam says. "I recite it often. My rinpoche instructs me to do so."

This environment and the people's devotion inspire me to develop a meditation routine. Several times a day I return to my room for half-hour sessions, but the foreign sounds and sights swirl turbulently in my mind forcing me to revert to counting my breaths like I did when I first started meditating: count each inhalation starting with the number *one* and start over when I reach *ten*. I had stopped using the method years ago but now I need it again—as a beginner in a new land.

It helps to be in the midst of people committed to studying the mind. This is sangha, the community practicing together here at the stupa in Boudhanath, Kathmandu. I've made the transition from tourist in India to practitioner in Nepal.

It's a sun-baked noontime when I leave for Kopan Monastery. As I hike, the dense groupings of gray, stone buildings in Boudhanath thin out, and become fields of rice. Women work the fields with sickles as men steer large oxen from behind a wooden plow. This is a land of contrasts: cell phones are used alongside centuries-old farming methods.

Along the way, I see a family of four sitting in their dirt yard around a stone altar. They're offering a daily ritual of flowers and water. Devotion—the practice of honoring—is everywhere.

The quiet, narrow road drops into a valley and I glimpse the monastery on top of a small—in comparison—mountain. The broad rectangular structure, pale yellow with deep red trim, is surrounded by trees and bamboo stands. This will be my home for the next month. I'm a long-time Zen practitioner but know little about Tibetan Buddhism. I've read some of the Dalai Lama's writings, I've even seen him speak. Impressed, I'm here to understand this tradition in greater depth.

I sweat profusely as I climb the steep trail. Two ten-year-old boys approach me and insist on carrying my duffel bag. When I arrive at the monastery somewhat spent, I offer them a tip, but they decline.

"No sir. Happy to help," they say smiling.

Surprised and impressed, I bow.

I'm a day early to settle in and get oriented. The office attendant, a monk in his twenties, wears the traditional maroon robes and a bright, spirited smile. "Is it raining outside?" he smirks, eyeing my sweat-soaked cotton shirt.

"Yes, it's raining badly," I join in. He smiles.

With some scribbling in his registry book, I'm given course materials and linens. A teenage monk escorts me to a four-person dorm room where I'm surprised to find one man already settled. He stands attentive as I enter.

"Hi, my name is Thinj," he says pronouncing his name as 'Thine.' "I guess we're roomies, eh?" He speaks with a thick European accent. His muscular tattooed arms bulge out of a tight tank top. He has a twelve o'clock shadow on his face and a shaved head. He's thirty-something and looks intimidating. He's a yoga instructor, fresh out of the military and on his way to Thailand to learn more yoga.

"I stumbled upon this Buddhist course and it grabbed my interest," he says. "I don't know about Buddhism except that it involves meditation and since yoga is also about mind I figured I should try."

Thinj looks tough but he's gentle and honest. He offers to teach me yoga during breaks, which I'm thrilled to accept.

Over the next two days, my other two roommates arrive. John is a lawyer from California, and Drew is a young man from Iowa City. Drew reminds me of my son, Matt. Close in age, they're both reserved and good-hearted. Drew took a courageous financial and spiritual risk to journey from his quiet Iowa hometown to Nepal to explore Buddhism.

The monastery has the ambience one would expect from being perched on a mountain peak overlooking the countryside of Tibetan Buddhists. I'm treated to a 360-degree view of snow-capped mountains in the distance and rice fields below. The whisper of the wind is as persistent as the call of eagles gliding overhead. Young monks chant in their classrooms while ceremonial trumpeters and percussionists practice.

Wandering the grounds, I find a spot tucked at the end of a narrow pathway. It's a flat, manicured, circular lawn at the peak of the mountain, strikingly similar to a putting green. It offers a nearly unobstructed view of the city and countryside—a perfect meditation spot. I sit on the soft grass and concentrate on my mind for a half-hour. I feel relaxed and content, and I'm able to concentrate well, the first stable meditation I've had since leaving home.

I think this cozy 'putting green' will be my go-to destination when time permits.

I'm fascinated to watch the daily activities of resident monks. By day, monks of all ages scurry between their duties, their

Monks in evening ceremony at Kopan monastery
Kathmandu, Nepal

classes, and their practice. At night, the faintly lit compound is dotted with young Tibetan monks sitting cross-legged on the cobblestone walk around a glowing candle. They rock fore and aft reciting chants in the deepest octave they can muster which echoes off the concrete walls.

At dinner the second night, I see a familiar face. It's Jeffrey whom I met my first day in Delhi. We spent a day together touring and getting acclimated to the culture. This time Jeffrey suggests another adventure.

"I'm going to a monastery tomorrow morning, about a one-hour walk, where a nine-year-old boy will be enthroned as a reincarnation of a deceased lama. Since the course doesn't start until later tomorrow, would you join me?"

"An enthronement!" I gasp. "Of course!"

Early the next morning, we hike through chilly, dense fog to the monastery, intermingling with locals flocking to the event. This enthronement is internationally significant; there's a diverse crowd of formally dressed westerners, renowned lamas, an infinite number of maroon-robed monks all mixed with casually dressed locals. The place buzzes with excitement as flashy new SUVs and Mercedes Benz limousines arrive with dignitaries.

Twenty monks assemble next to the entrance. Each monk plays a monotone note on a trumpet or horn. Other monks strike odd-shaped drums using arched sticks. On the temple roof, two monks blow into a pair of ten-foot-long brass and silver trumpets, called Dungchens, while drums and cymbals clash with increasing tempo.

We're directed to a large colorful tent with folding chairs and a video screen. The procession begins outside with the young boy seated upon an elaborate golden throne resting on poles carried by monks. Once inside the monastery, the boy sits on an oversized golden throne, fully aware that he's the center of attention.

For the next hour, the boy sits with impressive calmness while a series of lamas, monks, and officials give dharma talks in Tibetan. A procession then forms to place gifts at the throne: polished conch shells, Buddha sculptures, books, flowers, and a small mountain of incense.

Finally, the head lama begins an hour-long session of deep, monotone chanting and the temple reverberates. The grandeur and pomp of this ceremony rivals those in the English monarchy.

Hiking back to Kopan, Jeffrey says, "That boy will have his own personal teachers and great effort will be put to transferring knowledge from the best teachers of our day. What is really great about it is that he will readily absorb his teachings since he *is* a reincarnated lama. He will quickly pick up where he left off in his last life."

> **Author's Course Notes:**
>
> **"We can only experience someone as an enemy if our mind causes them to be in that category."**
>
> **—Venerable Dondrub**

"Do you really believe he's a reincarnation of a lama?" I ask.

"Certainly! That boy was selected from many children. He was put through numerous tests to discern if he is a reincarnated lama. Typically the children will be asked to pick out personal belongings from their previous life. Often the examiners will lay out a half-dozen different eye glasses and the child will pick out the correct pair. The Dalai Lama, when only a little toddler, picked out his correct eyeglasses and walking cane from a large assortment. Even at Kopan there was a young reincarnated lama who led examiners to his previous room at the monastery. There are many accounts that substantiate this. Yes, I do believe," Jeffrey says.

As the course begins, there's more than two hundred attendees—westerners of all ages and walks of life. Venerable Dondrub is seated at a colorful altar of sorts, and participants sit on the floor on meditation cushions. Some of Ven. Dondrub's material grabs my attention like a magnet. Sometimes, though, discussions on ritual and religious aspects of the tradition leave me struggling to keep my eyes open.

A 5:30AM bell rings and I jump from my sleeping bag and sprint across the hall for a shivering cold shower. Each day is filled with three hours of teaching, brief sessions of guided meditation, discussion groups, and an optional, early morning session of one hundred prostrations.

We learn the fundamental principles of Tibetan Buddhism: the concepts of impermanence, loving compassion, respect for your teachers, death and rebirth, and karma. Of the four traditions of Tibetan Buddhists: Gelugpa, Kagyupa, Nyingmapa, and Sakyapa, Kopan is of the Gelugpa tradition, which is widely known for its analytical approach. Sam, the English Buddhist I met in Boudhanath, told me that Gelugpa should blend well with engineering. He was right. The teachings are analytical and detailed.

We spend several days discussing reincarnation, a concept I've not yet come to accept. But reincarnation has a profound impact on Buddhist perspective because, when viewing life in the context of infinite lifetimes, one acquires a more sensitive outlook not just to other humans, but to all creatures. Tibetan Buddhists

> **"The amount of calm at the time of our death has an important impact on the quality of our rebirth."**

Venerable Dondrub,
Course Teacher at Kopan Monastery
Kathmandu, Nepal

believe that having been reincarnated an infinite number of times, each person, each animal in fact, was at one time or another, our mother and we must therefore treat all beings with love. And since accumulating bad karma could result in an animal form of rebirth, we come to appreciate how extraordinarily rare and precious it is to be born human. I'm gaining a richer appreciation for each breath of life.

"Our lives have no guarantees," says Venerable Dondrub, an Australian-born monk, the course leader. "Most of us can easily say 'I'll die someday,' but it's really quite different to say 'I'm prepared to die at this moment'."

Quite a struggle —is more like it. "Our life is hanging by a silk thread," he goes on. "The thread of life can snap at any instant: a bomb, earthquake, heart attack, or accident." I feel the significance settling in. If I live every day, every moment in fact, as if death were imminent—as if my heart were to fail this instant—would I act with greater intention?

> "Things do not appear to exist as dependently arising—they mistakenly appear to 'truly exist.'"

Tibetan Buddhists are sometimes criticized for their focus on death—of taking such a negative perspective. I don't see it that way. Why put blinders on? "But what that focus does," Jeffrey says at dinner, "is drive home true realization of our mortality and expose the uncertainty of the time of our death. We then execute our daily actions with greater precision."

Okay, so I'm *not* facing the reality of death with the sense of urgency that it deserves. Not in the way that I'd face it should a physician tell me, "This scan shows a large tumor on your brain." The subject feels uncomfortable to me but I recognize the value of focusing on it.

Jeffrey challenges me to meditate on death. "Dedicated monks will spend a years meditating on it," he says. He suggests that I visualize my last moments, my last thoughts, and my last breath. "This helps us be more prepared when that last breath arrives."

Somehow the whole subject feels taboo. Our society hides death behind closed doors. Other than attending a few wakes, I have to admit I've had little direct exposure.

"Go to Pashupatinath," Jeffrey says. "It's a Hindu temple of the Lord Shiva located on the banks of the Bagmati River, a forty-five minute walk from Boudhanath. Every day Hindu bodies are cremated at the edge of the holy Bagmati River. Go to Pashupatinath, sit there, watch bodies turn into ashes, and visualize your body being cremated."

Well that's pretty darn morbid! I think. But, I add it to a "must-do" list when I finish the course.

> "In general, the way one lives, is exemplified in the way one dies."

Back at Kopan, hundreds of monks often circumambulate a much smaller stupa holding 'Mala' beads, spinning prayer wheels, or chanting a mantra. Once I saw a nun circumambulating the stupa holding a cage with a white rabbit! Most unique are evenings when a hundred monks gather in pairs in a courtyard where they practice 'debate.' One monk out of the pair stands, the other sits. The monk standing has to convince or challenge the monk sitting about a Buddhist doctrine arguing loudly and dramatically. He loudly slaps his hand to emphasize his position. Then the pair switch places. The courtyard takes on the sound of a riotous crowd.

> "Our mind is our one tool to perceive sight, sound, smell, taste, touch, to think, to use intellect and most importantly to give conscious awareness of self. Based on all this, should we not find it critically important to develop the mind to its fullest?"

Each day, I escape to the 'putting green' for meditation. Always mosquito-free and with a 70°F breeze, I sit with my eyes slightly opened, watching my shadow creep across the grass as the sun sweeps the sky. I'm frustrated with my faltering concentration, but the frustration is tempered by the pleasant tropical environment. Butterflies flit by in

> **"Meditation is like a war against your attachments and delusions."**

a delicate dance while cackling birds seem to cheer me on.

This course is demanding! We're busy from the 5:30a.m. bell until 9 p.m. seven days a week. Yet I volunteer to teach English twice a week to three teenage monks. I use a conversational approach and the sessions become rich cultural exchanges.

Monks on Kopan Monastery mountain rooftop
Kathmandu, Nepal

"What is your favorite activity?" I ask Dashi, a fifteen-year-old monk with an incessantly bright smile and sparkling eyes.

"Dharma me like read," he answers.

I smile. "I like to read Dharma," I correct.

He smiles and nods his head *yes*.

"No, please repeat," I say smiling. "Say 'I like to read Dharma'."

He repeats correctly while his friends chuckle.

Seventeen-year-old Drukpa is next. "What's your favorite subject?"

"I like study a debate," he says, struggling.

"I like **to** study debate,' is correct English, Drukpa."

By counseling while conversing, their skills are advanced while we also learn about each other. They take turns questioning me about my lifestyle and beliefs.

They each joined the monastery at five years old; they see their parents a few times a year. Each of them is remarkably well-balanced with a great sense of humor and a miniscule ego. They accept my corrections eagerly, chuckling over their own mistakes.

The close nurturing given by teachers and senior monks seems to have made them content and happy. Conspicuously missing are material goods. These teens have no phones, computers, televisions, or electronic games. They do not seem to desire any. What they genuinely crave is Dharma teachings.

"Drukpa, what do you want to be in ten years?" I ask.

"Geshe."

"Say it in a full sentence, please."

"I want to be a Geshe."

"What is a Geshe?"

"Geshe is high degree in Buddhism. It is like doctor degree. I'll be Geshe in ten years."

The other two answer much the same. They've a genuine yearning to reach their highest potential in Buddhism.

My roommates and I have stimulating discussions every evening.

"Why do we turn great teachings into religions?" Thinj complains. "The Buddha was a great teacher of mastering the mind. But man has added deities, bowing, dogma, chanting, and blazing colors to his teachings. Same for Jesus. His teachings are sensible, and easy to understand. Why does man then embed layers of rules and regulations?"

Before anyone can respond he continues, "And this karma thing is too complex. Why focus on clearing bad karma from previous lives and creating good karma for future lives? I say we should focus on this life—now. I don't know about my next life or even if there will be one. But I do know about this life, here and now. I think it's much simpler to 'Do unto others as you wish them to do unto you.'"

"Thinj," I say, "I understand. But what if reincarnation is reality? What if your next life is impacted by what you do in this life? Doesn't it make sense to prepare?"

"Sure, I'll prepare but for a different reason," Thinj says. "I believe in goodness, I believe in being good here and now, for this life."

> **"Anger is almost always associated with an attachment."**

"It sounds like it makes no difference whether you believe in reincarnation or not," Drew interjects. "Your behavior's the same. You say you'll perform good actions for the benefits of this life. The Buddhists say to do the same but for the benefit of your next life. It's the same action, just different intentions."

John joins in. "It's the same action, but you take it more seriously if you believe you'll be reborn into a lower life if you have bad karma." John's a quiet guy and a deep thinker. He's the type of guy you listen to because you know his words have been well-thought-out. "With the potential consequence of being reborn as, say a dog, a whole different focus is placed on this life and the good or bad karma we create. I think we take our actions much more seriously if we believe karma affects our next rebirth."

> **"Be harmonious—if you are not harmonious then no spiritual progress can be made."**

Thinj is not convinced. "This sounds too much like Catholic guilt," he says. "'If you misbehave you're going to hell!' I was raised that way and don't believe it. Why don't we just focus on what we're doing now?"

"I was raised Catholic and know what you mean, Thinj," I say. Karma raises similar guilt feelings."

"Same here," says Drew. "I rebelled when I reached an independent age. That drove me to look at other religions and find Buddhism."

John is quietly engaged. "We must be careful not to meld past experiences into the current issue or let our upbringing influence us. Otherwise, we can misjudge any Buddhist teaching that puts consequences on our actions saying it sounds like imposed guilt. I also had a Catholic upbringing, but I must not let that influence every decision."

"I'm not doing that," Thinj says, getting defensive. "I'm just saying it sounds similar and wrong."

A thoughtful silence descends as we lie in our bunks. I relish the way the four of us interact. The tempo is sometimes rapid, perhaps even heated, but we respect one another and anger plays no significant role. No dominant ego steers the discussion. Thinj is open, honest, and uninhibited; he speaks his mind clearly yet respectfully. Drew gives a more humble perspective, with a touch of idealism. John has almost a priestly quality, filled with faith; he is deeply intellectual. I may be learning as much snuggled in my sleeping bag each evening, as I do from the course itself.

Our conversation is especially lively on the last night.

"I'm going to study Zen," says Thinj, sounding frustrated. "Zen is so simple. I don't need all this religion stuff. For me Tibetan Buddhism has too much ritual and superstition."

"It sounds like you won't come to Kopan again," says John.

"No sireee," Thinj responds. "Take today! Five hours of bowing, chanting, visualizations, and all that. It's not for me."

> "The five senses are a problem because we label pleasurable sensory perception as 'happiness.' Pleasure is not happiness."

"Zen is simpler, Thinj," I agree. "But you'll still be exposed to bowing and chanting. Try Zen if you want to question your perspective of self, but don't expect there to be no rituals."

"I know," Thinj says. "Zen's focus on the mind will help with my yoga. I'm going to open a yoga school. Maybe I'll include some Zen."

In addition to Venerable Dondrub's talk on death, the one thing he said that I hope to always carry with me is that as we come to appreciate how

Lama Zopa Rinpoche,
Spiritual Director of Kopan Monastery
Kathmandu, Nepal

everything is interconnected, we'll come to respect, care and have compassion for all beings. That sounds like a formula for having a profound impact on everything I do.

The course ends and I bid farewell to my roommates, the monks, and Jeffrey. I'll miss them all. Thinj will take yoga training in Thailand. John's taking another course at Kopan. I'm heading up the Himalayas, and Drew's going to tour Nepal then head home. I'll also miss Venerable Dondrub, the course instructor. My notebook is scribbled with pages of profound quotes that I'll continue to contemplate. I've grown to respect him. I've learned fundamental Buddhist principles that will help me progress in understanding of *self*. The course has challenged me to view my existence from different angles. I've laid a new foundation from which I can construct a fresh perspective on life. I have new tools to help me deal with life's challenges. I've strengthened my ability to evaluate situations from a more selfless perspective. More than ever, I realize the importance of living from integrity.

Next, I'll travel to Lawudo Gompa, a monastery high in the Himalaya mountains where I plan to immerse myself in contemplative solitude.

But first, I'll keep an appointment. Tomorrow, I'll visit Pashupatinath to face what I have not faced for fifty-three years. I think of it as a date with death.

Chapter 6

A Date with Death

Pashupatinath, Kathmandu, Nepal

Even if we accept that we will die, most do not accept that it could in fact be in the next moment.
—Venerable Dondrub

It's 4:00AM when the mystical sound of trumpets awakens me in my Boudhanath guesthouse. I feel a fleeting desire to rise and meditate, but shun the monastic routine, roll over, and let the sun awaken me an embarrassing four hours later. I find my way through a still-foggy alley to a chilly open-air café where local men munch warm grub. I mentally prepare to meet death as I sip a hot chai and devour spicy potatoes.

Pashupatinath is an hour's walk through rural villages. On my way, I pass a community water spigot with villagers brushing their teeth, washing clothes in buckets and showering in their clothes. It's a social gathering spot for the neighborhood, almost like a coffee shop, where people work, lounge, and socialize.

Pashupatinath is a large park surrounded by a tall, wrought iron fence. There's a wooded hill in the center but it's the ancient temple and the holy Bagmati River that lure the devoted.

Along the grey, stone walkway, numerous stone pillars are shaped like pagodas and Hindu deities including the elephant-headed Ganesh. It's a cemetery-like ambience. Two Sadhus—ascetic yoga practitioners—observe me from where they sit on bare stone. They have long snarly beards, tightly braided hair, and a single saffron garment wrapped below their waist. Their faces and bodies are painted white, yellow, and orange, and the white paint around their eyes has the effect of an overpowering stare. One Sadhu peers at me and I quiver. He looks scary. Yet I know that his aim, like mine, is spiritual enlightenment.

The holy Bagmati River reveals itself at the base of a hill. The slow, creeping river is barely one-hundred-feet wide. It's the dry season, so it is shallow with islands of weeds. A plume of smoke rises from the opposite bank. I know from where it comes.

An arched stone walkway spans the olive green water. A ghat—a series of steps leading down to the river—hugs the river's side. From the ghat, three young children push a small, wooden plank topped with marigolds into the water. They jump excitedly as their modest ship carries their prayers to their god.

The color grey dominates the walkways, buildings, ghats, walls, shrines, and even men's clothing. The river itself is lifeless and drab. The only color in this scene is the brilliant saris worn by Hindu women. A small group of people stand at the river's edge scrubbing clothes and washing dishes. A few women sit on the last step, leaning their heads into the river, shampooing their hair. A young family with two small children enjoys a snack in the morning sun.

And there it is! Across the river are seven brick and mortar platforms, ten feet above the river's edge where human bodies transform into dust. Two of the platforms have active pyres flaring with intense blazes, while columns of grey smoke rise upward. Family members congregate about the inferno. There my date waits.

Crossing the river, I make my way down the narrow walkway that runs beside each platform. It's lined with wooden benches for grieving families. Ten or so family members are gathered at each of the burning pyres.

I'm careful not to gawk or be disruptive. I only seek to expose myself to the raw reality of death and to let it sink in deeply. Will I be able to encounter my own death here? I've only known my body as dynamic and

Cremations at the Pashupatinath pyres on the Bagmati River near Kathmandu, Nepal

full of life, so it's difficult to imagine it lifeless. I'm here to capture the reality that one day my body will be stiff and lifeless. I'm coming face-to-face with a stiff and lifeless body. How else can I realize that my destiny is ashes than to feel the heat and hear the sounds of a body as it transitions to ash? I've expressed to my family my wish to be cremated—so here I am at my future.

I take a seat twenty feet from the blazes, inconspicuous from the grieving family. The pyre to my left has two layers of logs stacked in a body-size shape, and has been burning a while; the flames are four feet high and the core is intensely hot. Loud crackles and pops come from the center, sending streams of sparks upward and even outward. The inferno raises beads of sweat on my face and I slide a bit farther down the bench. The body is well consumed and indistinguishable. Yet, two calves and bare feet protrude, untouched by the flames. They look unsupported and I'm concerned that they'll soon topple off the pyre. The family grieves as the body vaporizes.

A male attendant wears grey pants rolled up to his knees and a faded blue, collared shirt; his feet are bare. He uses a five-foot bamboo pole as his only tool as he silently alternates between conflagrations. The body is nearly half consumed when the attendant notices the legs sticking beyond the flames. Using his bamboo pole, he jabs the sole of one foot in an attempt to push it into the glowing embers but the bone snags on something and won't go in. With the pole still jabbed into the foot, he flips the calf and foot upward and over, breaking the brittle knee joint. I hear a crunch. The foot and lower leg land in the hottest part of the fire. He does the same with the other foot but the knee bone disconnects and the lower leg rolls to the side nearly falling into the river below. Awkwardly, he manipulates the pole to finally get the lower stump into the inferno.

This is a blow to my senses. Ripping a human limb from a charred joint, like a cooked turkey leg from its carcass? That goes against what I consider proper treatment of a body. It's a sensual experience, though—I watch the body turning to ash, hear the joint cracking, and smell the flesh burning. So my body is an assemblage of components. My body is not me—that's what I'm thinking. That limb that almost fell into the river is not that person who has died. The limb is simply a nonfunctional body component that has expired. It's so easy to confuse the limb with a person. If our leg is sore in life, we are sore. This experience jars my perception of *self*.

The family watches the attendant manipulate the extremity into the fire. They appear unmoved as the attendant twists, shoves, and manipulates body parts within the inferno. Are they impacted as much as I am? Does their culture place a different significance on a corpse, which would make the experience we view together less shocking?

I visualize my body in that pyre. I allow the sights, sounds, and smells to anchor the reality of my body's impermanence. *That's me and this is my destiny,* I tell myself. *Let it sink in.* If it does, I hope it will affect the way I live—aware of my unavoidable destiny so that I might not waste a moment of life.

The cremation to my right has been recently ignited and the flames are weak but growing. An elderly female body rests atop three carefully stacked layers of logs, with straw loosely tucked into gaps to accelerate the flames. Logs have been placed around, but not on top of the body. The flames spread onto a sheet draped over her and to a layer of straw spread on top. Two middle-aged men, dazed, hover near the flame peering in. A half-dozen people sit on the bench a few feet away.

The fire becomes intense, the body blackens. From the inferno come loud sizzling and crackling sounds. The family appears resigned as they watch the body they've known in living form transition to nothing. Then the old woman's hand swings free from her side and limply dangles over the edge of the pyre. The family doesn't react as the attendant manipulates it securely into the flames with a strategically placed log.

Farther to my right, a battered pickup truck maneuvers to a platform where a man is already stacking logs. Two men in their early twenties hop from the truck and lift from the open truck bed a wooden stretcher carrying a linen covered body. They place the stretcher on the ground. Casually and without fuss, they lift the small body by the ankles and shoulders and place it on the gravelly concrete walkway next to a puddle from hosing down the last cremation. Without discussion they return to the truck and drive away, leaving the unattended body on the dirty walkway.

I'm uncomfortable with their treatment of the corpse. My cultural tradition typically clothes the corpse with the finest garments and uses a professional's skill to make it look as it did in life. We place it in an expensive casket with comfortable cushions and delicate lining. We keep the body clean and elevated from the ground. We rarely touch the body, but if we do, we do so gently.

This cultural tradition is opposite. Here, they seem to be saying—through their actions—that the body is not the person and of no real account. The person is gone and the body is just something that must be dealt with.

Several family members appear and walk to the small body on the walkway. They pull back the linen and I see a young boy about ten-years old. He has a severe trauma wound to his upper left temple. His face has color and his body is pink and flexible. The still-liquid blood glistens red. He died very recently.

Only a few hours ago this boy was playing, learning, loving, and full of hope. Now, his body lies in the dirt, drying up, and getting cold as preparations are made to burn it. How quickly and unexpectedly life can end! This could easily be my fate in a few hours. Sad as it is, here is a real life demonstration of Venerable Dondrub's teaching at Kopan: "Your life is hanging by a thin thread that can be broken at any moment." That is the truth in front of me—a young boy whose thread *was* broken in an instant when nobody—not he, not his family—expected it. Suddenly, unpredictably, and violently. I let it sink in.

The pyre is completed and two youths, perhaps his older brothers, lift and carry the cadaver ceremoniously three times clockwise around the pyre before placing it atop the wood. The attendant dips a small metal container down in the river and scoops some holy river water. He carries the container of water to the young boy's corpse and, as a ritual, sprinkles the head and body.

A woman weeps; I assume she's the boy's mother. Where's the boy's father? Where are his aunts and uncles, his friends and friends of the family? Will the father come home tonight to find that not only is his boy dead, but his body no longer exists? I wonder what my children are doing right now. How would I feel should I return home to such horror?

The ceremony is short. The mother sprinkles marigold buds on the boy's face. The brothers place bags of rice as an offering. The mother and brothers pace three times clockwise around the body and then step back as the attendant stuffs more straw at the base and over the top of the body and triggers the flame with a match. The mother staggers backward and bursts into tears as the brothers stand stunned.

Over to my left, the inferno of the first body is now only a few glowing embers and a pile of ashes. Several bags of rice and a handful of oranges left as offerings still remain at the platform base. The family huddles as the attendant sweeps the hot ashes into the river. Returned to nature. Finished. Gone.

From the other side of the river, two boys about ten-years-old wade across to the freshly deposited pile of ash probing for remnants of jewelry or metal they could sell. Simultaneously, a half-dozen, chubby monkeys jump from a nearby building and scurry onto the warm platform to feast on the fruit and rice.

For two hours, I witness the conversion of bodies to gas and ash. At times, I'm only five feet from the crackling sounds and smell of charred tissue. I watch bodies delivered to be burned and their ashes swept into the river. I experience the certainty of my death. I see the conclusion of my body. It all sinks in.

On the hike back to Boudhanath. I'm quiet and solemn. I stop at the monastery from which comes the daily 4:00AM trumpet call. It is near Kopan but I'd like to observe their morning ceremonies, perhaps join them for meditation. At the monastery's entry to the temple I find two monks in their twenties. Their English is poor. I can't get a clear answer when I ask if I can join their early morning ceremonies. But, with hand gestures and simple words, they nod their heads. I interpret this as a *yes*.

I head back to the guesthouse with a heart heavy from my tumultuous date with death. During evening meditation, my mind replays the scene of the attendant breaking the lower leg at the knee joint and flipping it into the hot coals. I don't think I'll ever look at my limbs in the same way. They're not me. Yet to fully come to grips with death will take much more effort. Monks spend years meditating on their own deaths.

The 4:00AM horns interrupt my sleep but this time I'm determined to join the monks at the monastery. I jump off my cot, throw on warm clothes, and head into the dimly lit alley. No one is awake and I can hear the crunch of each footstep on the gravel pathway. My breath leaves stagnant clouds of fog in the chilly air. It's only a short walk, but when I get there the main gate is chained and padlocked. Damn, I didn't expect that.

Off to the side a small, sliding gate swings open with a heavy tug. I feel uncomfortable entering but I've been invited—right? From the temple, horns sound again so I head across the large courtyard toward the temple. No one is in sight but candles at the temple doors provide a dim glow.

Halfway across the long courtyard, I freeze. A large black guard dog moves in the shadows. Has it noticed me? I stand perfectly still and realize my situation. To the black dog—and to any monk here—I'm a tall, white-skinned foreigner strangely prowling in the shadows. Surely, I'd be taken for an intruder.

If the dog sees me, I'll have to race it to the nearest tree, which is in front of the Temple, at the far end of the courtyard, which will surely end with a tightly clamped jaw on my calf. The commotion would fracture the stillness and summon an excited group of monks, none of whom speak English. Things are not in my favor. *What am I doing here?* And, *how do I get out of this situation?*

I stand frozen for several minutes, my heart thumping as I try to control my breath. The dog finally wanders around a corner and I use the opportunity to run quickly to the safety of the temple door. The door is open but no one is around. I enter the temple and wait beside the flickering candles. I'm mindful and awake, but the 'at peace' part is missing.

From the shadows, two monks in maroon robes casually walk toward me but don't yet see me. When one monk does, a startled, confused look crosses his face. The second monk halts, alarmed. I bow to them with my hands clasped and they return a tentative nod. Not knowing what to do, they hesitantly continue their routine taking positions on opposite sides of the door. They glance at me apprehensively then raise to their lips the 'trumpets' I hear each morning. The 'trumpet' is in fact a polished pink Conch shell with a blow hole carved at the center of the spiral tip. The monks raise the shells to their lips and sound another long, drawn-out announcement that reverberates through the area, echoing off the concrete walls, summoning the community to practice. They work hard to draw out a continuous note that seems to last for minutes. Simultaneously, they taper down and stop in a coordinated effort. They turn and reassess me.

"I come to join you for practice," I explain pointing to the temple. "I come yesterday and other monks say okay."

Their eyebrows furrow; one of them shakes his head *no*.

"No what? No you do not understand, or No I do not belong here?"

They look at me concerned, but say nothing. Then one monk moves back into position and the other monk grabs a striker and takes his place next to a large suspended metallic gong. One monk frowns at me and deliberately shakes his head *no*.

Oops. I made a bad call. Perhaps I misinterpreted the signals from the monks yesterday. Maybe this is not an open ceremony. Without a doubt, these monks don't understand a word I'm saying but their frowns tell me I'm out of place.

I step outside and scan the courtyard for the dog. He's not in sight so I nervously head to the gate, prepared to sprint at the sound of a growl. As I cross the courtyard, a single Conch horn sounds along with the rhythmic pulse of the gong.

I open the sliding gate and exit. Safe from the big dog, I stand in the tenebrous alley and soak in the ceremonial sounds that penetrate the morning stillness. For ten minutes I listen to the shuffling of the monk's feet through the courtyard, smell traces of burning incense, feel the brisk air on my face, and the firm, rooted feel of the earth under my feet. Looking at the brilliant stars piercing pinholes in the black sky above, I experience my breath flowing into and out of my lungs as smoothly as a tiny yearling feather falls through the air.

Though I missed an opportunity to practice with a community of Tibetan monks, standing alone in this dark alley, I feel the opposite of alone. Here, now, "I feel one with everything around me."

Chapter 7

Climbing High and Away

Nepal Himalaya near Mount Everest

Don't wish for things to be different. Accepting the way things are without labeling them as good or bad is an important ingredient to happiness.

—Venerable. Dondrub

The eighteen-seat, twin-engine plane departs Kathmandu two hours late after the pasty morning fog finally lifts. With Kathmandu at the plane's tail, the dusty city streets below quickly turn into green, terraced rice paddies that stretch across rolling hills. From up here, they look like an artist's brush strokes encircling the declivitous mountain. How do these mountain people farm these steeped slopes? The plane climbs and levels off on its way to Lukla, a small village deep in the mountains.

The plane shudders from the wind as we fly over a crotch in a ridge. Looking down, I see the wheels uncomfortably close to pine trees nestled on a ridge top. The plane banks hard and begins a sharp descent. From my seat, I look up the main aisle into the open cockpit and wonder if what I overheard at the airport is true: "Lukla is the most dangerous airport in the world. There was a fatal crash just two months ago. Seventeen people were killed!" Will today be my *for real* date with death?

I see the pilot in the cockpit and beyond, through the front window, a steep mountainside—with a small patch of land and a short, tiny runway sandwiched between a rocky drop-off and a steep cliff. There's no option for a second landing attempt. I guess what I overheard was right. It's do or die.

I exhale as the plane touches down with a thump. The wheels grab the paved runway and hard braking brings us to a stop with a sliver of runway to spare. The pilot did it. I sigh, glad to be alive. The plane pulls to the side and our doors fly open to a cool mountain breeze.

Lukla is a tiny village of 250 people. It's tacked onto the side of this, Himalayan mountain at 9,400-feet altitude. A day's hike away is Sagarmatha National Park, a protected region with the highest mountain in the world, Mount Everest. But my destination is Lawudo Gompa—a tiny monastery that clings to a mountainside in an obscure valley a stone's throw from Tibet. I want to experience the unspoiled culture of the Tibetan mountain people and to meditate at Lawudo. It's a three-day hike from here—up a mountain with no roads. I've seen my last bus, taxi, motorcycle, and rickshaw. This tiny airstrip is a link to civilization but I won't see it again until my departing flight, a few weeks from now.

Back home, it's Christmas Eve and children lie in bed dreaming about presents under the tree. In Nepal, it's Christmas day. In this Buddhist land, Christian celebrations are absent.

I yank my backpack and duffel bag from the plane's compartment and wander into the small town. Lukla's main street is a gravel trail dividing a string of two-story stone buildings all trimmed in bright turquoise. Few power lines are visible.

I can see my breath in the cool air but I'm grateful there's no snow. I worry about trekking the high mountains this time of year. Snow is unpredictable and there's a risk of avalanches that would make the trails impassable and isolate me. But time isn't a concern; I can wait out a snowfall—I accept the risk. I've rented a large duffel bag loaded with down-filled garments including a bib pant set, booties, gloves, jacket, and a -20º F sleeping bag. If need be, I'll just hunker-down.

I enter a building with a hand-painted sign: "Sherpa Lodge." With westerners frequently passing through in pursuit of a Mount Everest adventure,

English is prevalent. Inside the lodge, I find a short, robust man in his fifties. I greet him and say, "I'm in need of a porter to help me carry gear."

"Where you go?" he asks.

"To Lawudo Gompa. I have a backpack and duffel bag."

I'm an experienced backpacker having hiked mountains in Utah and Wyoming. A thirst for adventure tempts me to carry my own gear. However, the extra weight of my rented equipment, the risk of severe weather, and the need to acclimate to the high altitude make me cautious.

"I can arrange. Need short time. You wait here, ok?" he says.

I slide an unpadded chair across the wood plank floor "Sure, I can wait."

"Want lunch, sir?" he offers. His wife peers around the corner.

"Please. I need energy for the hike."

He chats with his wife and disappears. Soon she emerges with a steel pan of Dal-Bhat, a staple food of the Sherpa people. It consists of split beans, peas, and lentils in a soup with rice and stir-fried vegetables. As I finish the tasty meal, he returns with a hardy-looking, middle-aged man.

"This is Zhetta. He is Sherpa Porter and carry you luggage to Namche Bazaar." Namche Bazaar is a village halfway between Lukla and Mount Everest. It is the spot where people can acclimate to the altitude.

"His English is okay," the man says about Zhetta. "He spend two or three days help you."

Zhetta wears a winter jacket, a rather nice pair of blue jeans, rugged hiking boots, and a blue baseball cap. His skin is slightly dark; he's only about five-feet tall. I know better than to underestimate his physical abilities. This man could carry me up a steep mountain if need be. I introduce myself extending my hand. His handshake is soft but intentional.

"Hello, me Zhetta. I porter for you. Help you go Namche Bazaar." He speaks softly, smiling slightly. "OK leave right away. I need stop my village nearby. Need tell wife leaving."

We step outside and I grab my backpack leaving the duffel bag for Zhetta. He reacts quickly. "No, no, backpack I carry. Bag I carry also. No problem I carry both," he says.

"It's okay, Zhetta," I say. "I'll carry my backpack for a while and we'll switch back and forth. Okay?"

"Okay, but no problem for me. I carry all."

Zhetta's not used to sharing the load. He's a Sherpa Porter, after all, and he has a reputation to uphold. I'm a backpacker though, and used to hiking with a large load. I'll acclimate to the altitude more quickly with physical exertion. I don't want to hurt his feelings but I only need his help when I'm tired or the trail is steep.

Loaded up, we hike out of town and follow a meager dirt trail carved into the side of a moderately steep slope. The sound of the white water rapids, out-of-sight below, is ferocious. The distant peaks to the North have deep and jagged spires barren of trees. Beyond those lie the greatest peaks in the world; the snowcapped, high, and dangerous Himalayan range centered about the magnificent Mount Everest. At journey's end, I'll be amidst those behemoth beauties.

Zhetta leads the way. Occasionally we pass local foot-traffic. Teenage girls carry large straw baskets filled with grain on their backs. An elderly man in flip-flops leads a pack of mules saddled with burlap bags full of goods. Each mule has a cowbell and the clarity of the bell's ring makes me realize just how quiet it is.

Zhetta stops and chats with two women, both wearing red saris, head-dresses, and sandals. Their voices are so crisp; I'm perceiving sound more vividly. There's no "nuisance" noise here like speeding cars or trucks or flashing lights. People don't hurry about. Am I seeing improvement in my concentration from my meditation practice? Or is it just this mountain environment? I'm not sure.

After hiking twenty minutes, Zhetta stops at a branching trail. "To my village," he says. "We go my home. Give tea. Then leave, cannot stay long. Need get next town before sunset." On the way, Zhetta tells me that he came here for work. "I'm porter and guide. More work by airport," he says. "I guide trekkers and mountain climbers. I guide anywhere. Two months ago, I guide over mountain pass more than 23,000 feet. I carry load that high. No problem."

We approach a village of a dozen stone homes with green, corrugated metal roofs. We stop at a two-story, unpainted wooden house with few windows; it looks like a barn.

"My home," Zhetta says. Then he yells in Nepali.

From loosely swinging wood doors, his wife emerges holding a toddler. "My wife, Ashmi," Zhetta says. She looks downward bashfully.

Ashmi looks fifteen years younger than Zhetta. She is quite attractive despite an absence of makeup or jewelry. Her head tilts with a touch of sadness while they talk in Nepali. I assume he's telling her that he'll be away. She speaks to me and Zhetta translates.

"You like lunch here, Mr. Mark?"

"I just ate. Thank you, but no."

"You sit with us, okay?" Zhetta asks.

"I'd like that."

My Sherpa Porter, Zhetta (center), and his family
Lukla, Nepal

Zhetta leads me across a dirt floor in his home to a stairway that's more like a steep ladder. It's dark and a bit musty. On the second floor, he removes two wood planks that cover a window and the room brightens. The unfinished wood floor is simple and sturdy. The walls are vertical planks with splinters of light seeping through. There's a single bed with layers of blankets spread out as a mattress, and a child's bed beside it. The cooking area is a three-by-three-foot-square slab of baked mud on the floor with a small depression where pods of yak dung are smoldering. This is the first I've seen dried yak dung used as fuel; I'm surprised the smell isn't offensive. It's like a wood campfire. Five cooking pots hang from rusty nails irregularly spaced across the wall and metal bowls and plates are stacked on the mantle. The room is open and free of clutter. Their primary possessions are cooking utensils.

Ashmi pours water from a metal bucket into a blackened teapot and hangs it from a hook over the fire. She pulls out a jar of pre-cooked rice, chops a few vegetables, and mixes them in a pot.

A layer of smoke hovers in the room and seeps out the window. Zhetta's son runs back and forth across the room.

"You go to Lawudo for many days?" Zhetta asks.

"Three or four weeks," I tell him.

"Monastery only? No trekking?"

"No trekking. I'm a Buddhist and I visit the monastery for training. What religion are you?"

"I Sherpa. Of course, I Buddhist."

"All Sherpas are Buddhist?"

"Almost all," he says. "Always been Buddhist. Many Buddhist shrines along the trail. Stupas. You will see."

"Stupas like in Boudhanath?"

"Same like Boudhanath but smaller. People build stupa along trail for safe travel. Often stupa have remains from great lama or monk inside. Also mani carvings on stupa and on stones."

"What is a mani carving?"

"People carve famous mantra into stone. 'Om Mani Padme Hum.' You know this mantra?"

"Yes." I often heard it in Boudhanath and someone said I'd encounter it everywhere.

"It's part of meditation practice," Zhetta says. "People spend lifetime carving mantra into 'mani rocks'—stone tablets, boulders, and stupas. They get great merit."

Climbing High and Away

With a warm smile, Ashmi hands me a glass of chai.

After lunch we head outside. Ashmi has a peaceful way about her. They strike me as a very close couple, contented and unashamed of—what westerners would consider—a substandard lifestyle.

I wonder what it's like to always be 'without.' I look at the glorious scenery, the rushing river below, and the stunning peaks above, and wonder if nature's 'soul food' compensates for the missing comforts. I wonder, just like I did in remote India, what impact having few possessions has on one's outlook. Zhetta and Ashmi have no car to service, no carpet to vacuum, and no furniture to clean. Outwardly, they seem content. I think about my comforts back home and wonder if they're worth the price of stress. Perhaps Lawudo Gompa will yield an answer.

"Namaste," I say, bowing to Ashmi before Zhetta and I hurry off. We've only a few hours before the sun dives behind the mountain peaks.

The terrain is steep and the trail's edge precipitous. I kick a baseball-size rock over the edge and watch it plunge hundreds of feet, kicking loose other rocks in its wild tumble ending in a hard impact into the torrent far below. This trail has been the only mode of travel and trade here for centuries. Zhetta and I are on a main artery that leads to many villages and ultimately Mount Everest.

As Zhetta said, signs of Buddhist practice are everywhere. A white stupa, looking like a smaller version of the one in Boudhanath, is in the center of a tiny village surrounded by those large inscribed boulders—the "mani rocks." Huge boulders, some more than twenty feet around, have the entire surface carved with Tibetan characters painted black on a white background. Hundreds of stone tablets carved with *Om Mani Padme Hum,* line the trail. Each represents someone's meditative labor to discipline the mind and dissipate negative karma.

The quiet settles into my core. The sounds I hear would be unheard in a city: the rushing river below, cow bells on the yaks, distant voices on the trail, even my own footsteps and heavy breathing. I'm hearing simplicity. It speaks to my soul.

A herd of seven yaks approaches, led by two male porters. Zhetta steps off the side of the trail and motions me to do the same. These ferocious-looking beasts struggle by as they carry crushed rock in canvas sacks that swing on their sides. Each breath from their monstrous nostrils releases a foggy cloud into the late afternoon coolness.

"Are yaks dangerous?" I ask Zhetta.

"Not dangerous," he says. "No problem with yak. Only problem if yak very tired, hungry, or hot. Best not go close. Okay?"

"I'll stay far away," I say. He recognizes my fear and smiles.

As we progress, the trail becomes perilously steep and rugged. Tall steps are carved into the face of a boulder and frequent switchbacks zigzag up the declivitous mountain. I sweat from effort and breathe heavily to squeeze oxygen from the thin mountain air.

There are no railings to prevent a deadly fall from the slippery and loose gravel and stones. With fifty pounds on my back, it'd be easy to lose my balance on the carved stone steps tilted and irregular in height, polished smooth from centuries of use. I'm responsible for my safety here so I step with care. A broken bone would mean a painful and lengthy trip being carried by porters to the airport.

Danger makes me more mindful and focused. I once read this: "Walk through life with mindfulness as if you are balancing a bowl of hot oil on your head." I think about it now on this climb. I put it into practice.

Porters pass in both directions hauling loads of vegetables, wood, and clothing. A solitary porter wearing flip-flops struggles downhill with an eight-foot metal column strapped on his back. Other porters carry full hind-quarters of oxen, unwrapped and dripping blood.

"Carry to market for sell," says Zhetta. "Big market tomorrow."

The sun drops behind the mountain peak and the valley fills with shade. A layer of clouds descends on the great peaks and those clouds will soon swallow us too. We approach a tiny village nestled just above the river and this is where we'll stay.

"Zhetta, please choose an inexpensive place," I ask.

He looks surprised. "Okay, I know good place."

Even the best guesthouses are inexpensive to a westerner. But I want to live with the locals and learn the culture. I don't want to be pampered.

"This place here," he says pointing to a two-story wooden house. "Not expensive. Only porters here. It okay?"

"Perfect!"

The lower-level walls are granite block. A crooked door at the trail's edge hangs partly open. The second story walls are vertical wood planks and the roof is loose planks, with large stones holding the planks in place.

Darkness has come and a thick fog has wrapped around the village and filled the valley below. The temperature has been plummeting and the breeze is chilly and clammy. The room has no linen or personal toiletries; it's unheated and already cold. My heavy down sleeping bag should be warm enough. I offer Zhetta my warm liner and lightweight sleeping bag.

The next few weeks, I'll stay in unheated rooms. Wood fuel is precious and supplemented by dried yak dung. People here are acclimated to bitter cold, but I've been pampered with a gas furnace that pumps unlimited warm air. I can feel the heat drain from my body and I wonder if I'll be able to handle constant cold.

Downstairs, Zhetta mingles with the owners and helps prepare dinner while I'm directed to a sitting room. I wander to the kitchen to mingle, but they're uncomfortable and insist I relax in the sitting room. This is a porter's house where they don't normally socialize with my "class"—the people they porter for.

I step outside and enjoy the darkness. Few people are out. The muffled sound of a man chanting *Om Mani Padme Hum* seeps from the open gaps of a nearby home. From up the trail comes the rapid ringing of a cow bell, and I'm startled when a horse in full gallop rounds the corner with a bare-back rider. Horse and rider gallop by with a swoosh and pass into the darkness; the sound of the bell tapers away.

Famished from the arduous hike, I wolf down Dal Bhat and noodle soup. When a second rice serving is offered, I nod but realize too late the rice is limited and it's taken from their portions. Here, they give freely to others even if it means sacrificing a meal. I feel like a glutton.

"Get good rest tonight, Mark," Zhetta says. "Today easy climb.

Tomorrow walk one hour then very big climb. Cross river on cable bridge. Then very steep, many steps. Take much hours."

"Do we need ropes?" I ask.

"No ropes. Sometimes use hands pull up. Very tiring. Namche Bazaar at top. Spend night there."

I'd been advised to spend at least one day in Namche Bazaar because of the dramatic altitude change. I ask Zhetta what he thinks.

"Definitely," he says. "I spend one night and go home but you spend next day." He pauses. "If feel sick in Namche Bazaar must drink lots of water and rest. If not better must come down to here immediately."

"Do people often have to come back down?"

"Yes," Zhetta says. "Cannot tell who. Some no problem, some big problem. Altitude sickness very serious. Can die from. Sometimes carry person back airport."

"Do you ever get altitude sickness?"

"No, I Sherpa. No problem. Sometime go very high. I been 26,000 feet. Sherpa no problem."

I ask how far Lawudo Gompa is from Namche Bazaar.

"Only five hour hiking. Only difficult at end. Must go up mountain. You hire porter help you."

The meal warms my body, but I quickly chill again. The altitude and the strenuous hike claim my energy. The never-ending river melody serenades me to sleep.

A knock on the door awakens me. I glance at the window and see a dawn-lit glow behind the mountain. "Get up now, please," Zhetta says. "Breakfast downstairs. Then go. Long hike."

Again I'm ushered to the sitting room. "I want to eat with you and talk," I say. A few Nepali words are exchanged and there are smiles. It worked. Zhetta directs me to the crowded but cozy kitchen where we eat family style. As I down a bowl of porridge, I watch the community activity. Heavily loaded porters occasionally pause on the trail, open the door, and greet the family while puffs of thick fog roll into the kitchen and across the floor. This tiny village is friendly and intimate.

The strenuous hike offsets the morning chill. The sun is still tucked behind the mountain. Large blackbirds dive in and out of the milky grey fog looking like fish swimming in an aquarium. The scene is surreal and full of life.

It's a long, steep climb from our 8,100-foot elevation to the 10,730-foot Namche Bazaar. It becomes particularly steep at one point and crosses a long rope bridge. The bridge is well-constructed, made of thick wire rope, aluminum floor slats, and metal chain-link sides. Tibetan prayer flags flap from the cable hand rails.

Just before I cross, Zhetta stops me to wait for porters to cross with a load. Emerging from trees on the other side are fourteen heavily loaded donkeys. After hours of climbing, we encounter another rope bridge—this one extraordinarily high across a rugged gorge. *This is no bridge* I chuckle. A bridge goes *over* something. This gorge looks bottomless! The ends of the bridge are fastened to perpendicular, sheer-faced bedrock. Tibetan prayer flags strung across the handrails flap fiercely in the wind as cold grey clouds charge through. Roaring, turbulent whitewater echoes from far below. I'm reluctant to step out, but Zhetta strides forward—and I follow, tentatively, with short, careful strides. I hold onto the swinging rope railings with both hands as the bridge sways with the gusts of wind. I'm afraid I'll get blown off.

I force myself to concentrate on every step. I practice a meditation skill I learned at my hometown Zen temple: pay attention to each footstep, feeling my foot touch the metal slats. I become one with the present moment, fully immersed only in walking. As Craig, my Zen teacher back home has instructed many times: "When you walk, just walk." Or, as I interpret it, be fully applied to whatever I am doing in the moment and keep tight rein on the wild stallion of mind. So crossing that swaying bridge, I just walked.

Here I am, hundreds of feet above rocky whitewater, mountain cliffs on either side of the gorge, and an icy wind swinging the bridge I'm on—and I'm practicing Craig's advice. It's easier here—to just walk—because my life depends on being mindful. But during much of the hike, it's been difficult to keep my mind present, to not let it wrestle with details like where I'll sleep tonight or whether I'll get snowed in.

In this treacherous situation, I also remember something Venerable Dondrub said at Kopan: "Don't wish for things to be different. Accepting the way things are without labeling them as good or bad is an important ingredient to happiness." So on this bridge that feels shaky because I'm shaky, I practice accepting the experience.

As I step onto solid rock on the other side, I feel relief—but it's temporary. I look at the trail and my heart drops. The trail on the other side of the bridge is incredibly steep and traverses the side of the precipice, weaving across carved steps wide enough for only one person. A trip means a freefall to the rocks below. *Don't wish for things to be different* I think. I check that my heavy backpack is tightly strapped to help me maintain balance. Zhetta carries the clumsy duffel bag.

Zhetta is looking at me. "You okay? Need a rest?" he asks, yelling above the wind.

"A couple minutes, okay?" Leaning against a tree with the frigid wind blasting into my face, I question the wisdom of getting into this situation.

I think Zhetta senses my fear. He looks after me carefully as we scale the precipice. I'm glad I brought a pair of trekking poles for balance. I force myself not to look over the edge; I might seize from fear.

Twenty minutes into our climb, I hear the familiar cow bell ringing from above. Sure enough, from around the rocks comes a slow-moving train of six yaks with a pair of porters encouraging them with a "Hohhh" command. I'm amazed. How can a heavily loaded yak come down this steep trail without stumbling to its death?

To let them pass, Zhetta squeezes into a small corner butting up to a pine tree, but my position forces me to stand on a rock overhanging the gorge; if I lose balance, I'll be swallowed by the abyss. I stand only a few inches off the trail and as the yaks pass, I feel their warm bursts of breath on my face. Their horns swing just inches from my body. I remember Zhetta's comment that yaks are "only dangerous when they are tired, hungry, or hot." I don't know about hungry, but they certainly look tired and hot. All it would take would be a small thrust of one head to launch me flying. I don't know if contentment and acceptance apply to this situation, but I've no choice but to wait and let them pass.

After they pass, Zhetta seems a little shaken. He nods, prompting me to proceed. For the next two hours we navigate segments of the mountain that feel appropriate only for professional climbers. Finally, the slope levels, the trail widens, the barren rock transitions to tree and shrub.

Eventually we find ourselves on a gentle peak looking down on the village of Namche Bazaar. The horseshoe-shaped village rests in a mountainside saddle with a flowing stream through the center. About one-hundred buildings, mostly two-story guest houses and shops—are painted white with blue or green trim giving the village distinctive character.

Namche Bazaar Village, Nepal

It's now late afternoon; the sun falls behind the mountain and the temperature takes its predictable plunge. The village appears already bunkered down for the evening. I'm physically exhausted and the thin air makes each step a struggle.

I follow Zhetta to a guesthouse. It's the off season and we're the only guests. My room, at the end of a dark hallway, has three deer carcasses hanging on the wall, drying. Icebox-like temperatures thankfully prevent any odor.

The family prepares noodle soup and we eat perched around a small wood stove with yak dung burning, but the warmth reaches only the first couple of feet. An elderly man sits alone in a cold corner fingering prayer beads and mumbling a mantra.

I awaken to the sight of a magnificent snowy mountain peak glowing orange in the sunrise. I love mountains. My thermometer reads 29º F. I want to meditate but my warm sleeping bag holds me captive. I compromise: I keep my lower body in the sleeping bag and put on my down coat and hood. Not the greatest meditation posture, but I'm able to concentrate for a half-hour.

"You go tomorrow to Lawudo Gompa," Zhetta says at breakfast. "People help find porter. Today I return Ashmi. It long walk but Ashmi need help with children. Okay for you?"

"Sure. Thanks for your help, Zhetta. It was fun hiking with you." He smiles. I've grown fond of this humble and hard-working man. He looked out for me, asked often if I needed rest and always made sure my needs were met before his own.

Now I'll begin a new phase of my journey. I'm on my own now. Once I reach Lawudo Gompa, I'll be in solitude, a meditative retreat I'm looking forward to.

By mid morning I'm feeling weak, and have a pounding headache – symptoms of altitude sickness. I take medication and decide to stay put two days instead of one.

When I feel better the next day, I hike up a mountain to view Mount Everest. I hit the trail early, knowing that view-spoiling clouds will roll in by noon. At the edge of the city is a dusty dirt path with a steep ascent, slightly less strenuous than yesterday's. I carry only a day pack with a drink and snacks. The village below shrinks and the air becomes cooler and breezier. An hour-and-a-half climb and numerous wrong turns bring me to a forested summit. I cross through a pasture and pine grove and arrive at a small guesthouse with a view to the north. And there it is—the magic mountain! Mount Everest, the highest mountain in the world, is the dream peak of every mountain climber. It's magnificent! Clear and cloud free, it stands well above other peaks, the crowned king of the Himalayas. As I watch, a local snowstorm begins to form on its downwind side and within minutes clouds wrap around the peak. I was just in time for the last glimpse of the day.

Sharp, jagged snow-covered peaks are in every direction. The air is so crisp and clear that it seems I can reach across the valley and touch the other side. It's an incredible view and I see an opportunity. I'm on a mountaintop with few people. Why not meditate? I return to the pine grove to search out a spot. As I do, the weather changes. Clouds form from out of nowhere and within minutes a mass of clouds comes charging up the valley, wrapping around the mountaintop. I become engulfed in a breezy, cold, and deep grey cloud. But I'm dressed for it and stick to my plan.

I choose a tuft of grass beside a rhododendron bush, whose leaves are curled from the frigid winter. I sit cross-legged, surrounded by yak dung patties. Pulling my insulated hood over my head, I close my eyes and concentrate on my breathing. I let my mind and body become calm. Thoughts arise but this time I let them fade. I have mental quietude that I haven't experienced for some time. It's not a trance but an absence of mental clamor, making me keenly alert. I pay attention to the sounds around me. The wind kicks up slightly and a fine sleet starts to fall. All I hear are tiny frozen pellets hitting my hood, bushes and rocks. It's a relaxing sound like listening to rain hit the roof while I sit cozily inside.

The thought comes that I could get snowed in. It's a realistic thought. I make an intentional decision to disregard it. I'll take the risk. I sit for thirty minutes as the sleet gets heavier, then lighter, fluctuating in intensity before subsiding. I continue my meditation and let the environment around me change and evolve. I focus on my breathing. The wind is soothing. It's pure stillness-within and without.

Suddenly, a twig snaps—it sounds like a large animal. I open my eyes and see a Nepalese woman collecting dried yak dung patties and placing them in a wicker basket. She glances my way and jumps, startled to see a bundled up Caucasian sitting in the pines among yak patties. To break the awkwardness, I clasp my hands, bow and smile. She returns a nervous smile but hurries away. Now, I realize it's late and getting dark. I rise and head down the mountain.

Clouds—a bright milky white to a deep ominous grey—roll across the landscape. Suddenly, they descend on me and I'm immersed in a dense fog that feels as if I have to push it out of the way to move. It's a long hike back and I feel vulnerable. This is a different side of the slope than I hiked in on. I've a reasonably good idea which direction to go, but as I begin walking, I can't see in the distance, and I can't tell if I'm heading in the right direction. It's desolate and there's no one to ask.

From out of the murkiness, I hear cow bells and a string of yaks emerge led by a lone, middle-aged woman in a traditional black, full length skirt. "Namche Bazaar?" I ask, pointing down the trail. She nods *yes* with the slightest smile.

I enter a pine forest with a maze of Tibetan prayer flags stretched overhead. The forest opens onto a broad plateau where I begin a steep descent that should lead to Namche Bazaar. I come across a man in his early forties, He's leaning against the steep slope. He looks troubled.

"Are you okay?" I ask. He shakes his head *no*. I'm surprised he understood me.

"Hurt," he says, pointing to his stomach.

A small bag of vegetables lies next to him and his thin clothing seems inadequate for the cold. He's rubbing his hands for warmth and his nose is dripping heavily. I assume he's on a return trip from Namche Bazaar to buy vegetables and is heading to the small village a half hour behind me.

"You go?" I say and point toward the village. He nods *yes*.

"Need help? I help you go," I say pointing.

"No help. Rest only. Stomach no good. Many time stomach no good," he explains.

I sit next to him, to keep him company until he gains strength.

"You need doctor?" I ask.

"Doctor already," he tells me. "Me go Lukla doctor. No good. Village doctor better. Tomorrow I go village doctor."

I offer him an energy drink; he accepts and drinks with vigor. I pull out an energy bar, which he also accepts. I take off my gloves and give them to him to help him warm up and I scrounge some tissue paper for his runny nose. We sit conversing as he munches, rests, and gains energy.

"My name Mark," I say.

"I Ngodrup," he replies.

After twenty minutes, he appears to be improving, but he's worried about the time. Finally, he pulls himself up.

"I go family."

"I help you go," I offer again.

"No need. Okay now. I go."

I give him another bottle of water. "You keep," I say, pointing to the gloves and the bottle. He's surprised and a smile breaks across his face. He nods slightly. We bow to each other and he moves on.

Mountain life might be peaceful and simple, but it's hard. With limited access to modern medicine, diagnosing and recovering from illness can take so much longer—if one recovers at all. What is for me a simple task of driving to the local grocery store for vegetables is a laborious trek over the edge of the mountain for Ngodrup. Access and quality medical treatment from doctors are rare. I yearn for such simple living yet it surely has its downsides.

As I continue down the trail, the slope steepens and I worry about slipping on loose scree. It also branches in many directions and I stand there—still deeply immersed in fog—trying to guess which branch is correct. Darkness is settling and, like Ngodrup, I'm worried about time. Walking through clouds is walking blindly but twenty minutes later a hazy glow from Namche Bazaar filters through the cloud cover. I sigh with relief.

After a warm porridge breakfast the following morning, I hike to a small house with a red roof where I'm to meet a porter named Happa. A young woman in her mid-twenties answers. I introduce myself, expecting her father will be my porter. In broken English, she introduces herself as Happa, my porter for the day. I'm embarrassed. This petite woman, about my daughter's age, and only two-thirds my weight, will be carrying my bags. She asks me in and shows me her one-year-old son. She's arranged for a babysitter so she can make money. She wants to leave quickly so she can return by dinner.

The trail heads west into a more remote valley. I'm pleased to find it more level, less rugged, and less traveled than Zhetta's trek. Each small crest we climb and each mountain we round delivers yet another grand view.

The trail is dotted with small stupas adorned with white khata scarves, a symbol of purity. Happa is careful to walk only clockwise around each stupa, following Tibetan tradition, at times climbing over small boulders to do so. Attractive and feminine, Happa is rugged. She hauls my backpack without complaint while barely breaking a sweat. After several hours, she points to a mountain a few miles away. "Monastery there. See up high?"

The mountain is mostly barren of vegetation but two-thirds of the way up—and much higher than we are now—is a patch of pine trees and a couple of small white buildings. That's Lawudo Gompa, my destination. Above the monastery, the terrain turns into jagged rocks with brilliant white peaks.

"Over there trail go up" Happa says. "Very steep hard climb. But no problem. We go slow. Take rest. No problem I carry for you."

An hour later we're climbing what I would call a goat trail. As Happa promised, we stop often so I can catch my breath and dry my sweaty face. With each step, my eagerness and anticipation grow. This is a holy land where sages have mastered their minds over millennia. The beauty is pristine and the solitude extensive. I've explored parts of Asia over the last month; now I'm ready for inner exploration.

Another hour of climbing brings us to the monastery at 12,700 feet. Only the flapping of Tibetan prayer flags breaks the silence. The wind is picking up and clouds embrace the peaks. The trail ends at a wooden gate that leans to one side. A large pair of carved mani boulders are painted white, blue, black, and red.

I'm alive, and I've arrived at Lawudo Gompa.

Chapter 8

A Cave in the Clouds
Nepal Himalaya near Mount Everest

The aim of a Dharma practitioner is not to live a happy life, but rather to live a meaningful life.
Venerable Dondrub

Happa and I walk through the monastery courtyard, past a colorful temple, to a two-story building with red, white, and blue trimmed windows. Happa opens the door and yells in Tibetan; an invitation is hollered back. We follow a dark hallway with a disorganized array of pots and kitchen supplies until we come to a dimly lit kitchen with smoke-stained windows and a worn wooden floor. An open fire burns atop a rock pillar near the center of the room and a suspended layer of smoke tickles my lungs.

At the only table sits Ani Samten. "Ani" means "nun" and is the proper way to address her. She's the only nun here, the sister of a famous lama. Ani is short, slightly stocky, and in her early sixties. She wears traditional maroon Tibetan robes composed of a long skirt, heavy jacket, and a woven head cap. She smiles kindly.

"I'm Mark. I've come for a retreat if you have room."

"Yes, have room," Ani says. "We have small cabin that very quiet." She speaks softly. "But first rest. You want chai?"

Happa nods. "That sounds great!"

Ani Samten instructs a young, petite woman who's tending the stove. "Mark, this is Sangmo," Ani says. "She help monastery."

Sangmo wears lay clothes with a maroon headdress. She has a beautiful smile, eyes that are full of life, and a palpable sense of humility. "Do you live here?" I ask.

"I sleep here most time. Live in valley and go home often," she says.

"Are you studying to be a nun?"

"I study with Ani and Norbu, the head monk. I like to help but not sure about being nun." She smiles

Lawudo Gompa is more of a tiny retreat center than a monastery. A small temple just inside the entrance is ablaze with color. It has an elaborate altar and walls draped with symbolic images. It can hold about thirty people. Like Kopan, Lawudo Gompa practices Tibetan Buddhism and follows the same Gelugpa tradition.

This kitchen serves as a dining room and gathering place. Close by are three small retreat cabins, a barn of sorts, and a small residence house for the monastics. Norbu and Ani Samten are the 'keepers' who tend to duties like gardening and feeding the cows and serve retreatants who venture up this mountain.

Ani walks into the other room. Her body's wobble tells of her pain. She comes back with a small plastic bag, opens it, and extends it. "Here, smell. What you think?" As we sip chai, Ani tells us that Lawudo Gompa is famous for a mixture only she can make for a special incense that is sent to a nunnery in Kathmandu, where they make incense sticks. "Twice a year, I climb mountain," Ani says. "Climb very high and pick special plants, can only pick at right time. My mother show me and only I know. But I get old and my knees hurt climb so high. Still, I do."

Happa rises to go. I pay her and thank her. Then Ani escorts me down a short, steep trail to a stone cabin on a narrow terrace carved into the side of the slope; pine trees wrap around the back and sides. The six-foot walls are painted white and the corrugated metal roof is red. Tibetan prayer flags are strung from the roof to the pine trees.

Inside the cabin is a single but sizable window facing the valley and the majestic, 20,000-foot Mount Kungde. The room is eight-foot square, bright, clean, and thinly carpeted. On a shelf are candles, and a small sculpture of Buddha, draped by a white khata. The bed is a wooden platform with a three-inch foam mattress. In the corner is something I've not seen before—a three-foot square meditation box. The simple box of finished wood has a cushioned bottom and comes with a stack of blankets for warmth. *That'll be my spot*, I think.

There's no electricity and no heater. *I'll deal with the cold*, I think.

"I've come here to meditate, Ani. This secluded cabin is perfect."

Ani smiles. "Toilet around corner. Very close," she adds. "You settle. Dinner at 6:00PM. Come and meet head monk and other two people on retreat." Ani has a kind and relaxed nature. I feel comfortable around her.

As she leaves the cabin, I step out the door to take in the view. The three-foot stretch of grass in front of the cabin ends at a short stone wall. Beyond that is a steep, mile-long slope to a raging river below. I can barely hear or see the river because clouds fill the valley. Jagged snow-covered peaks face me with puffs of clouds scattered about. I'm truly in the clouds. I'm in heaven.

I can barely contain my exhilaration. I unpack before trying out my "box." I put the mindfulness techniques I've read about into practice: I move slowly, giving precise attention to unpacking, feel the book in my hand; my hand's movement when I place the book on the end table. Moving like this is unusual for me. The faster the better is how I operate. But this cabin, this environment, the long climb, have calmed my mind.

I try out the meditation box. The sun's rays have been beaming through the window warming it, so I leave the window cracked slightly. It'll soon be cold so I put on my coat, place a thick blanket on my lap, and assume sitting posture. This peaceful environment has calmed my mind and so when thoughts do surface, I quickly notice them. My breathing is slow and calm and concentration is strong. I think about dinner, catch myself, and come back to my breath. After twenty minutes I begin to feel cold. I begin to shiver. Then the sun sinks behind Mount Kungde and the room instantly chills. I grab some blankets stacked next to the box and arrange them behind me against the cold outside wall. I resume practice but within five minutes I'm shivering again. I grab another blanket, tuck it behind me and resume. Just as I settle my thoughts, the wind kicks up, pushing a frigid breeze into the room. Frustrated, I remove the blankets, get out of the box, and close the window. Meditation ends. I'll have to develop better strategies to handle the cold.

A frozen morning at my mountain retreat cabin
Lawudo Gompa, Nepal

The basic outhouse is a stone's throw from the cabin. The handmade door is constructed of bound wood branches. When the door is closed, it's dark inside, so I leave it open. The walls are loosely constructed stone with a corrugated metal roof. A simple hole is cut in the wooden floor that overhangs the hillside.

A few minutes before dinner, Ani and Sangmo are busy in the kitchen. "Sit, Mark, sit," Ani says when I walk in. "You want chai?"

"Yes please. I'm chilled." I realize it sounds like a complaint.

"Yes," Ani says. "Wintertime cold here. Sometimes get snow. Sometimes deep. Not often. Maybe you see snow." Ani pulls out a thermos, pours a glass of chai and hands it to me. "You like room?"

"Very much," I say. "It's quiet and beautiful." Suddenly I'm hungry. "What are you cooking?"

"Thukpa," Ani says. "A vegetable soup. Have thick noodles. Make noodles myself."

A large, worn kettle sits atop a metal grate on the stone fireplace over a small wood fire that's just hot enough for cooking. As the fire dwindles, Sangmo grabs a dried yak dung patty from a straw basket with her bare hands and feeds the fire. Without washing, she returns to cooking. Her poor hygiene is disturbing but there's limited water for washing one's hands and the cold dry air limits bacterial growth. This is how food has been handled here for centuries.

As I sip my tea, a man enters. "Hello! Hello all. How is everybody?"

"Hi, Arpi. I do fine," says Ani with a smile. "This is Mark. Sit down by Mark, okay?"

Arpi is from Budapest. He's traveled through India and Nepal to study with teachers and to advance his spirituality.

"You and I have similar quests then," I tell him. His deep, dark eyes match his thick black beard. He's unreserved and assertive, his smile broad, and his eyes sparkle. Arpi is six feet tall and looks like a big friendly bear. I presume he's in his mid-twenties

I tell him my story, ending with "I really don't know when I'll be going home." The kitchen door opens again and a younger nun enters, also dressed in maroon robes. She's short and has a gentle smile and a soft walk.

"Ani, this is Mark. This is the man I was telling you about." says Ani Samten. "Mark, this is Ani Dechen. Please sit, dinner ready."

Ani Dechen sits across from me. She's from Singapore and came to Lawudo at the direction of her guru. "I've been spending all my time in my room practicing," she says.

"What type of practice?" I ask.

"My guru instructed me to recite the mantra 'Om Mani Padme Hum' 1.1 million times. When I'm done, I'll go to another monastery and do 100,000 prostrations," she says.

"1.1 million times? How do you keep track?"

"It's quite simple," she says, with a lovely smile. "I know how many I do in one hour. I just keep track of time, it's simple math. I'll finish in two days and then leave."

I can't help from asking the obvious. "Ani, what are the benefits of reciting a mantra so many times?"

"Purification, Mark," she says. She is soft-spoken. "We all have negative karma accumulated from bad deeds and bad intentions. These accumulate from this life and previous lives. If we don't purify bad karma it'll come to fruition in the form of suffering. You might get into an accident, acquire an illness, or die an early death from bad karma. By purifying karma and not creating newer bad karma, we avoid suffering." She studies my face. "Does this make sense?"

I hesitate. "It sounds a bit like saying a rosary to wipe away sins in the Christian tradition, in which I was brought up."

"It's similar," she agrees, "but with karma there's no judge that punishes. Karma is carried with you, even between lives. When you die, only your mind continues and your karma is carried with it."

"I'm sorry," I say. "I didn't mean to dive into . . ."

She smiles. "I enjoy talking about my practice, Mark. It's my life. It makes me happy."

The glow on her face tells me that's true.

Ani Samten dishes out the food. I'm famished. Across the room I notice a small sink with a plastic spigot. The spout is wrapped in plastic. I turn to Ani Samten. "Ani, if your faucet isn't working, I can fix it for you."

"Faucet is working but frozen," she says. "No can use in wintertime."

There are a several large water jugs by the sink. "Where do you get your water?" I ask.

"Sangmo and Norbu carry from nearby spring. But we have problem." She pauses. "Soon spring will dry up. Maybe in two months no more water. After that must go to spring far downhill and carry up. Very difficult. Must do every day from March until June rainy season. Not always like that. Just few years ago spring never dry. Less snow now—that is problem: less snow."

Carrying my backpack up that hill was torture! I can't imagine carrying five gallon jugs of water. "Tomorrow I can help you carry water from the spring," I offer.

"No, no," Ani insists. "You here to practice. No worry about water. Very important to practice."

Once again the door swings open and in walks Norbu, the head monk. He's around Ani's age and just shy of six-feet. His head is shaven. He's serious looking. After speaking with Ani in Tibetan, he turns to me with his hand extended.

"Hallo, Hallo. Welcome be here."

I thank him and bow. He pokes around the kitchen, grabs a bite to eat, and leaves.

I wipe my bowl clean with roti, flat bread similar to Indian naan. Ani walks over, and sits.

"I see you serious about meditation, Mark. Your room is good place for you. Also can use cave nearby. Cave is very holy place. Much energy!" She stretches out her arms. "Before monastery, a famous lama meditated most of his life there. When die, they find his reincarnation in three-year-old boy in valley below. Boy want to go to cave and be lama. When only three-years old, he say that is *his* cave. He become lama. When grow up he build this monastery. Build many monastery. He is my brother."

"I've heard of your famous brother, Ani."

"Yes, so it good for you meditate in cave. Cave have locked door. Key there." I heard about the cave and its framed-in front, but am surprised about the lock. "Use anytime." She looks at me. "Now eat more. Must eat more," she says.

I'm full but I have more roti and then excuse myself. I'm tired. It's dark and much colder as I follow my headlamp beam down to my cabin. It's eerily quiet. I peer into the blackness of the valley. There's cloud cover above and no moon. Only a couple of light dots shine from the valley. I feel alone on this mountain.

As I've said, this is a nearly perfect setting for meditation. There's nothing to attend to so I've little excuse to let my mind wander. I dress in warm gear, organize the blankets, and crawl into my box. My preparations pay off—too much! After fifteen minutes, I'm hot and steamy. I try to unzip my jacket but have to first move blankets and then yank off my gloves. Each move is cumbersome wearing so many clothes. I make adjustments and continue.

I mentally prepare myself for the cold night. I've camped in the snow without a tent in 15° F temperatures. What I've not done is live and meditate for an extended period of time in such a cold climate.

I crawl into my cocoon-style sleeping bag and quickly nod off. I wake several times during the night from the shock of inhaling bitter cold air. Each time I wake, I pull the cord tighter around my face until the opening is barely the size of my mouth. Usually one only needs to wear lightweight clothing in cold weather sleeping bags, but light clothing is not enough here. At 2:00AM I quickly add a wool sweater, heavy pants, and wool socks. That does the trick.

My alarm goes off at six and I peel off the sleeping bag and head to the bathroom. The frigid outside air is perfectly still. The pine trees surrounding me are coated with glistening frost.

The simplicity of the outhouse is appropriate. It brings me into union with this mountain in an elemental way. It's another example of the power of simplicity. My mind is content with being here in the moment. My hands tremble from the cold, but that doesn't matter, at least not right now.

My morning meditation begins with a new routine of finding the right combination of garments and blankets for comfort. The thought of a warm breakfast chai helps me maintain mental clarity.

Mealtimes here are social events. "Ani, do you know that these mountains are still growing in height?" says Arpi. "Someday this monastery will be much higher."

Ani Samten gives him a disturbed look. "No good," she says. "No can live higher. Not enough food, not enough water. Very difficult."

"Oh, but you have a couple of cows you can live off of," Arpi says.

"Cow no good during dry season," Ani says. "Very dry and no grass growing so cow not have milk. And little cow is big problem," Ani says of the monastery calf. "Always worry snow leopard come and get."

"Snow leopard!?" says Ani Dechen, alarmed. "I didn't know there are snow leopards here. Am I safe?"

"No problem. Safe," Ani assures. "Leopard no want people. Want small cow only. Not big cow. Not people."

After breakfast, I grab the key to the cave and tell Ani I'm going there.

A narrow dirt path climbs a rock stairway and ends at the foot of a sheer fifty-foot rock. In the shadows at the base is an ornate, white adobe façade. Four windows have frames painted in blue, red, and yellow. The door is barely four feet high and similarly painted. It looks like the front of a small house built onto the side of a huge rock. But it's the cave. It even looks a bit sacrosanct.

The inside is clean and cared for. It's eight-feet deep; the grey rock ceiling slopes to only two-feet high in the back. The walls and floor are varnished wood. In back, an ornate ledge holds photographs of lamas who've meditated here. In the center is a picture of the Dalai Lama. Numerous silk paintings of the Buddha fill the space. In a corner is a stack of sitting cushions and a tall bundle of blankets. It's slightly warmer in the cave and smells fragrant. It's dry with no draft.

This cave is not the clammy, musty, dirt-floored room I'd pictured. It's comfortable and even more perfect for meditation than my cabin. I feel a powerful energy, the kind of energy I've felt in other places where worshipers have practiced over centuries, such as the ancient Catacombs in Rome and the Wailing Wall in Jerusalem. I light an incense stick and a column of smoke flows straight upward. Placing a soft cushion in the center, I wrap myself in a heavy blanket and begin meditation. The cold is challenging but not overbearing. It's incredibly quiet. Not even a bird's song penetrates this rock. I can almost hear my heart beat.

I sit forty minutes before my knees pound and my mind has wandered twice around the globe. Frustrated, I question myself: *If I can't concentrate in this pristine environment, how will I ever?* I remind myself that a stallion is not trained overnight—and that applies to the stallion of the mind. It takes perseverance and consistent effort.

After breakfast the next morning, Ani Dechen says goodbye. She has completed the 1.1 million recitations of the mantra. I congratulate her.

"I think this mantra is now your mantra for your lifetime, yes?" Arpi says to her.

The facade of the Lawudo Gompa meditation cave, Nepal

"I boil now," she says.

Wood and yak dung for heating are also scarce.

She boils one liter of water and pours it into a thermos.

Standing in the afternoon sun outside my cabin, I wash. Heat from the water is whisked away instantly. Not only is hot water precious, but using it to wash outside is a waste. Swiftly, I finish the job and wipe myself dry. I'm freezing. Fortunately the dry mountain air instantly dries me so I can dress quickly, leaving me shivering but invigorated and refreshed.

I decide to take a short hike after morning meditation. In the box, the sun radiates onto my back, but I still I can't concentrate. My mind keeps hiking up that mountain ahead of me. My make-it-happen nature insists I control my mind and master it—hold it in place. I'm an engineer and I use my mind to solve problems. Yet every time I try to concentrate on a simple task—like observing my breath—my mind soon wanders. My frustration escalates. Though I know it isn't helpful, I yell at myself internally: *If I am my mind, but cannot control it, then who am I?* Who is this mind? What is this mind? Maybe I'm at a disadvantage because I don't have a guru like Arpi and Ani Dechen. Ani Samten and Norbu are certainly highly trained monastics but they're busy running a monastery. I think about Panditarama in Lumbini, Nepal. I've read the teachers meet daily with students. Did I make a mistake in coming here first, without the guidance of a guru or teacher? Maybe I wasn't ready for this kind of solitary practice.

Restless and disappointed in myself, I leave the box. Perhaps the hike will calm my mind. I might as well go since my mind is already climbing. I swing open the front door—and am aghast to see a full-sized, jet-black yak facing me—not even three steps away. He's huge. His dark eyes are about the size of eggs. Each nostril is bigger than my wide-open mouth and the steam from his breath makes him look like he's breathing fire. His enormous head is as big as my torso. His right horn is broken off, leaving only splintered stubs but the left horn is long, curved, pointed—and quite threatening. I jump back, slam the door, latch it tightly, and step aside fearing he'll ram it down. My heart is pounding. I wait listening for movement, but hear none, so I look out the window to see his huge dark eyes glaring back at me. I pace the room and keep looking out the window, but he doesn't move. He remains just outside my door.

I'm safe in my cabin. . . I think. I decide to read, relax, and wait him out. I sit on the bed reading Venerable Vivekananda's meditation book, but I can't help jumping up to see if the beast is still waiting for me. I try to read but every few minutes I check on the monster. He hasn't budged. I begin to think irrationally: Maybe he's not as ferocious as I think. Maybe I can walk past him without being gored. Maybe his ferocious looks are deceiving and he just wants to be petted. I finally settle down and read another twenty minutes. When I look again, he turns and strolls away. I give him a little time to get a safe distance away before I step outside.

Ani told me about a narrow and loosely defined footpath that leads up the mountainside, weaving amidst hip-high bushes. Eventually I cross a precipice with a steep drop at my feet and a remarkable view of the entire Himalaya range.

The sun is high, the morning chill is gone, and a breeze cools my perspiration. There's plenty more mountain to climb but it's not why I'm here. A flat rock on the edge of the bluff calls to me. It's cold, hard, and uncomfortable, but for centuries people made do without cushions. So can I.

Deep blue sky fills between the white jagged peaks and I can see fifty miles in any direction. A mile below is the river valley; a mile above is Mount Kungde. Below me, the monastery looks like a couple of tiny boxes. I feel alone; it's a "good" alone. I feel part of nature, part of this massive scene. Like the eagle soaring above, the grass growing on the slopes, the bug fighting the wind as it tries to land on me, and the very boulder on which I sit—I'm part of this. I feel integral to the whole setting and totally contented. Is this meditation? Feeling at one with everything?

I meditate for about forty-five minutes, but I'm not sure as time seems to tick differently here. My mind still wanders, but instead of focusing on the future, it analyzes my situation: *What kind of bird is that? Is this granite I'm sitting on?* Frustrated again, I become curious about the questioning nature of my mind. Venerable Dondrub said that we always feel the need to label things, but he advised us to let them be as they are.

"It's an illusion to label things," he told us. "Labels are not inherent to the object; a woman might be beautiful to a young man but she's a patient to a doctor and viewed as food to a lion," he said. "Just let things be. There's little need for labels."

Zen teachers call it "non-duality," but I've never quite grasped the concept. My mind wants to label and name the bird, the height of the mountain, the type of rock. I've been taught to label since first grade; applying labels to persons, places, and, things. I want to understand non-duality. Perhaps someday I will, but for now I understand that my mind wants to label. I see that clearly because at the moment it obstructs my meditation.

Late morning clouds are rapidly forming, manifesting, and evolving into being from changing conditions. A puff of haze beside the mountain grows, deepens its hue, and before I know it, a huge grey cloud materializes before my eyes. Before long, much of the valley is cloud-filled like a bowl of creamy soup. On my right, a small grey cloud the size of a tree scuttles up the mountainside as if it were running away from the others below. And to the left a thin sheet of white puff flows down the mountainside as though someone spilled a can of off-white paint.

The dynamic, three-dimensional scene is like watching a movie. Every part is changing with every instant and the whole conglomeration seems like a living being. It reminds me of something Venerable Dondrub spent a few days discussing. He explained "all-encompassing impermanence" as applicable "from the smallest atom to the largest galaxy. Everything is churning, morphing, and evolving," he said. "Nothing stays the same, nothing at all."

The turbulent sound I hear from the river below is the sound of this immense mountain shrinking. It tells the story of change, of boulders being ground into sand, mountains being washed away, carving the valley every moment. It's the sound, quite literally of moving this mountain I'm perched on into the ocean. Yet how illusory is our perspective, for the mountain seems so solid and invincible.

Acknowledging impermanence means accepting change rather than struggling to keep things the same. If I become attached to anyone or anything, I'll suffer, for people and things change. My suffering reduces to the degree I can simply observe change and watch it flow—with acceptance and awareness. I sit on the mountainside, in unity with the mountain range. I think about labeling things, what change is, and about life and death. All the reflecting I'm doing makes me miss that inclement weather is imminent. Suddenly, I'm engulfed in clouds and I've lost sight of the monastery. Fortunately, the way back is a rather straight line down the mountain.

The next few days, I stay on monastery grounds. I spend the most time in the cave mediating where I sense the presence of previous meditators. I'm able to sit longer but there's little improvement in my concentration. I start skipping lunch because I'm tired from too much food. With less food, my meditation improves. But I have Ani Samten and Sangmo to contend with.

"You come lunch this time, okay?" Sangmo says after breakfast. "No good for you not eat. You come."

"I love your cooking. I really do," I say. "Please understand. I meditate better with less food."

The delicious food is part of the problem. My favorite, Sherpa stew, is a hearty combination of thick noodles, peas, carrots, and potatoes in a spicy sauce. She also serves Mo-Mo, delicious dumplings filled with vegetables, steamed with a spicy sauce.

"No eat lunch, then no carry water. . . " Ani Samten sighs. I've been helping them carry water from the spring. They're uncomfortable accepting my help but the forty-pound jugs are too heavy for an aging nun, a monk in his sixties, and a teenage woman.

It's been several weeks since I've washed my clothes. High in the mountains, it's normal to go long periods without washing because of limited resources. Fortunately, the dry, cold mountain air inhibits bacterial growth so cleanliness is more of a visual than an olfactory issue. Still, I decide to hike down the mountain to the nearest running spring. All I need is a bucket, soap, and one liter of hot water. If I leave after breakfast, I'll be back by noon so my clothes can dry in the remaining sunlight.

The spring is not a rambling natural brook. It's a two-foot-high concrete block with a protruding pipe that spurts a continuous flow of water. I throw several garments in the bucket, sprinkle powdered soap, fill the bucket, and plunge my hands into the near-freezing water and wash. I drain and rinse a few times. Easy enough, but I underestimate how cold the water is. It's bitingly cold, and it takes huge willpower to keep washing and rinsing. I'm glad I brought hot water! When I finish the first batch, my fingers are numb and my hands tremble. But the sun reaches this parcel of land, so I lay my clean wet clothes on the rocks to dry. I'm doing the final batch when around the corner comes a yak herder leading eight of the beasts. The first yak looks at the flowing water and heads toward it. I assume the herder intended her animals to drink before they graze. I panic that my wet, clean clothes strung across the rocks will be trampled. I motion to her that I'll move the clothes, but she shakes her head *no* and tries to nudge the leading yak away. The yak is reluctant and forcibly resists. It wants water. Still apprehensive around these animals, I step behind an abutment and wait. Using her staff, the herder coerces the lead yak away and it retorts with a throaty moan. I feel bad. The animal needs water. The yak finally moves away but each following yak makes a similar attempt giving the herder a tiring task of moving each animal away.

When it's time to head back, I collect my clothing only to find each item frozen to the rocks. I feel like an idiot! The water is near freezing and the rocks are colder than the water, so of course my clothes would freeze! The hot water is gone, my shirt sleeves and pant legs are wet, and I'm shivering. I can't wait several hours until the sun thaws my garments—if it will. The solution jumps out at me. I use spring water to unfreeze my garments, slowly pouring water over a sock while carefully pulling it from the rock.. It works! I peel one item. The only casualty is a slightly torn shirt. Lesson learned.

When I return to Lawudo Gompa, I hang my clothes from tree branches around my cabin, turning them frequently to fully dry them before the sun sinks behind the mountain. If my hat and gloves aren't dry by tonight, I'll have real problems, but they do dry

I've been here a couple of weeks and I'm still spellbound by the beauty, the solitude and by the caring people. The cold is another issue and the freezing climate is affecting my practice—though I never expected that outcome. It never gets above 60°F—and only briefly before the temperature plummets. Holding a book and turning the pages in heavy gloves becomes complex and takes nearly herculean effort while meditation is a constant test of endurance. I've tried numerous strategies to stay warm while I practice. I've been trying to be patient as I acclimate and adapt to the cold. But really, I'm growing weary.

Sure it's helped to be here in solitude surrounded by beauty and I've improved my practice by learning how to endure the frigid air —but not as much as needed. I can't seem to concentrate and need a master or guru to coach me. Panditarama in Lumbini has teachers who meet with students weekly. I decide to leave Lawudo to further my purpose in making this trip. To advance further I need to move on. I announce my plans at dinner that night.

"We'll miss you, Mark," Sangmo says. "You should come back when it's warmer."

Ani Samten looks down and frowns. I suspect she's questioning if she's helped enough.

"Ani, you've helped me tremendously but you can't change the cold. I've plenty of blankets and you often give me chai. I'd like to return sometime."

Her posture relaxes. "You're welcome anytime, Mark" she says.

I ask Ani Samten if she thinks I need a porter to hike back down.

"You go slowly, it no problem," she says. "Take two days I think, no problem." She looks at me. "Did you know I was porter when young?"

I smile, surprised. "I can't picture you as a porter, Ani!"

"As teenager, I porter. Come, look at groove in my head."

She shows a deep impression across the top of her head from the strap porters use to support the baskets loaded with anything from rocks to food.

Arpi turns to me. "Before you leave, I'd like to hike with you. I saw a route up a ridge where we can view the western valley. The climb looks reasonable and I'll bet we can be back by lunch. Would you join me?"

"Sure, I can stay an extra day to explore."

I've grown to like Arpi. His conversations are always spiritually oriented. He never engages in mindless chatter, and I'm learning from him.

Early the next morning I stuff my daypack with essential items: a compass, flashlight, bandages, energy bars, and water. My hiking boot recently tore so I have to wear tennis shoes.

Our route follows a yak trail that traverses a steep slope and squeezes through dense brush. As I scramble over a thick bed of rock, I inadvertently step on a loose rock the size of an automobile tire, which breaks free and tumbles down the steep grade hurtling twenty feet into the air then continuing its chaotic downward plunge. Arpi and I watch until the rock tumbles from sight. The sound of it impacting rocks comes from far below. I look at Arpi suddenly, shaken. "I hope there's nobody in its path," I say.

"Watch your footing," Arpi says. "One slip and we'd tumble forever."

"A mantra for this hike is. 'Don't slip,'" I say.

"I think your mantra should be positive," Arpi says. "How about, 'we are safe.'"

"Good point!"

The trail wraps around a bluff and begins to ascend. Lawudo is now out of sight and our meandering direction makes it hard to know where we are. We can't plan our path because the jagged topography blocks our view. Arpi finds a passage and moves ahead. I follow but freeze in fear when I'm about to cross a narrow segment with a sheer drop. There's nothing to grasp and I have to admit to this youngster: "Arpi, I'm 'chicken.'"

He looks disappointed. "No problem, we'll find another route." he says.

The views are stunning as usual. We negotiate the irregular route another forty-five minutes. Hungry and weak, we break for a snack and chat. We're slightly above 14,000 feet.

Our conversation turns to meditation. He tells me about a technique called '"listening meditation" learned from his teacher in Hungary.

"It's very effective," he says. "I simply sit and listen. Instead of paying attention to breathing, I focus on sounds. There are more sounds than you think."

"Do you try to hear more *sounds?*" I ask.

"No, the objective is to experience," he says. "Just as with breathing, I don't think about sounds. I don't make any effort to identify them. I just absorb the sound experience."

"Is it disturbing when you hear unnatural sounds like people talking or airplanes?"

"Not at all," Arpi says. "It's just a sound like all other sounds. It's part of the world around and I don't prefer one sound over another. I passively accept all sound. In letting go, I don't get caught up in analysis, labeling, or associations. I'm just present to life's experience, without thought or preference."

In India, Arpi also explored "dark room meditation."

"I was placed in a very quiet, dark room for twelve days. I could hear almost nothing else. Food was given to me through a slot in the wall but no light entered. I did not talk, nor did I see anything."

"How extreme," I say. "Was it helpful? Did you learn anything?"

"It was very enlightening," he says. "I saw my own mind. I saw things that were unexplainable. The purpose is to deprive you of sensory input to simulate the Bardo State—which is the state your consciousness enters after death but before reincarnation. I think I want to do it again, next time for thirty-nine days."

Arpi was also in an Indian Jain meditation community. "They wore simple robes and went to great lengths to make sure they did not hurt any beings," he says. "They literally broom swept in front of them as they walked so as not hurt insects. They were absolutely wonderful people."

He amazes me. "Most people your age are caught up in socializing and materialism," I say. "How does a man in his mid-twenties end up so deeply spiritual?"

"My mother and father motivated me spiritually," Arpi says. "My mother was especially spiritual and encouraged me to be the same."

When Arpi finishes his retreat at Lawudo Gompa, he'll return home to write his second book of poetry. "But spiritually I cannot predict my next step, Mark," Arpi says. "People have a scripture written within them. If they pay attention to it they can live that scripture. I'm listening and will continue to listen. I'm going to live out my scripture fully."

"Is your 'scripture within' the same as 'intuition' or 'having a calling,'" I ask

He nods. "It's the common thread of the heart."

Arpi's well-rounded, intelligent, humorous, and playful. He loves his family and is a great listener. He could easily be a role model. I'd call him "exquisite."

Another hour-and-a-half and we find ourselves at nearly 15,000 feet. This is the highest I've ever been but we are not yet at the view we sought. It's cold and windy. We aren't at snow level but we're close. Though the climbing is strenuous, I still feel cold. Only a light snack and a liter of water remain. Clouds are starting to form and our view will soon be lost-making finding our way back difficult. "I'm feeling like we're out of our safety zone, Arpi," I say. "What do you think?"

"I agree," he says. "People die going beyond their limits. Let's stop."

Just then I wipe my nose to find a small bleed. We're too high already.

Our downhill descent is easier said than done. The slope feels steeper going down than it did climbing, when we could use our hands. And there's another frightening aspect: looking down to place my foot, I see the valley two miles below. Houses are just specks. It's disorienting and intimidating; I feel I could fall straight off the mountain.

The terrain looks completely different coming down, which makes it difficult to recognize the route back. What looked like a dark gray, jagged precipice from below looks like a grass-covered rock from above. To make things worse, boulders and cliffs block the view, making it difficult to plan. We stop frequently.

"I think we came over that left ridge, didn't we?" I say, pointing.

"No, I don't think so," Arpi says. "Wasn't it over there?"

Just then we hear a loud roar from miles across the valley. Looking up we witness a cloud of dust form in a mountain gully. "That's a landslide!" I blurt.

Arpi stares. "It's beautiful, amazing, unlikely to be seen," he says. "And it adds to the uneasiness of our situation."

We confer constantly discerning the route. We're getting colder and I'm getting shaky. I feel panic building. I'm a little dizzy, probably from stress and the thin, cold air combined. I'm glad I'm with Arpi; his memory is clear and together we find our way back in mid-afternoon, well past lunch. Sangmo knew we'd be hungry, and has thick potato soup hot and ready. I never see Sangmo do anything for herself until everyone else is satisfied. I've seen her eat only two times, both after everyone else had eaten. She even hiked to my cabin once when I was late for dinner to make sure I was ok. Sangmo and Ani Samten are both examples of Bodhicitta, the highly treasured Tibetan Buddhist virtue of seeking to relieve others of suffering through compassionate caring.

While Sangmo serves the soup, Ani Samten washes dishes reciting the Om Mani Padme Hum mantra. It's then that I realize that the monastics have little time for meditation. Not once have I seen her going to or coming from meditation. Later, I ask her about it.

"I do little bit meditation," she says. "Very busy so difficult do sitting meditation. Much work to run monastery. My meditation is chant 'Om Mani Padme Hum' while work. Every day, while cooking, cleaning, and in garden I chant. Also before go to bed. This is my meditation."

Now I feel guilty that I have so much time for meditation while she, a nun, must squeeze her practice into her work. But she is practicing Bodhicitta; doing what she loves, serving other people.

That last night I awaken to a howling wind storm. The corrugated metal roof groans and rattles, pine trees emit a ghostly howl, and the Tibetan prayer flags flap violently, sounding like sizzling hot grease. Neither snow nor rain falls. The next morning, the sun jumps into a pristine blue sky as if nothing unusual had happened.

High spirits—Sangmo, Ani Samten, Ani Samden, and Arpi
Lawudo Gompa, Nepal

I have mixed feelings as I stuff my backpack to leave. I'm ready to advance my practice at the Panditarama Meditation Center, and I'm certainly ready to be warm again. Yet, I may never again experience a Himalayan monastery, or meditate in a cave, or experience the virtue of Tibetan Buddhist people.

My friends gather in the sunshine after breakfast to bid me off. Ani Samten hands me a bag with cheese and my favorite roti bread for the hike. Norbu honors me by draping a khata around my neck. Sangmo stands with her hands clasped and sweetly bows. Arpi shows his tender side by giving me a big bear hug. I take a few steps away, turn and bow to these human beings of purity. I'm richer having known them.

I'm glad not to have a porter going down. Alone I can process my experiences. What did I learn here? I've learned that quiet, solitude, and nature's beauty help me become more aware. It's clear why so many have mastered their mind living and meditating in mountain caves.

Also endurance. Although my departure is partly due to the climate, I've learned tolerance by sitting perfectly still for hours in the bitter cold. I've increased my ability be content with what is.

I've had another good dose of simplicity at Lawudo and realize again how little I need to survive! I think simplicity is, as Arpi would say "written in my scripture."

Chapter 9

Diving Deep
Lumbini, Nepal

> Mindfulness is awareness without ego, unreactive awareness.
> Venerable Vivekananda
> Panditarama International
> Vipassana Meditation Center

No one's in sight when I arrive at Panditarama. By entering through the gate, I'm committing to thirteen hours of daily meditation. I'll wake every morning at 4:00 AM and I won't talk to anyone except the teachers—and then for only a few minutes each day. I'll also be agreeing to only two meals a day with nothing past noontime. It's going to be difficult but I want to see if it could lead to a better understanding of my mind.

I've traveled from Nepal's cold Himalayan mountains to its southern tropical plains—a big change. I left behind Tibetan Buddhism, prayer wheels, prayer flags, and the drone of horns. There the focus was on rituals that address karma and foster selflessness whereas here, in the Vipassana tradition, the focus will be deep exploration into consciousness. In both traditions, the result is the same: the betterment of humanity.

A passenger van carried me down the mountains where exotic sights yanked me out of mindfulness and into dazzled amazement. At one stop, three men were holding a freshly decapitated goat upside down to drain the warm blood onto the dusty roadway. Then I chuckled to see a half-dozen goats enjoying the breeze . . . on top of a full-sized bus traveling down the highway.

I'm excited to be back in Lumbini. About six weeks ago, I stopped here for two days on my way to Kathmandu. I made arrangements with Venerable Vivekananda to stay at Panditarama and to study with Vietnamese monk, Thay Minh Do at a nearby Vietnamese Temple. I've five weeks left on my Nepal visa, so I plan two weeks at Panditarama, then a few weeks with Thay Minh Do.

It was a mile hike from the van drop-off point, in intensely hot sun. Just a few days ago, I was struggling to keep my fingers warm. As the sun sinks to the horizon, jackals hiding in the expansive meadows yelp and howl as if in pain. It's an eerie sound and I pause to absorb it. I'll be isolated here. I'm not to have contact with anyone—not even Jayne. I had occasional phone contact when I was in the mountains, but Vivekananda says I'll progress more swiftly if I remain secluded. I spoke with Jayne last night and she accepts this separation. But I have a cell phone, and I plan to speak with the master about calling her occasionally. My spirits perk when I talk with Jayne and I'd really prefer not to go without talking like I did at Kopan. I think about all these things as I walk toward the gate. Then I open it and let myself in.

The modest and unadorned setting of Panditarama is a striking contrast to the colorful trim, fragrant incense, and gold sculptured statues of Tibetan Buddhist temples. It's pretty clear that I'll be learning a distinctly different Buddhist practice. This Vipassana practice is based on Burmese Theravada principles about which I know so little.

The schedule is pinned to a bulletin board and I know it's time for meditation but I can't enter until I register. I wait on a bench outside the meditation hall. At 4:30, practitioners filter out of the hall. I watch as yogis—male meditators—and yoginis—female meditators, walk by. They move slowly, some more so than others, their gaze fixed on the walkway as they meticulously place each footstep with anchored attention. No one glances about. Over ten minutes, twenty people emerge from the hall and find their own isolated spot for an hour of walking meditation. I dare not interrupt.

Hearing shuffling behind me, I turn and find Vivekananda approaching. He motions me to silence and we walk around the corner.

"Welcome, you're Mark, right?" he whispers.

I'm delighted to see him again.

"We've been expecting you. We've quite a few people here but I saved you a room in our three-person dormitory. I think you'll like it."

"Our other teacher, Venerable Bhaddamanika, will provide pamphlets for you to read," he says. "She'll also provide instructional recordings. It's important you review these. The more exact you are in following instructions, the quicker you'll progress. Ask if you don't understand. The instructions are for your benefit; don't expect that we'll police them."

He smiles; there's great depth in his green eyes. "I must go. I'll give a dharma talk at 5:30 in the meditation hall. Perhaps you can unpack and attend."

He leads me to Venerable Bhaddamanika's room. She's a short nun, about forty years old, with a round face, large, sparkling eyes, a gentle smile—and a cat in her arms. She wears the traditional Burmese nun's attire: a pink full-length robe with matching long-sleeved shirt and a woven cap stretched over her shaved head.

The cat turns toward me and I'm stunned to see empty eye sockets. Bhaddamanika notices my shock. "This is Bhouki," she says. "He and his sister were born without eyes. I care for and protect them both; they'd never survive on their own. It's compassion, you know." She speaks clear English.

Vivekananda asks her to show me my room and then excuses himself. She escorts me down a wide, red-tiled walkway lined with palm trees. Branching footpaths lead to single-level, brick residence buildings. We enter a unit facing woodlands and from the window I see monkeys frolicking in the trees.

The room is tidy and clean, plenty of room for three people. It has white concrete walls, a thinly carpeted floor, and a five-foot privacy partition by each bed. Each area has a bookcase and a wooden cot. That's it. Neatly folded are two quilts, a thin blanket, and a pillow. One of the quilts I can use as a mattress. A rectangular mosquito net is draped around the cot. The room is empty and I assume my roommates are in meditation.

"Mark, this bed for you," Bhaddamanika says pointing to one corner. "The man in this bed, Pieter, has been practicing over four months. He'll leave in a few weeks. Sleeping over here," she says pointing, "is Deon who's been here one week and will stay two more. Remember, no talking please. It may seem awkward, but you should be 100 percent focused on being mindful of your actions, your mental processes, and perceptions. The same is true for your roommates so kindly always be silent."

"Of course," I say.

She points to the bathroom. "The solar heated water is warm only in the afternoon so please be considerate. This may not have the comforts of home," she says, "but we hope you have what you need to support your practice. We try to remove the distractions from practice that you normally encounter in worldly life," she continues. "Here you don't need to worry about cooking, paying bills, or maintaining housing. We take care of that so that you can focus on your practice. Diligent practice is hard, Mark. Hopefully you'll achieve rewarding insights. Here's some instructional reading for you." She hands me two photocopied booklets.

"Breakfast is at 6:00AM and lunch is at 11:00AM. The Buddha taught not to eat after noontime. Also, every day you'll have a ten-minute interview with Venerable Vivekananda or myself and that schedule will be posted. Any questions?" She pauses with a soft smile.

"Can I call my family once a week? They have your phone number for emergency use, but I'd like to check-in once a week."

She pauses. "Yes," she finally says. "However, it's best for your practice that you not call. If you do, please talk as little as possible. You'll progress much quicker with uninterrupted mindfulness."

I understand her point but don't like it. It seems to pose a conflict in being a serious Buddhist and having an intimate relationship.

"You'll see that it's for your benefit. There's a phone in the kitchen if you need."

She's relaxed and intentional. "One other thing, Mark," she says. "Nepal is a poor country and the electrical system is fragile. There's eight hours of electricity a day and power can go off at any time." She looks apologetic. "In the evening and morning we use candles. Do you have a flashlight?"

"Yes."

"Okay, please get settled. You can join the dharma talk if you hurry," she says, before leaving.

Just as I finish dressing for the dharma talk, one of my roommates walks in. He glances my way and I feel awkward. It seems rude not to introduce myself.

"Hello," he says, beating me to the punch. "I'm Deon. Welcome."

"I'm Mark. I'll be here a week or two. I'll do my best to be quiet."

"No problem. I'll be here two more weeks. Welcome again and goodbye as well. We'll not talk again."

He slowly walks to his bed placing each step with concentrated intention. Trying not to stare, I observe the technique. To put on his shirt, he extends both hands with definite purpose, grips his shirt, and *slowly* inserts each arm. His motions are as slow as an elderly man's and each movement is deliberate. It takes him ten times longer than normal. As I purport to be adjusting my own clothing, he walks across the room at a turtle's pace, gripping the door handle and ever so slowly letting himself out.

The movements look unnatural. I'm sure the booklets will explain the value of moving so slowly. As I change I try to re-enact his movements. It's difficult. I quickly, impatiently resort to my familiar hurried motions. I've been frustrated with my uncontrollable mind and now I have a disobedient body to contend with as well.

The sun sets and the air cools, but nowhere close to the numbing cold of Lawudo Gompa. On the main walkway, seven people walk a painstakingly slow pace toward the meditation hall. They hardly move ten feet a minute! My impatience glides me right past them. *What a waste of time!* I think. My lifestyle has been on focused productivity—and it's become a habit. I get from point A to point B as fast as possible—and why not? It's more efficient. Now I force myself to move slowly like my fellow yogis. I position myself behind a tall man with long black hair and walk his pace. It takes fifteen minutes to reach the hall—which isn't even a two-minute walk at a normal pace.

The meditation hall is triangular with a red-tiled floor, white concrete walls, and a ten-foot concrete ceiling. A glass block wall allows the dwindling rays of the sun to sift in. A soft breeze from four screened doors cools the room, which is still hot from the day. Mosquito nets hang from supporting wire strung from the ceiling and drape around thirty sitting cushions. Women sit on the left, men on the right. At the apex of the triangle, on a small altar, is a modest two-foot statue of Buddha, a candle, and a vase of flowers.

I find an open cushion, sit cross-legged, and drop the mosquito net around me. Looking about, I realize my movements were coarse and rapid compared to others. I hope I wasn't disruptive. Yogis are still approaching and slowly sitting. They move with such engaged concentration. Then I realize I'm the only yogi glancing about—and I quickly look down? The experienced yogis focus their minds only to their own experience. *I have some learning to do.*

Twenty-five practitioners are seated when Vivekananda enters. He sits on his cushion, settles his belongings, and pauses for a long moment to glance intentionally at each individual. Vivekananda's dharma talk is about dukkha, the unsatisfactoriness of life that we all experience. He often quotes directly from texts, speaking in English. Dukkha, he says, is the suffering inherent in life, including sickness, old age, and death. But "unsatisfactoriness" comes closest to the true meaning. To properly describe dukkha in English would mean using a variety of nouns such as frustration, affliction, anxiety, anguish, etc. Even happiness can be dukkha for all happiness is eventually displaced by impermanence. Yes, and I think it's safe to say that dukkha includes my annoyance with this pair of mosquitoes seeking to feast on my neck right now!

That evening, I cuddle in my sleeping bag and read the pamphlets that explain Vipassana as an ancient technique believed to be what the Buddha himself practiced twenty-five-hundred years ago. It falls under the Theravada school of Buddhism; Theravada means "The Teachings of the Elders" because of its exacting conformance to scriptures.

Each student is to make a mental note of each and every act of consciousness. When taking a step, one notes clearly that he's taking a step; when tasting food one clearly notes, when seeing, one notes. The same is true for touching, thinking, smelling, and hearing. Everything one sees, perceives, or thinks must be noted continuously and unremittingly. A practitioner is to make each movement very slowly so he or she can label the act, feeling, or thought. Do I really have to do this? It seems so tedious.

If in pain, we're instructed to detach, observe, note the pain, and restrain our tendency to alleviate it. Students can make great strides in improving concentration if they mentally observe pain. When sitting in meditation for long periods, pain may arise, giving opportunity to focus and observe its *nature*, the changes in intensity, feeling, and type.

Hmmm . . . "great strides in improving concentration"—that's what I'm after.

By labeling—or noting—every act over an extended period of time, the student becomes more aware of the nature of his or her own consciousness and the relationship between consciousness, thought, and the body. *Hmmm.* I continue reading: "With this new awareness, we begin to perceive *self* as a series of continuing and successive acts of consciousness rather than as the distinct individual we usually think we are—one who exists independently from childhood until death." *Self as continuing acts of consciousness,* I paraphrase. I haven't thought of myself that way. Ever.

Such focus on bodily movements results—according to the pamphlet—in a series of insights that lead the student to understand, through direct perception, the teachings of the Buddha. I wonder if these are like the 'breakthrough realizations' that Tibetan Buddhists talk of.

These insights occur in a predictable sequence that includes the realization of impermanence, dukkha, cessation of sensual cravings, equanimity, and ultimately enlightenment. I'm a bit different. I strive for a deeper understanding of the concept of "no self"—a teaching common to all Buddhist traditions.

As I read, a jackal screams a solitary complaint that's quickly picked up by a dozen others. They break out in a unified crying concert. I peer between my window's security bars at the star-filled sky, then finish my reading and burrow into my sleeping bag just as my roommates enter and do the same.

I'm awakened at 4:00AM by deep reverberations of a huge bronze bell struck four times. I'm motivated to start. I spring up and throw on my shirt before I remember to move slowly and with awareness—and to note. I flip on the light switch but the room remains dark—a power outage. I dress slowly, noting every movement: lifting my hand, gripping my pants, and pulling them on.

Outside in the chilly fog, we begin a walking meditation session. One person is already doing walking meditation. At the far end of the walkway, in a garden area, a small bonfire burns warming a grey-haired watchman slumped back in an old wooden chair. A low-lying fog glows orange from the campfire creating a mystical aura. I make out the soft glow of a half moon through the fog. The walkway has been lined with candles all the way to the main hall. Through the dark woods, from a neighboring temple, come the sounds of a slowly struck gong and, from another direction, I hear the knock of a hollow wooden striker at a tempo like a heartbeat. As if complaining of the noise, a pack of jackals wail and whine.

All over the world, while most people sleep, Buddhist practitioners rise early to perform rituals, ceremonies, and meditations to improve their minds and to benefit humankind. I normally despise waking this early, but I'm committed to this program.

I walk more intentionally than ever. The cold morning chill wins over my grogginess, yet I struggle to walk at this snail's pace. The forty-degree, foggy air makes my fingers tingle and my nose run. It comforts me some to recall the frigid Himalayan air.

Gradually all students filter onto the long and wide walkway, and find their own patch of solitude in which they pace twenty steps forward and twenty back. Applying the pamphlet instructions, I catch my thoughts and make mental labels. It's an awkward exercise. Predictably, my mind wanders. *I wonder what Jayne's doing? Is she is angry that I'm isolated? I'm getting hungry.* Eventually I catch myself, note that my mind's wandering, and bring my attention back.

At the session's end, the yogis flow toward the meditation hall like cold molasses spilt on a table. Claiming what's now my spot, I sit, still using abrupt movements. *Habit* I note. The hall is unheated so I wrap a blanket around my winter coat. It's now 5:00AM and I'm among twenty meditators in a room lit by two candles and, silent except for the occasional sniffle.

I apply my labeling instructions: breathing in, breathing out, feeling cold air in my nostrils, hearing a sniffle, breathing out, smelling breakfast cooking, feeling hunger pangs . . . *Hmmm, I wonder what's for breakfast? Are portions limited? Hope they have fried eggs . . . Stop!* Return to noting: Wandering mind, feeling frustrated, breathing in, breathing out. What an amazing creature the mind is! Who's running this show anyway?

Pain hits in my right knee. *Pain,* I note. It's not serious but everything in me wants to reposition. The pamphlet says to "observe it." I do. "Sharp," I note. "Tighter," I note. "Stabbing," I note. *I don't like this. This is stupid!* With a quick shuffle, I reposition my knee, abandoning my effort to endure. The pain instantly vanishes. It lasted less than a minute. I could have endured longer, which is what the pamphlet encouraged. I feel weak-willed. How am I to enjoy this mind-over-pain contest?

Now a different pain sets in. I haven't eaten since lunch yesterday and I'm feeling weak and shaky. Fifteen minutes are left in the meditation session. My mind keeps jumping to the dining hall as my mouth waters over images of waffles, syrup, and an imaginary cup of coffee. "Craving," I note. I fight my mind's wanderings, but when the session ends, I don't get up and join a couple yogis who rise to leave. I linger on my cushion, not wanting to be seen as ravenous for food, which I truly am. Rather, I join the next group as we slowly rise and step our way to the dining hall.

Breakfast is buffet style with a healthy selection of cereals, yogurt, fruit, and bread presented with warm milk, and coffee. No waffles, syrup, or fried eggs. We sit in pre-assigned seats in groups of four. There's no eye contact, no good-morning greetings, no smiles. It feels awkward, but it enables me to note the goings-on in my mind.

I'm thankful the genders are separated. There are some attractive yoginis who'd surely distract me. I've been sexually abstinent for several months and I don't need another challenge to contend with.

As instructed, I note my eating experiences. *Sweet,* I note when tasting honey. *Crunchy* when I bite into an apple, *swallowing* when downing a bite. This is to be my life for the next two weeks—note, note, note.

I follow the schedule of alternating walking and sitting meditation until it's time for my 10:20AM interview. I wait outside the small interview hall with another yogi, who I know to be Yusef from the posted schedule. The door to the hall is open and I see Vivekananda sitting cross-legged on a woven carpet as a yogi sits facing him; they're talking.

While still speaking to the student, Vivekananda rings a small hand bell. Yusef walks in, bows and sits next to the other yogi. When the interview ends, the yogi rises, bows, and exits. Yusef's interview begins.

Ten minutes later the hand bell rings again, I enter and take my seat next to Yusef. Vivekananda is finishing Yusef's interview and I feel uncomfortable listening.

"But I cannot determine which object to note," Yusef says in a strong accent I can't place. "They're appearing and disappearing quickly. There are so many."

"Ahhhh," says Vivekananda, "just pay attention to the dominant object that arises in your consciousness. Many will come but you must let the dominant one settle and then note and observe that object."

Yusef's interview has extended beyond the ten-minutes allotted. Vivekananda turns to me. "Okay, Mark," he says in a bubbly manner, "How are you this morning? Are you settled?"

Yusef rises, bows, and exits.

"I'm doing fine," I tell him. His cheery nature puts me at ease.

"Ahhhhh, good, good," he says. "Do you have any questions about the instructions?"

"I think I know what you mean by 'objects' of consciousness, but could you clarify?"

"Objects of consciousness are simply that which the mind grabs onto in any instant. It may be a bird flying, a loud noise, an emotion you're feeling, or a thought . Your mind can *only* hold one object of consciousness at a time. It may not seem that way because the mind can jump between objects so rapidly it seems you're paying attention to many things at once. But that's not so, and you'll come to realize this as your perception becomes refined."

Before Panditarama, I'd never heard of noting. "And so I must simply pay attention to what I'm paying attention to?" I ask. My question seems odd.

"Yes! Be aware of what your mind is grasping. Do that continuously and unremittingly without resting. This can be enhanced by moving ever so slowly, Mark."

"I watch the yogis move slowly. I'm trying to mimic them but it's hard."

"Follow the process, Mark. Note everything. Note your intention to move even before you move. Say 'now I will turn' before you turn. If you do this consistently you'll find it easier. It's then that insights will evolve and your perception of reality will become clearer and more accurate. Any other questions?"

"Yes. The instructions say it's crucial to have continuity of mindfulness. Can you help me understand this?"

His eyes are locked on mine. "Mindfulness can be stated as unreactive awareness. It's awareness without ego—bare awareness. This is important to remember. Mindfulness is not thinking, not a feeling or emotion. It is pure awareness. We strive to be mindful of everything we do and at every moment."

The words "not thinking, not a feeling, or emotion" gives me a twinge of repulsion—it sounds inhuman and sterile. Yet, I know many sages over millennia have said the same, starting with the Buddha himself.

"Now here are your instructions: during sitting meditation give microscopic examination to the feelings in your abdomen. What are the feelings when your abdomen rises with the breath? Note feelings of fullness, pressure on the skin, clothes sliding on the skin, warmth of blood circulation. Be precise and detailed. Do the same when the abdomen is falling as you exhale. Be aware of everything you feel and sense in the abdominal area. I want you to note those feelings at the beginning, middle, and end of both inhalation and exhalation. That's how detailed I want you to be."

"So I should be aware of every feeling and note them all?" It seems like a boundless task.

"Be scientific about it. After your session, take notes and report them to me in an exact manner."

"How about walking meditation? Shall I focus on slowing down?"

"Yes, but I want you to give microscopic examination to the feelings in your feet. Observe the pressure in your heel, the ball, and the sole of your foot. Do you feel sagging or pressing, rubbing or sliding, hot or cold? What textures do you feel?"

As he talks he lifts his hand bell, and rings it to prompt the next person. "Also break the step into segments of lifting, moving forward, and placing down. Know the sensations in each of those phases. Again, be scientific, detailed, and exact. Report the dominant feelings and sensations at our next meeting. Any other questions?"

"No. It sounds like a lot to pay attention to," I say. Which I think of as an understatement on my part. A fellow yogi, much younger than I, approaches, bows, and sits.

"Since Bhaddamanika and I alternate interview days, it'll be two days before we next talk. Every hour of sitting is sixty minutes of observing feelings in your abdomen. Every hour of walking is sixty minutes of observing your feelings of each step. That's a lot of time to be mindful, observant, and precise. Be mindful," he says as his final instruction before he turns to his next student.

I rise and slowly, slowly leave.

Vivekananda is friendly, caring, and cheerful. He speaks fluent English and gives exacting instructions. He inspires me. Everything seems right here.

My routine is simple: quiet, slow, quiet, slow. The more I practice the more I become committed. I note and note and note. When I entered the front gate, I worried about keeping up with the difficult meditation schedule. Now, a mere week later, I find myself looking for every opportunity to sit and walk in meditation. I become the first to rise in the morning and the last in bed at night.

Chapter 10

Inner Explorer
Lumbini, Nepal

> Don't identify with your thoughts. They are only thoughts.
> Ven. Bhaddamanika
> Panditarama International Meditation Center

I've been at Panditarama now for almost two weeks. Things feel right here—the practice, the environment, and especially the teachers. My priorities have shifted. I shave only when the stubble itches and, even though the days are hot, I shower every other day. That gives more time to focus on awareness and note the objects of my mind—what my thoughts are.

But today I need a haircut. I borrow an electric shaver and decide to shave my head. I prune my hair one swipe at a time. Suddenly, with only one side of my head shaved, the power goes out. I can't finish the job. I burst out laughing. I use scissors to balance my appearance until I can finish the job.

When I got here, I was worried that I'd not be able to sit in meditation for one hour. I'd never done it before and, truthfully, couldn't imagine sitting one hour watching my thoughts, following my breath. But I've surprised myself. I now sit for as long as an hour-and-a-half. I can hardly believe it!

My teachers, Vivekananda and Bhaddamanika, strongly suggested that as I observe the pain in my knees—rather than getting up or moving my body—that deep observation of pain would improve my concentration. And it has, slightly. One time during sitting meditation, as I observed the sharp pain in my knee, a pack of jackals broke into a fury of yelps that sounded like the scream that should have come from me—the same scream that I want to let loose. I nearly laughed out loud. As the days progress, I mentally befriend those jackals with their ghostly howls.

I've also become fond of the huge tropical cranes that soar overhead, the melodic and colorful parakeets, and the frogs that liven up the evening with their deep base. I'm still unable to befriend the nuisance mosquitoes.

I've made an unexpected discovery at Panditarama. I've unearthed the precious treasure of the pre-dawn hours. Even at Lawudo Gompa, up in the Himalaya, I never knew how precious the predawn could be! Until now, I despised waking early. But now, with that first strike of the bell, I leap from my dreams into a state of calm awareness and make my way outdoors into the tranquil stillness, where I begin walking meditation.

Pre-dawn in this nature preserve that houses Panditarama is like a magic show. Thick fog has engulfed the compound and often Bhaddamanika has lined the walkway with candles. Foggy water droplets glow from the flickering candles, looking like a miniature aurora borealis. The droplets appear so large that candlelight makes them seem like tiny lustrous BBs hovering against gravity.

I'm immersed in silence; my footsteps, however gently placed, sound loud against the stillness. Percussion is added when a symphony of dew droplets cascade down the trees and hit the walkway sounding like a tap-dance. I feel part of this percussive music. A slight breeze cracks an opening in the fog and moon beams slip through. A large bat with a five-foot wingspan flies overhead leaving an impressive shadow on the walkway. A single bird sequestered in the bush performs a flute-like melody that awakens a pack of jackals who howl a morning serenade. Looking down, a tiny glow from the garden's edge turns out to be a fluorescent snail leisurely crawling across the dew-covered earth.

Every day I feel more driven to become ever more consciously aware, especially as my daily interview nears. Although I often vent about my continuing frustration with my concentration, the teachers assure me I'm improving. I always leave the interview richer from their wise advice.

"I want you to continue paying attention to feelings Mark," Vivekananda advised again two weeks into my retreat, "Begin noting the lifecycle of your mental state. From the moment you rise until you go to sleep, note how your emotions, attitude, and energy level evolve. Note both physical and mental states and do so with pure observation and acceptance. Take special note of wholesome and unwholesome thoughts."

"Unwholesome thoughts? Like anger or jealousy?"

"Unwholesome thoughts include laziness, criticizing, and judging. It also includes desire. Take note of cravings and desire in an unattached way. Don't act on these thoughts."

"Then wholesome thoughts include kindness and caring?"

"Yes, yes," Vivekananda says in his musically enthusiastic voice. "And it can include contentment, commitment, and inspiration. Note all of these mental states."

"Shall I record them in my notebook?"

"As you wish. But lastly guard your senses. Don't let interesting sights pull your mind away. If you hear a conspicuous sound, don't let it pull your attention, just observe and note it. Guard all of your senses." There is a sense of urgency in his voice and manner. "And, as always, maintain continuity of mindfulness."

I re-read the pamphlet, which tells me that by observing our constantly changing internal emotions and feelings, the yogi comes to understand impermanence at a personal level. We begin to see that psycho-physical phenomena occur beyond our control. The "I" is redefined. My thoughts are not "I." My feelings are not "I."

Trained in the sciences, I'm a problem-solver. I look at clues, draw a hypothesis, test it, and execute a solution. Straightforward, no feelings and emotions involved. A scientific mind can logically link puzzle pieces. Part of what attracts me to Buddhism is its practicality and logic—even if it tends to be obscure and a bit fuzzy at times. The intellectual challenge of

Venerable Vivekananda at Panditarama Lumbini
International Vipassana Meditation Center
Lumbini, Nepal

assembling the clues that make the puzzle pieces fit together excites me. At Panditarama, I'm in a scientific study program, studying my breath, feelings, and the motions of my body while looking for something very obscure. By trusting the teachings handed down through millennia, I'm changing my perspective—of *self* and of the universe—which adds practical value to my life. These teachers monitor my progress and offer clues about pieces of the puzzle.

Panditarama has been good for me. I've been here two weeks. I decide to stay another week.

I can notice that I'm making progress. My senses are more receptive, my vision crisper, and sounds clearer. I'm more aware of touch and I notice even internal sensations such as digestion. I'm growing in awareness. I'm getting stronger in maintaining mindfulness. I lock onto whatever task is at hand, instead of watching my mind jump around distractedly. Sometimes during meditation, I experience periods of great stillness. My mind is an empty field where nothing comes or goes. My best description would be "pure awareness with a sense of peacefulness." Sometimes during meditation I feel a gentle smile of contentment blossom on my face.

Without fail though, that deep stillness evaporates and peaceful contentment eludes me as I fall back in the trenches battling an inability to concentrate my mind.

My body is a similar story. It's not yet under my control. I catch myself moving quickly without intention or mindfulness. Vivekananda advises me to continue my efforts and accept where I'm at—yet I still get frustrated.

My nervous habits, though, are nearly gone. My fingernails are long since I don't pick and bite them. Rubbing my tongue inside my cheek, I feel a smoothness I haven't felt in years. Becoming aware of chewing the inside of my cheek enabled me to stop. My dentist will be pleased. Even the slight twitch in my eye from job stress has vanished. Just two weeks of intensive meditation has overcome habits I've battled for years.

I sometimes gauge a snippet of my own progress by observing newcomers. A new person mindlessly yanks out a chair and loudly plops himself down. That was me two weeks ago.

Vivekananda encourages me to observe every desire and aversion that arises. It's fascinating to note how salivation is stimulated at the sight or smell of delicious food. I observe my body's desire for moderate temperatures, my aversion to mosquitoes whining in my ear, my aversion to using the squat toilet. I've come to see at a deeper level how desires or aversions drive my behavior.

Although I can see that I've made progress, I still have meditation sessions plagued with 'wandering mind' —I return to Lawudo, cycle back to Delhi, drive into work back home. When it happens I become quite frustrated—which doesn't help at all to fix the problem.

"This is impermanence, Mark," Bhaddamanika says with a smile. "The mind is always changing you know. Focus on acceptance. We're really training on the Four Noble Truths, right?"

I mentally revisit the Buddha's fundamental teachings: 1) Life inherently involves suffering; 2) Suffering arises from attachment and desire; 3) Suffering ceases when attachment and desire cease; and, 4) One can eliminate suffering by practicing Buddhist philosophy.

"Your desire for a concentrated mind is causing suffering" she says. "Impermanence happens not only in physical phenomena, but also in your mind, body, and feelings," she continues. "You must accept that the mind will have difficult times."

So, I desire a disciplined mind, yet I can't ultimately master it? Is that it? Wow! Is the stallion essentially untamable? Is she saying I'll always struggle with an uncontrollable mind? I feel panicky. "Isn't it a Buddhist goal to develop strong concentration and mindfulness?" I ask.

"This is a common paradox," Bhaddamanika says. "You're attached to achieving results. You want to achieve a disciplined mind. That's attachment to a desired outcome and it's resulting in suffering. You've experienced calm peacefulness through deep practice, which has produced a desire for more of that experience. Be careful of this, Mark."

She's right. My ego wants control. "But I'm here to master my mind!" I tell her. "What's wrong with that?"

"It's a paradox," she repeats. "Don't be attached to expectations. Just follow the instructions. Be diligent in your practice and let go of the outcome. This method has been proven over centuries. You must have faith."

She's right again. I expect quick results. I have to figure out how to let go and accept what is.

I stay a third week and it slips by all too quickly. My work feels far from complete but extending my time here means abandoning my other plans. My Nepal visa expires in three weeks, and I don't want to lose the chance to train under Thay Minh Do, the monk at the neighboring Vietnamese temple. I felt a strong internal message to spend time with him when we met three months ago. But my practice here at Panditarama has been going so well that it's put me in a quandary: Should I stay here longer or go resume practice with Thay Minh Do?

I feel the need to discuss this with Jayne. It'll be great just to hear her voice. Besides, I really value her opinion. She doesn't get caught up in analyzing but goes by her instinct and intuition, which is almost always right on.

"You've talked about Thay Minh Do numerous times since you met him," Jayne says. "I think you should spend time there. Besides, you can always go back to Panditarama, right?"

She nailed it.

During my next interview with Vivekananda, I ask him, "Is this a bad time in my practice to depart?"

I surprise myself by surrendering my decision into my teacher's hands, but I've deep respect for him.

"Ohhhh, Mark," he begins with his usual melodic launch into a discussion. "You've made good progress and will do well if you stay. But you're on a committed path and can continue practice after you leave. This is a fine time to depart and you're welcome back anytime."

"I'll leave in two days, then," I tell him. "I've plans to visit the Vietnamese temple nearby and must make arrangements tomorrow."

"Ahhhh, do you know the master at that temple?"

"I only met him for a discussion. He invited me to practice there with his senior monk."

"The master there is very good. They're not normally open to visitors. It's a good opportunity."

With Vivekananda's permission, I excuse myself the next afternoon to make arrangements. Slipping out the front gate, I walk three-quarters of a mile to the isolated Vietnamese temple. The path cuts through the center of the preserve, along a nearly dry canal, through a wooded area, and across a somewhat marshy prairie. The metal gate is locked with nobody in sight. The sign still reads "Closed for Construction."

"Hello," I yell several times before someone approaches from the dense tropical bushes. It's Thay Minh Do. It's been more than three months since we met. My heart warms to see him. I smile, clasp my hands, and bow. "Thay Minh Do, I am Mark."

"Yes," he says, smiling warmly. "You Mark. I know."

He radiates peacefulness and I feel it no different than before. I'm delighted he remembers me.

"I wait for you. Glad you come," he says. Inwardly, I chuckle that his English has not improved. "How your practice Mark? Learn meditation?"

I tell him about Panditarama. "I've been in meditation from four in the morning until ten at night, Thay. My practice is improving."

"Very good," he says but hesitantly. I realize I spoke too rapidly.

"I want to practice with you," I continue. "I can come in two days." I don't want to presume the invitation is still open so I ask, "Is it possible that I stay here and learn from you?"

"Must ask master. Master not here," he says.

I met his master, Thay Huyen Dieu, who was very kind when we chatted three months ago. "You come back 7:00PM and ask master practice with me. Okay?"

I hesitate. It's already dark by seven. Most of the preserve is vacant and I'll be hiking alone. It's also an awkward time to leave the meditation center as things are settling down. But I'm uncomfortable asking him to adjust to another time for my convenience. I'm also confused why I need to ask again. Communicating all this will be difficult so I decide to follow his suggestion.

"Okay, Thay, I'll return at 7:00PM."

"It good," he says with a smile. "You explain Thay Huyen Dieu you want practice here."

"I'm very happy to see you again, Thay."

"Yes, very happy too," he says.

That evening, after the dharma talk, I alert the watchman that I'll return in one hour.

"Go?" he asks, looking puzzled.

"Go Vietnam Temple," I say. "One hour come back."

He nods, still looking puzzled.

I find my way up the dark jungle path using my flashlight. The route is simple, but looks different at night with thick dark woods to my left and a canal to my right. I hear voices and movement in the woods but see no one. Rounding the corner onto a narrower path, the area becomes even darker. I'm now questioning the wisdom of going through such a deserted area at night. Usually, dogs roam this path by day and at night, I'm afraid one will attack.

I recall a posted sign: "This reserve contains dangerous wildlife such as monkeys, jackals, snakes, and dogs. If you are bitten please report it immediately."

I try to dismiss my fear—but I note it—as I continue to walk. After ten minutes, I hear footsteps. I turn to see a dark figure a couple of hundred feet behind me, walking in my direction. I can't see clearly but the figure appears to be a man wearing a hooded shirt. He's leaning to one side, walks with a limp, and occasionally grunts. He carries no light, yet his pace is brisk, so I pick up my pace. If I walk any faster though, I'm sure to trip on a tree root, or one of the many deep ruts. The figure slowly gains on me.

The gravity of my situation sinks in. I'm in a poor region of a foreign country. I don't speak the native language. I'm in an unlit, heavily wooded area, alone without identification. There's no authorities for miles. I'm unarmed and if I were to disappear I'd not be found for days, if at all. My heart races like a galloping horse.

Panicky, I pick up a brick for security, and continue my fast pace. Now I feel uneasy because of my potentially violent response to an attack. I've spent weeks in meditation fostering inner peacefulness and here I am, holding a brick, ready to smash it into another person. I don't feel like a Buddhist right now.

I continue on, brick in hand, for the next fifteen minutes with the grunting dark figure striding behind. I'm convinced that he's the pursuer and I the pursued. Finally, I see the glow of the Vietnamese temple ahead and am relieved as I turn onto the side path to the temple gate. The "villain" behind me continues on the main path without even glancing my way.

Relieved but embarrassed, my heart is racing so I lean against the gate to catch my breath. I don't want to meet with a Buddhist master while visibly panicked. When I regain my composure, I summon a worker to open the gate. He's surprised to find a visitor at this hour.

"Thay Huyen Dieu," I say.

"Yes, yes," he says and leads me past a lake to a residence building. Only a few lights are on.

"Master come. You wait," he says.

A few minutes later the master appears, dressed in a traditional Vietnamese silk evening robe embroidered with Buddhist symbols.

"What can I do to help you?" He looks sincere.

I introduce myself again.

"I remember you, Mark."

"I'm interested in staying here for two weeks to learn meditation from Thay Minh Do. We talked today. I can pay and help around the temple."

He pauses a moment. "We not open to the public, we under construction," he says. "But I talked with Minh Do and he tells me you're a sincere man."

I smile.

"You may stay and learn from Thay Minh Do. He's a good monk."

I clasp my hands and bow. "Thank you. Please let me know if there's any way I can help."

"Just practice diligently, Mark," he says.

"I'll arrive in two days. Okay?"

"Yes. I'll be traveling, Thay Minh Do will be here."

I'm relieved. My remaining time in Nepal is planned.

The spectacular evening is cool, clear, and starlit, but I'm uneasy about my return to Panditarama. I fight with my fear about attackers and wild animals and briskly retrace my path to find the guard ready to let me in.

I practice diligently during my remaining time at Panditarama. But my concentration is off as I anticipate my next step to Thay Minh Do as my teacher. I'm reminded of one of Vivekananda's dharma talks in which he spoke about exercising determination, persistence, and effort to overcome obstacles. I've coined myself an acronym, DPE, to help me remember this advice, and I use it whenever I feel internal frustrations about my practice.

The mental work here can be grueling. The other day in the meditation hall, I watched a yogi lower his head to the ground and put his face in his hands in mental exhaustion. Two days ago my roommate, a twenty-five year old Nepali man, came into the room and lay on his bed crying. I wanted to help but I know I'm unqualified; these are matters that Vivekananda can best handle.

My last day arrives. I have a 10:15AM interview with Vivekananda, who's had a bad cold for days. His nose is red and running, his voice is hoarse, and he fights a persistent cough. I've been watching him conduct his duties with a display of happiness that I probably would not be able to manage. Though the air is cold, he wears his traditional monk's robes with fully bare arms, calves, and throat. He hasn't changed the schedule for his dharma talks or his interviews. He practices what he teaches: DPE—determination, persistence, and effort. I respect him.

During our final interview, I ask a question foremost in my mind: "Venerable, can you advise me how to carry the mindfulness I've gained into my home life? I'm afraid I'll just get tangled up in my job and daily responsibilities; I'll lose this hard-earned mindfulness. Can one live a mindful Buddhist lifestyle in a western society?"

"This is an important question," Vivekananda says. "Whether you progress, maintain, or fall backward is dependent on your commitment to practice, Mark. Time demands can be difficult for a lay person but if you commit to three to four hours every day you can maintain and perhaps advance your practice. This is a good goal. But if you're only able to commit one hour per day, maintaining will depend on the quality of your sitting."

"Do you mean the quality of mindfulness?"

"Of course that too, but I mean sitting. Be aware that a sitting hour is extremely precious. Sit down with firm determination to instantly apply courageous effort. Try to put forth concentration immediately so as not to waste time. Be consistent every day. It's easy to make exceptions and if you do they'll grow in frequency. Remember Mark, effort. Heroic effort."

I've spent several weeks under Vivekananda's direction. He's a model of self-discipline, purity, and goodness. He directs his students as if he's guiding his own son through a life and death situation. He's studious and his teachings are meticulously extracted from textbooks. I've no problem clasping my hands, and bowing three times to show respect. And that is what I do.

Moving on again, I feel like a nomad, and I see value in being one. Traveling as a nomad I enhance my understanding of impermanence.

Saying goodbye to people I admire and places I appreciate helps me recognize that nothing belongs to me. I merely pass through experiences in the same way that phenomena pass into and out of consciousness. Are we not all nomads just passing through the universe?

The stallion analogy depicts—to me—the effort involved in training the mind. I got the stallion of my mind out of the meadows—where he wandered haphazardly—and into a training corral. I met him face to face, looked at him, stroked his snout, stared into his dark eyes, and told him we could cooperate. He's smart. Many times, I've thought "got him!" but then I loosen the reigns and he's gone for the meadow. Whoosh, just gone. Often I don't even know he's gone until I suddenly realize that the stallion—my mindfulness—is not with me.

I'm departing a good trainer and headed to another—Thay Minh Do. Eventually I'll climb on the stallion's back and gently lead him along without reigns—perhaps someday soon.

As I walk to the Vietnamese Temple, I walk slowly. So many rare and precious people dwell in these surrounding temples, all of them striving to better their minds for the benefit of humanity. I feel their presence in this sacred land.

Chapter 11

A Humble Monk
Lumbini, Nepal

Stick and see one thing, nothing else; no stick and see all.
Thay Minh Do
Vietnamese Phat Quoc Tu Vien Temple

"Thay Minh Do not here. He sleep," a worker says when I knock at the Vietnamese Temple and inquire for my next teacher.

I know better than to think Minh Do is asleep. At 2:00PM, it's more likely he's in meditation.

"Sit here until wake up," the worker says, leading me into the compound.

I ask the worker his name.

"I Talagram," he says. He looks to be in his late thirties with curly hair and a receding hairline. He's in a long-sleeve shirt that's too small and nylon pants that are too short. He's barefooted, and his dark eyes are curious and interested.

"I'm Mark. I'll stay two weeks to meditate with Minh Do."

"Yes, Minh Do tell me," Talagram says. "He ask me clean Lake Temple for you. Nobody use Lake Temple in long time."

I'm impressed to hear Minh Do remembered how much I admired that small temple centered in one of the lakes.

"Must go now, must work," Talagram says.

I make my way to a concrete platform situated above the Lake. To get there I cross a dozen concrete lotus flowers that span the lake. This is tricky; there are no handrails and it's difficult to balance on the curved sculptured lotus flowers. Yet I manage to make it across to the platform without falling. From here, I can see the main temple, a magnificent three-level structure with a center staircase of one hundred red tile steps. The handrails are sculpted dragons with fierce teeth, blazing eyes, and reptilian feet. To my right is that special "Lake Temple" perched atop a ten-foot pillar on an island with lotus flower pads leading to a small door at the pillar's base.

Somebody pinch me, I think. I'm immersed in bamboo groves, above a quiet lake, serenaded by tropical birds, cranes, and frogs. Bananas grow above me and brilliant colored flowers fill the gardens. It's like Adam and Eve's paradise.

Suddenly, a loud, trumpeting scream comes from a pair of Sarus cranes wading in the water. Their bluish-gray bodies transition to red at their necks. They bugle an elephant-like sound for almost a minute and I use it as my cue to return to the lobby.

"Oh, yes. Hello Mark," Minh Do greets me. He keeps the *r* in my name silent.

"Thay Minh Do!" I almost gush. "I'm happy to be here."

"Yes, yes," he nods with a big grin. "It good you come practice."

It takes him time to process sentences. His English skills are limited. I wonder how effectively we'll communicate as student-teacher.

"I'm excited to learn from you," I tell him." He pauses as if he's thinking and then responds. "Mark, I no teacher. No teach." He shakes his head to emphasize. "Only share my knowledge."

I'm not sure if that's a sign of humility or if there's a regimented structure that limits who can be called "teacher." It doesn't matter.

We enter a hallway off the lobby and he points to the first door without stopping. "This room mine. You need, knock anytime." He continues to the last room and lets me in.

"Not much," he says. "It small. It okay?" He looks at me hoping for approval. The private room has one window near a bed with a mosquito net draped around. There's also a four-drawer wooden chest and a small closet. Out the window, a dense bamboo grove filters most of the afternoon light. The attached bathroom is clean and bright.

"Perfect" I say.

The overhead light is dim and the bathroom light doesn't work.

"Power out," he says. "So sorry. Only few lights from generator."

"No problem, I have a flashlight."

He suggests I rest and then meditate. "You remember how I teach meditation?" he asks.

"Before inhaling, say 'now I'll inhale' and before exhaling say 'now I'll exhale,'" I say. "I used this in the mountains."

He smiles and tells me I can meditate in the main temple, the Buddha Room, or at the Lake Temple. "Workers clean Lake Temple for you," he says. "Use anytime." He tells me that another monk uses the main temple for chanting as do visitors. "Dinner at 6:00PM. You meet visiting monk and volunteer cook. I no eat dinner. Breakfast and lunch only. Now I go."

Free of Panditarama's regimented meditation schedule, I feel mentally uneasy. Dinner is two hours off so I head for the Lake Temple. Like a tightrope walker, I gingerly step across the stone lotuses, reach the island and open the miniature door. I squeeze into a dark circular shaft and

Thay Minh Do,
Phat Quoc Tu Vien Vietnamese Temple
Lumbini, Nepal

climb a homemade bamboo ladder through a trap door onto a tiny platform halfway up. I'm crouched inside a dark cavity with only a sliver of light from the door I left open. Another ladder leads to a narrow door and into Lake Temple.

There's only one room, about nine feet square. It's surrounded by sliding glass windows with a full view of the lakes and gardens. In the center of the room sits a magnificent hand-carved, wooden sculpture of Quan Am, the multi-armed female Bodhisattva of Compassion, whose many hands symbolize helping all beings. The figure is brightly painted and all the hands are gold. On the same pedestal, at the foot of Quan Am, is a small tiled pad with an ochre cushion, just large enough for one person to sit cross-legged.

Stepping stones to "Lake Temple"
Vietnamese Temple
Lumbini, Nepal

I slide open a large window and step onto a red tiled walkway that wraps the periphery. I lean on an ornate bamboo railing admiring a Sarus crane fishing for dinner near workers tending a garden. I go back inside and sit on the cushion. Directing my consciousness inward, I apply Minh Do's instructions: 'Now I'll inhale . . . now I'll exhale . . .'

Minh Do, another monk, and a woman are at a hibachi-style wooden table when I enter the dining hall. The room could seat one hundred people, and it echoes with just the four of us. Colorful vegetable dishes are neatly arranged with a heaping bowl of steaming rice. Each place has a dainty ceramic tea cup.

Minh Do points me to his side. He introduces Nguyen, a monk from Ho Chi Minh City, who's been practicing here for two weeks, and Yen, a woman from California, who's a student of the master. Yen has volunteered to cook for the two months she's here. Nguyen, in his early twenties, is slender and nearly my height. Yen looks to be in her mid-sixties and in good physical shape. Minh Do motions for quiet. He lifts a small bell and rings it three times. He sings a short prayer with Yen and Nguyen joining in. When the prayer's finished, all three clasp their hands and bow in appreciation to all who contributed to bringing this meal to us.

"You eat now," Minh Do says. "Remember, eating for nourishment to keep body alive—not for enjoyment. Enjoy is okay. But not purpose. Must not be fussy eaters. Take what have and be thankful. Eat all, no waste. Buddhist never waste." He clasps his hands, closes his eyes, bows, and then rises to leave. Like Vivekananda, he's vowed not to eat past noontime.

"I see you in morning," he says to me. "Breakfast at seven, okay?"

I nod.

I address Nguyen, "How long have you been a monk?"

"Four years. Since eighteen. Live in very small monastery in Ho Chi Minh City. I learn from my master, he ninety-four years. Master send me here to practice."

His English is better than Minh Do's, but he still has trouble understanding me.

"Nguyen is a very diligent monk, Mark," Yen says. "He's been chanting the names of Buddha twice a day. You'll hear him in the temple."

Nguyen's face lights up. "Yes, I chant the names of each of 11,100 Buddhas and do prostration to each. This my project. Have book of names of each Buddha. When I finish, I leave." I can see his passion. "Maybe you join me," he says. "Okay for you sit and watch."

I accept his invitation.

The vegetarian stir-fry dishes, sautéed greens, and soup are healthy and look as good as they taste. In traditional Asian style, we fill a small bowl with rice, and then mix vegetables from the community dishes using chopsticks.

"Your cooking is delicious," I tell Yen.

"Thanks," she says. "With five children and four grandchildren I cook often. That's my way of giving to my family and others."

"Since I benefit from your work, how can I help?" I ask.

Nguyen kicks in. "We wash dishes for her, okay?"

After dinner, Nguyen coaches me at the kitchen sink. "This is opportunity to be very mindful," he says. "Place silverware in the basket with intention. No rush, no hurry. Take time and pay attention to every detail. Be exact."

Twenty-two-year-old Nguyen isn't coaching me on washing dishes. He's guiding me to be mindful and conscious during life's routine duties and I appreciate his courage to share with an elder student. He's sharing the teachings of his ninety-four-year-old master. "Do this way with everything," Nguyen tells me. "All day can do like this. Understand?"

I do understand. Practice at Panditarama brought me to realize that a huge part of my daily activities are mindless actions. But what is not clear is how to live like this in the fast-paced, working world. How do I respond mindfully when the boss needs a report in ten minutes? How do I remain mindful when an impatient driver blares his horn at me when I'm late for a doctor's appointment?

I'm in a deep sleep when I abruptly awaken at 1:00 AM. I'm disoriented and don't know where I am. I sit up and look around but it's pitch black and I can't see a thing. Not the slightest sound breaks the stillness to give me a clue where I am. It's the most unusual feeling—consciousness submersed in blackness. I'm acutely aware, but I've no idea if I'm in Nepal, India, or the United States. I sit keenly alert for what seems like several minutes, straining for some sense perception so I can place myself, but I find none—not a smell nor a touch to give me a clue. I just . . . am. I'm pure awareness. Just that.

I feel around for clues. I feel my body, my hands, and the warmth from my sleeping bag. I don't feel Jayne next to me, and I'm in a sleeping bag—those are clues. I feel the mosquito net ... suddenly, it all comes together—I'm at the Vietnamese temple.

My heart's pounding. I'm alarmed, alert, and unable to sleep. I lie down, thinking about that extraordinary feeling of being only consciousness. I felt almost absent of my body. The experience reminded me of Arpi's darkroom meditation. I wonder what this experience means. Is it tied to my meditation practice? Is it a clue to *no self*?

I awaken at 6:30AM feeling slightly guilty for sleeping past four. I'm a free spirit coming out of Panditarama's rigorous schedule. I get dressed while a small team of mosquitoes pesters me.

Minh Do and Nguyen are already seated and Yen is placing bowls of rice porridge when I arrive. Minh Do sings a thankfulness prayer.

"How you sleep?" he asks.

I consider telling him about my middle-of-the-night experience, but the language barrier seems too great.

"OK. I was tired."

"Practice this morning?" he asks.

"No, Thay, too tired," I say. "I'm getting adjusted. Tomorrow morning I'll get up earlier." I hope he doesn't think I'm lazy.

"I chant every morning before breakfast," he says. "Chant one hour, then sit two hours. Finish sitting, I come breakfast." He pauses. "I think good for you. I think you join me. It's okay?"

He's sincere –I know he's not pressuring me. Disrupting the early morning silence with chanting doesn't appeal to me, but I'm here to learn and I trust Minh Do.

"Yes, Thay, I'd like to chant with you. What time?"

"In main temple at 4:00AM, Mark. Awake at three-thirty and chant at four."

"And then sitting meditation for two hours?"

"I sit in Buddha room two hours. Okay if you join me, okay if not. You sit where you wish. Up to you."

"I've tried morning meditation with Thay, Mark," Yen says. "It's hard for me at that hour. It's too cold. I've my own practice in my room. But it's good for you to join him."

They speak in Vietnamese for several minutes. Nguyen and Yen listen attentively, as a student listens to a teacher. Once finished, Minh Do addresses me in the best English he can muster.

"There are different kind of mind you know, Mark?" he begins. "There are buffalo mind. Buffalo mind slow-moving. No aware of surrounding. Only aware of hunger, cold, tired. It go where want to go. It move when want. No aware." He shakes his head. "Only move in response to craving. Hot, move to shade. Cold, move in sun. Hungry, find food." His eyes brighten. "Buffalo mind can be trained. First put rope around neck. Can use rope to lead around. When good with rope then can ride on back. Slowly we steer where want to go. Eventually can even sing while riding Buffalo back. This is goal. This we can do."

I smile at the buffalo analogy because it's so similar to my analogy of my mind as a stallion—an image I prefer to the buffalo. A stallion is magnificent and beautiful. Its enormous strength can be leveraged for hard work when it's disciplined. These are qualities of a trained mind as well. Hearing Minh Do say we can harness and ride a buffalo while singing, gives me hope that I can indeed train the stallion and ride it—an accomplishment that too often seems impossible.

"Also monkey mind there is," Minh Do continues. "Monkey mind always jumping. Jump here, jump there. See banana, grab and eat. Feel bug in fur, itch right away. See girl monkey, go immediately. Monkey mind always jumping. When doing a daily duty don't be monkey mind. Be in yourself. Don't let monkey mind jump out of self. Then you lost! Stay in self. When walking feel feet. Look around. Take in what you see but feel your feet." He pauses to emphasize. "Stay in yourself. Don't let mind stick to things."

I'm engrossed. His passion invigorates me.

"Buddha said he cannot help us with this," Minh Do continues. "We have to do. Buddha say don't worship him, don't pray to him. He say don't ask him for help. Up to us. We must turn selves into a Buddha. We have to do work. Everyone can be a Buddha! You understand like this?"

All three of us nod, completely tuned in to his teaching.

"It's good. It's important. Stay in yourself."

He stops, pauses, rings the bell, and sings a Vietnamese chant ending his breakfast teaching.

"Lunchtime at eleven thirty, Mark. You okay until then?"

"Yes."

After washing dishes, I head to the Lake Temple, squeeze up the shaft and sit on the single cushion. Brilliant green parakeets chatter loudly, gliding between the trees. I feel like I'm in a ranger station overlooking a forest.

I adopt Panditarama's schedule and decide to alternate one hour of walking with one hour of sitting meditation. After sitting an hour, I slip onto the outer tiled promenade and slowly walk paying attention to sensations in my feet. I note objects of perception flow into and out of consciousness. I know the mental exercise well.

But on this narrow and elevated walkway, turning each corner delivers a scene of fresh beauty that steals my attention. I have monkey mind—and it's jumping from birds to the workers to the sound of the Nguyen's bell ringing in the temple. Grrrrrrr. My shoulders tense. I'm frustrated. My monkey mind is wildly grasping at beauty.

'Stay in *self*,' I mentally remind myself. When a bright, golden wasp lands on the railing next to me, my monkey mind locks onto it, 'sticks to it' as Minh Do would say, and for a brief spell, I lose broad awareness of all that is around me. I am "outside of self." It happens over and over again.

Besides preparing meals, Yen helps interpret Minh Do's teachings. She's a hard worker, clearly enjoying serving the monks.

"How your practice this morning, Mark?" Minh Do asks.

"Monkey mind was too active." I say still frustrated. Yen and Nguyen chuckle. I tell him about my experiences.

"So I stuck to the wasp, right?"

"Yes. Mind stick to wasp. But you catch. This good. Only stick little while. Okay to look, okay to see, see all, but no stick."

"Is it possible to not stick at all?"

"Yes. Must! Must always stay in self and no stick. Stick and see one thing, nothing else. No stick and see all. Understand like that?" As he talks his facial expressions and gestures convey a wisdom acquired through direct experience.

After lunch, I join Nguyen in the temple for his prostrations. The sun barrages through the temple door and the cool marble floor feels refreshing against the hot air. My pants and shirt stick to my body. I'm not thrilled to be doing prostrations now but its an opportunity to learn from him.

"I show ceremony first," Nguyen says. He strikes a bronze bowl. With his other hand, he grabs a small Vietnamese book and loudly sings two sentences. The sound resonates between the cavernous marble walls. The fragrant incense, burning candles, and beautiful statues, give the room a deeply spiritual ambiance.

"We show respect to ancestor Buddha," Nguyen says. "Prostrate like this." He kneels, extends his body forward, places palms, elbows, and face on his mat, and then while resting on his elbows turns his palms upward and raises them. He then reverses the sequence to end standing. I follow his example.

Back home at my Zen temple, it took years before I could experience chanting as any kind of entry to consciousness. At first, chanting seemed mechanical, but I now realize its value in training me in mindfulness. I've yet to find such value in doing prostrations, which feel like busy work to me. Yet all traditions have a place for prostrations. But why 11,100? Or, in Ani Dechen's case, 100,000? And why do them in the heat of the afternoon? But I'm here to learn so I use the ritual to put "microscopic attention" on each knee bend, each bodily movement, each placement of my hand. I keep my mind in *self*.

"Now we do for next Buddha name," Nguyen says. His book lists 11,100 names of people who've attained Buddha-hood in this tradition. He duplicates the sequence for each name. We repeat the sequence over and over. I'm breathing hard my clothes are sweat-soaked. Perspiring as well, Nguyen is focused on ringing, singing, and prostrating. He doesn't flinch. He ignores the stream of sweat flowing down his face. I admire his discipline. As we near one hour, I feel weak and fatigued while Nguyen continues strong. I'm ready to quit, and he soon does. With reverence he closes the book, places it on the altar, bows one last time, and we exit onto the shaded balcony to cool off. We rest together in silence.

Later, on my way to Lake Temple, Minh Do approaches. He smiles, "How go today?"

"I did prostrations with Nguyen. I followed his movements."

"He explain to you of prostrations?"

"I know how to do them but I don't understand why we do them. Buddha told us not to worship him. Yet, in so many places, I see Buddhists doing prostrations. Why?" I remember Ani Dechen's explanation at Lawudo Gompa—to remove karma from past lives, but I want to hear Minh Do's thoughts.

"Not bow to Buddha," Minh Do shakes his head. "Not worship Buddha. No. When do prostrations, you clean bad karma. We all carry bad karma. Everybody! Carry from past lives. Sometimes very much. Can undo bad karma here in this life." He looks toward Lake Temple. "We like mirror clouded by bad karma from past. Each time we meditate, or do good task, or do prostration we clean mirror. Every prostration clean. Many prostrations take much off."

Same basic response as Ani Dechen's. I'm still uncomfortable with the concept of karma from past lives. Everything else in Buddhism is tangible—it can be experienced in this life. Not so with karma, which is faith based. I don't believe in karma—I struggle with it but I can't explain this to my teacher. I'm afraid he won't understand me.

"I turned the prostrations into a mental exercise," I say instead, explaining how I focused on my movements.

"It good. When doing prostrations, you doing action outside but you inside your mind. Same thing chanting. When chanting eyes look at words but you stay inside. Everything like that. Practice stay in self."

I feel a warm friendship growing between us. Minh Do's accomplishments at taming the mind are advanced, although he'd never claim so. I'd be quite privileged and pleased if my stay left us with an ongoing dharma-based relationship.

Back at Lake Temple, I slither up the pillar and onto my personal lookout cushion. Over and over I become frustrated because I cannot bring my mind to silence. My concentration is pitiful. Once again I've been bucked off the stallion's back. If I felt comfortable saying "shit" out loud in a temple, I might do that. But I remain quiet. Good thing. Suddenly I hear noises and the door squeaks open. Nguyen enters, looking apologetic.

"Excuse," Nguyen says. "So sorry but Thay Minh Do say we clean main temple. You and I clean. Come with me, okay?"

I'm surprised. Minh Do had refused my previous offers to help. "We clean altar," Nguyen says. "Not for workers to clean Buddha."

The peak of the afternoon sun has passed and the temple's just beginning to cool. We use four pure-white linen cloths and crystal-clear water in two unstained buckets reserved for this task alone. The Buddha statues look well cared for. Feet bare, Nguyen climbs atop the altar, face-to-face with one life size Buddha likeness.

"I clean past Buddha, you clean present Buddha," he says referring to the left and center figures. The third Buddha is the future Buddha.

Starting at the crown of the head he dips the rag in water and gingerly wipes. "Do mindfully, Mark. No think, just do. To clean Buddha statue is also clean the mind."

That's why Minh Do asked me to help; it's part of practice. Maybe Minh Do, knowing of my frustration with meditation, is giving me an opportunity to meditate in a different way.

Nguyen works exactingly and his face glows with satisfaction. For him, there's no greater honor than to clean the Buddha statue. We work barefoot on the altar in silence for forty-five minutes. Soft streams of incense smoke trail by and the shrill sound of tropical birds echoes as we focus our minds on stroking the clean linen across, into, and through each and every crevice of the elegant figures. It works; switching mindfulness techniques helps me concentrate on the task at hand.

Mealtimes become precious not only because of Yen's delicious food, but because of Minh Do's teaching. With each teaching, a jewel is handed to me. This evening I learn his perspective on love.

"There are different kind of love," Minh Do begins. "Some based on wanting or need. This love causes conflict in family. Create disagreements, disappointments, and even fight. Not good in family to have love based on wanting."

"Minh Do, how about living in monastery?" I ask, curious about the monastic aspect. "Everyone depends on and needs from each other, right?"

"Ahhh, no," he says, shaking his head. "Monastery very different. Monk vows to follow 250 rules. All monks want other person be free of suffering. So put others first. In monastery others have food first, get comfort first." He pauses. "Then okay for monk do for self."

That's good in theory, I think. But I've heard that monasteries can have similar conflicts as do families.

"Wanting for self is not just family problem. Whole world problem. Cause many wars. Want power, want land, mineral, and oil. Kill because of want. Many die! Very sad. It all monkey mind. Mind jump here and then mind jump there. But!" he brightens. "If calm, if people calm, then different. People look inside, then no need for war, no need for kill. Must stay inside self."

His wisdom comes from experience. Vietnam has had many wars. He has first-hand knowledge both of war's insanity and how a calm mind promotes peace.

That night, I retire early so I can join Minh Do at 4:00AM. Intermittently during the day, I've pondered my experience of waking in the dark—and it stirs within me now in my room.

As I sit on my bed, I see the candle flame wave, bounce, and flicker. It occurs to me that the fragile flame is much like consciousness or *self*. I see the candlestick there just like I can see my body here but the flame is of a completely different nature. The flame is not the candle, nor is it part of it. The flame is not something solid that one can grab onto. Its presence is obvious but in no way an object. The flame is a process happening moment to moment, but only when the conditions are just right. If conditions are not properly supportive, the flame instantly disappears. It vanishes without a trace. It's that fragile and it can indeed vanish because it is not a thing—it's a process.

In the same way, my consciousness happens moment to moment. If the supporting conditions are just right, then consciousness continues. Take away essential conditions, the process stops, and all that remain are the supporting elements. When a flame disappears it leaves the wax, wick, and surrounding air, so too when consciousness disappears it leaves a body. Just as the flame appears to be an entity in and of itself—but is not, so it is with consciousness. We fool ourselves with the illusion that our *self* is solid, existing in and of itself. We think the body is *self*, that we exist independently. Maybe what we really are is that fragile flame burning and flickering . . . just being.

At 3:30 AM, I fight the temptation to stay in bed. After slipping in some stretching exercises, I step outside into the pristine pre-dawn. Standing alone, I drink in the wonder of the universe. All of creation seems locked in sleep; there's not a breeze, not a sound. Only stillness. Not even the jackals dare break the silence. I look up at the temple and see flickering candlelight leaking from the temple's large circular windows. Minh Do's already at practice. The black silhouette of the roofline dragon appears like a monster gliding through the twilight sky. A quarter crescent moon shines just above the dragon. It's an enchanting sight.

Climbing the long staircase allows me time to fully drink the morning's cool stillness. From the distance comes the 4:00 AM morning bell, and the deep, rich sound sweeps the entire preserve. It's the same bell that awakened me at Panditarama. Moments later, another bell rings out as Minh Do strikes the first of a series. A Sarus crane trumpets a call of alarm.

At the top, I swing open the massive wooden door. A single candle is lit on each of the three altars highlighting the statues' facial features in a way that almost brings them to life. Minh Do is lighting incense, the visible scent rising vertically into the stagnant air. He wears yellow ceremonial robes. He does not acknowledge me. Rather, he moves to the next altar and strikes a metal bell. The whole room becomes a large bell, reverberating with each strike. As the sound nearly subsides, he strikes a second time, and then a third, before prostrating three times. I do the same.

For the next several minutes, he steps to each figure, studies it as if to be reminded of its symbolic meaning, and then prostrates three times. I mirror his every step and try to follow his advice: "Stay in self, keep empty mind, feel your feet."

He moves to the 'ancestor altar,' which has framed photographs of people, young and old, both recent and from the past. Similarly, he lights an incense stick, rings a bowl, and fills a brass goblet with a water offering.

After the ritual at four separate altars, Minh Do returns to the main altar, assumes a lotus position on a small rug, places a chanting book on a stubby pedestal in front of him, lights a candle that illuminates the Vietnamese script, and then strikes a small brass bell. For the next forty-five minutes, he chants rapidly, simultaneously ringing the bell.

I can literally see the concentration on his face. His chanting alternates between a slow and a rapid-fire pace. He fluctuates between melodic and monotone. The bell is irregularly struck at specific syllables, sometimes in rapid succession. It's a detailed execution of a complex composition that could only happen with a fully present mind. And that's the goal of course—to train the mind to be fully present.

He ends an hour later, replaces the books, extinguishes but one candle, and bows—including to me. It's his first acknowledgment of me. His mind has been fully devoted to his practice. How can I not admire that?

We step outside and he whispers, "Now meditate."

This is my first time meditating in the Buddha room. It's a simple room with a wooden floor, painted walls, and a low ceiling. It can hold perhaps forty meditators. The altar is a wooden desk with a three-foot Buddha statue, candles, incense, and a bowl of fruit. A single cushion sits on the floor at the foot of the altar. I grab a cushion from the corner as Minh Do lights incense and a candle.

For two hours we sit illuminated by flickering candlelight. This is my first two-hour meditation session—ever. After an hour-and-a-half, I begin to squirm. Minh Do does not. My knees ache, my back is sore, and my mind is mentally fatigued. I endure because I want to practice with Minh Do. It feels good to be in his presence. Two hours pass and Minh Do quietly rises, prostrates to the Buddha likeness, and again bows to me.

"Breakfast now," he says softly.

Minh Do has given me a gift—a teaching not through words but through example. He's shown me his early morning routine, which is a mirror reflection of his words. I feel privileged to be at his side, and that goodness will come out of this.

At breakfast I admit that I had trouble concentrating.

To my surprise, he says, "It good, Mark. You aware of problems. Most people not aware of what they think or not think. You are aware what you think. This is an advance. This is step forward."

He's right! I've been using the wrong yardstick. I've been comparing myself to where I'd like to be and forgetting how far I've come. My frustration lifts.

"Also Mark," he continues, "be careful of trying too hard. Practicing is like guitar. If string too tight it break. If too loose not make right sound. If you striving hard then have expectations—attached to results. This mean improperly tuned."

Bhaddamanika said the same thing. I plead guilty. My expectations got me in trouble again.

Early each morning, I hear a drumbeat. I hear people marching along the path near the temple. I've heard it every morning at six, even at Panditarama. I ask Minh Do about it.

"That Japanese monks. Every morning walk path to Buddha's birthplace, do circle march, then sitting meditation at birthplace. Anyone can join."

"It's okay with you if I join them one morning?"

"Sure, it's okay."

Chapter 12

A Back Door Exit

Lumbini, Nepal

Must always know what I thinking! Must always know what I feeling.

> Thay Minh Do
> Vietnamese Phat Quoc Tu Vien Temple

I've been following Minh Do's advice to not push my meditation practice hard. My concentration still falters but I'm more accepting, not as frustrated. Bhaddamanika said that concentration will fluctuate and I only need to wait for improvement—but how long does that take?

I've been calling Jayne every other day on my cell phone. It's good to have the freedom to talk. Things are well at home.

"Do you know when you might come home?" she asks.

She asks every so often. I've been here five months.

"I don't know," I say. It's what I always say.

"Okay." She hesitates. "Where to next?" It says a lot about her that she doesn't push me.

"My Nepal visa expires soon," I tell her, "then I'm off to Vietnam."

"We'll talk before you leave, right?" she asks.

"Yes, I'll call soon."

Sitting for two hours every morning is a killer. I'm pretty dull in the morning and I need coffee to sharpen my wits. I borrow the temple's bicycle and ride to the village shop. I've been isolated for five weeks so I'm apprehensive about how this short jaunt will affect my mindfulness. It's an opportunity to put what I've learned into practice. I pass several women in brilliantly colored saris balancing brick-filled baskets atop their heads. *Don't stick to anything.* I remind myself to perceive the whole scene rather than "sticking" to any one thing. It takes effort amidst all the unusual sights. As I do though, it leaves a feeling of fullness, completeness, and contentment. It's good.

Near the village, the front tire strikes a sharp rock, pops, and flattens. A bicycle repairman in his late twenties sits on the roadside with a bicycle pump and a half dozen tires and tubes that he's placed on a dusty boulder. This is his career, his source of income. I show him the tire.

"No problem," he smiles. "Done soon, sir."

In a tiny village shop, I sift through old wooden shelves and strike it rich. "Yes! A box of coffee."

The village shops have electricity and there's an ancient computer available for rent. I grab the chance to catch up on e-mail. But once on the computer, I quickly get lost in thinking and analyzing. I'm out of the "self" Minh Do told me to stay put in. Occasionally, I become alert that I'm 'out of self,' yet I'm just as quickly immersed again in emails. Is it possible, I wonder again, to engage in thought-intensive work at my job and remain in *self*? This nagging question has broad implications for my career.

Back at Lake Temple, I experience a kind of connectedness that is new. It's a feeling of wholeness in coming back, fullness, and strong inward focus. I'm aware and rooted in my *self*. I feel full of life. It's incredibly refreshing. I wish I understood what triggered this state. Was it the trip to the village? The cup of coffee? Coming back? Could it be that my practice is paying off?

Before dinner, I come across Minh Do walking a winding stone path in a Feng Shui garden. I ask him, "Thay, I'll make lifestyle changes when I return home. I like my engineering career. The work is fun and challenging and I think I'm skilled at it. But it is thought intensive and I need to decide if I'll resume it. Do you think if I practice diligently that I could maintain strong mindfulness when working?" I pause. "If I do continue to be an engineer, I plan to use more of my earnings to help others."

There's so much I admire about Minh Do but at the top of the list is the way he stands facing me when we converse, his hands humbly folded in front, his deep dark eyes mindfully focused.

"That is good, Mark. Okay to work and help people. But not as good as teaching dharma or Buddhist practice. If teach Buddhism, it has major effects on universe. Helping is good but only temporary. It like helping beggar. Give beggar money then eat one night. But teach beggar how make money then have many dinners. Same with teaching dharma."

"Maybe I can be an engineer and help teach the dharma somewhere. But engineering has difficult mathematical problems. I literally get lost in thought. That's the only way I know to solve technical problems. How can I be mindful at the same time?"

He pauses again. "Not at your level," he finally says, and my heart sinks. "Very difficult to be mindful and fix problems. I think better for you practice. Practice number one priority because help yourself and others. Must be within your self!" His tempo picks up as he speaks. "Meditating on loving kindness is good. It does more good for the world than anything else. It like TV station. It broadcast and available for many people to tune in and use."

I'm uncomfortable. I love my work. I don't feel qualified to teach the dharma, and I'm not ready to focus on meditation and teaching. But I won't let this upset me. I don't have to decide the matter until my plane lands in Cleveland.

I've been here a week-and-a-half, and ask to stay the week-and-a-half that remains on my visa. Minh Do approves.

Nguyen completed his prostrations and left a few days ago. Only the three of us remain. I've found a good friend in Yen in part because of her good heartedness. She's like Sangmo at Lawudo Gompa, always serving others. When I've helped with dishes she's shared her life story, which is filled with hardship overcome through faith.

My reverence for Minh Do grows daily; he has an impeccable commitment to practice. Every morning, well before the faintest glow of the sun, I propel myself from bed for the opportunity to chant and sit with him. Now that Nguyen's left, Minh Do does the 11,100 afternoon prostrations and I frequently join him.

This afternoon, I'm with Minh Do while he's chanting. Talagram enters the temple, stands next to Minh Do with hands clasped, needing to speak. But practice being Minh Do's number one priority, he doesn't even acknowledge Talagram's presence. After waiting several minutes, Talagram leaves but quickly returns and places himself between Minh Do and the Buddha statue—a rather bold move. Minh Do continues both chanting and drumming until he finishes a segment. He pauses chanting but continues drumming while he addresses Talagram's urgent issue. Apparently the gate is locked and keys are lost. Minh Do instructs Talagram, who then leaves. Minh Do immediately resumes chanting. I don't believe Minh Do's response is rude. Rather it's a demonstration of determination, persistence and effort—the same DPE that Vivekananda teaches.

The next afternoon work is under way at Lake Temple, so I meditate in the Buddha room. I find Minh Do leaning against the second-floor railing, overlooking the grounds. I stand beside him. Black crows are screeching loudly and flitting between tree branches. The sun is beginning to set. The temperature is in the low eighties but the mild breeze makes it feel just perfect.

"It's a magnificent garden," I say.

"Yes, it good," he says softly. He seems extraordinarily calm—I haven't seen him so calm. It's unlike him, though, not to look at me. He continues gazing at the garden.

"I practicing seventeen years," he says. "Now just three or four months ago became satisfied with practice. Every second I come back. I know what I am thinking." He turns and looks at me. "Must always know what I am thinking! Must always know what I am feeling! And I do."

He's sharing his personal story and I'm surprised he's confiding in me.

"My mind come home. I come back into myself," Minh Do says. "No get angry. I return into myself, have no worries. Seventeen years!"

He's opening his heart to me, in no way complaining or bragging.

"But before that very hard to remember. Not remember to come home. It like knowing where the front gate to Lumbini is but forget about. Cannot find way back. But now—now I start to walk away from Lumbini gate and remember where is. I can go back. I go back immediately."

I see the analogy.

"Now, when I work hard, I not feel tired. I happy. I be working hard and hungry, no problem. I can be sick, but still happy. I happy only myself. No need people help me happy." He nods to himself. "Not sure when I can be Buddha. Don't know when I can reach that. Maybe next life, don't know."

He pauses again. "But I feel like I can remember at dying time. When I die, I believe can remember to be in myself, to come home to help with next life."

Buddhists believe that if you can keep your mind calm and aware during your last moments you'll carry the composure needed to select an appropriate body, preferably a human one, to be reborn into.

"Many people not realize they have what needed," Minh Do says. "They all have. It's like everyone, everybody, poor, sick, old, young, all people have a diamond right in them. Big diamond! They're very, very rich! But they don't know. They don't see. But always there."

"My teacher Craig, back home, tells me it's like you're dying of thirst but you're standing in water up to your neck."

"Yes!" Minh Do exclaims. "Yes, like that. Exactly, like that."

"I'm happy for you, Thay. Is it frustrating that it took seventeen years of effort?"

"You can do it. Must remember come back. Must remember come home. Every time come back into self. Very hard. Very hard to do. Until three years ago could not do. Must always, always remember to come back home."

"Thank you, Minh Do," I bow in gratitude. "You inspire me."

"Remember Mark, don't let things stick. You can look outside, you can look around but don't let monkey mind stick out there. Bring it back! Only see, not follow."

"I always worry that when I return to the city I'll get lost in thought and lose concentration."

"Body can go anywhere but mind not come, not go. Go anywhere but stay in empty mind. Don't let mind worry. If you worry, then empty mind becomes monkey mind. Just empty mind. That all."

Minh Do has passed me a key, something I can hold onto, something solid which will help me further develop consciousness. Seeing Thay Minh Do practice diligently and catching this glimpse of the rewards further motivate me.

Minh Do teaches through example and I've tried to do the same thing as a parent. He's a humble monk of incredible depth. I feel like he's holding candy in front of a child—me—and I want some of that candy. And he just told me how to get it.

I've sometimes noticed a slight fear when I look at Minh Do. The fear is buried a couple of levels down and I haven't been able to pinpoint exactly what it's about, until now. Fear stems from my admiration for this humble monk; I'm drawn to him as a person and I find his lifestyle attractive. But it's deeper than that. Finally, today I saw the fear clearly—the fear that I'm being called to become *a monk*. Something is simmering within me. I'm not sure what's next.

After breakfast the next day, Minh Do says, "Excuse please. Need you help me today."

"Sure, Thay." He rarely requests help.

"Need plants for garden. Want buy plants for near guesthouse. We go to city and buy. You help me pick, please. You good at garden."

Landscaping is my hobby and I've recently suggested a few things to Minh Do. We walk to the village to hire a taxi. It's a quiet walk; it's great just to be with him. As we travel from the tiny village to the city, it feels like a transition from Beethoven to Acid Rock. *Don't stick, stay in self,* I remind myself like a cheerleader. My personal task is to stay in observer mode as I help.

My sensory perceptions are crisp and colors seem brilliant. Sounds are sharp and the smells, pungent and aromatic—a result, I think, of being secluded in meditation. The taxi pulls into an empty lot scattered with loose bricks and logs and intermingled with haphazardly placed potted plants. As Minh Do converses with a gardener, I step to the street corner where the scene is noisy and chaotic. This is an opportunity to practice mindfulness in the midst of busyness.

I am pounded with sensory stimulation; Horns honking, motorcycles squeezing by inches away, loud trucks spewing dark soot into the air, beautiful women in flamboyant colored saris, and the tempting aroma of roasting peanuts from a street-side vendor. These sites, sounds, and smells compete for my attention. They're drawing me to 'stick' my conscious awareness on them. Holding my head still, I use direct and peripheral vision to perceive the entire scene while I apply Minh Do's advice: "no stick and see all." Observing in this manner, my mind remains detached and calm. I'm cognizant of the entire experience and also aware of my mind. It's not easy, but I'm doing it. I'm beginning to understand the significance of Minh Do's advice: I have a richer experience than by not sticking than if I'd allowed my awareness to be scattered.

Minh Do begins selecting plants and I move to help. He's randomly selects plants—and they are not the choices I'd make. I make suggestions but I don't steer the outcome. In the past, I'd have more aggressively pushed my ideas on him. But now there seems no 'right' or 'wrong.' I'm more accepting, which feels good in a peaceful way. I notice how easy it is to get lost in thought when making decisions. This time I'm able to catch thoughts quickly and 'bring myself home.' We load the trunk and as we head back and I share my street-corner experience with Minh Do.

"That's good. That's right thing. Was hard?"

"Yes, but I was carefully watching my mind—staying in self."

"Yes, good you not stick. Must be aware of self always. Very simple but very difficult. VERY difficult!" He shakes his head.

"When picking out the flowers, Thay, were you judging good and bad, right and wrong color, or size? How do you stay in yourself while making decisions?

"Just be clear you're making decisions," he says. "Be aware every instant what thinking. Danger is not being aware. When making decisions, know you making decisions. If angry, know you angry. If happy, know that too. Danger is you become lost. Must come back to self. You understand like that?"

"I'm beginning to."

"Good! For me seventeen years to get. All people different. Some more. Some less."

Tomorrow I plan another village excursion to make travel arrangements. I'm glad I'm tapering into the busy world under the direction of an accomplished monk. I didn't plan it that way. Again, I feel I've been led—as if my experiences have occurred in planned sequence, each step building upon the previous. I've become more aware of how life hands us events in an orderly way if we allow it.

This morning Minh Do and Yen remind me that a tour bus of visitors will arrive. "May be noisy," Minh Do warns. "Almost forty-five people."

Shortly after noon, a dust covered bus arrives and a whirlwind of activity erupts. Out of the bus come nuns, all wearing powder blue, full-length robes.

The temple grounds transition from placid to a beehive-like flurry as nuns weave through the gardens, chant in the temple, and converse in scattered groups. Few speak English, leaving little opportunity to mingle. I exchange my prime Lake Temple for the privacy and quietude of the secluded Buddha room. My concentration suffers.

At breakfast the next morning, the cavernous dining hall is full of life, almost raucous. Thay Huyen Dieu has returned with the group and I'm privileged to sit at his table along with Minh Do, Yen, and two nuns. Both nuns are friendly and acknowledge me with an occasional smile but they don't speak English. The senior nun, SuBa (which means Elder Sister), is short and much older. She wears oversized, baggy robes with an unassuming gray sweater on top and a brown hood that seems more for warmth than a sign of status. At her side is a five-foot, hand-carved wooden stick.

When she speaks, everyone listens intently, even Minh Do and Thay Huyen Dieu. She glances at me frequently and I return her smiles.

Conversations are solely in Vietnamese, so I stay in 'self' and observe. Later, I ask Thay Huyen Dieu if he has time for a question. We arrange to meet in the garden later.

"It's a pleasure to have you here," Thay Huyen Dieu says when I meet him.

I bow and thank him for his time, "You know that I'm traveling for several months learning Buddhist practices." He nods. "My life in the United States is usually busy. I plan to continue a strong practice at home and wish to bring mindfulness into my busy life. Is it possible to have a strong practice living a very busy life? I see you're involved in many things and can give me useful insight."

"Yes, of course!" he says without hesitation. "It's very possible. To do so you must build firm mindfulness. You must always be mindful. You must meditate daily. No exceptions. This must be your priority."

"I think I can do that," I say. Several people approach him and he notices.

"Good. Having a daily routine is essential. Also it's important not to stick things. You know what I mean by that?"

"Minh Do's talked about that."

"Okay, always remember that and you will have a strong practice."

Pressured to move on, the master rises. I bow and hand him a donation envelope. He returns the bow, and addresses the next person.

Within an hour, the bus loads and departs. The head nun, SuBa, and her personal assistant remain behind. Quiet returns, and I resume my practice.

I see Minh Do at the Lake Temple watching the Sarus cranes, so I join him.

"How you meditation? Concentration better?"

"Sometimes good, sometimes not good. But now I accept either. So it's better."

He pauses, thinking. "I think you try other meditation method, more advanced," he says. I feel a tingle of excitement; it's like I'm being promoted.

"Be aware of breath," he says, "but not focus on it. Focus on yourself and everything around. Feel, hear, be aware of everything. Very powerful and quick way to advance." He changes tone. "Most people start meditation have very bad monkey mind. Must count breaths, otherwise monkey mind jump away. Breath always moving so easier to focus. But when concentration stronger then can focus on being one. Can feel one with all. Not everyone can do. Once you get advanced state your practice move quicker. Can advance faster."

"So if I stay in *self* for a longer time, I can advance more quickly?" I ask.

"Yes, like that." He pauses. "Mark, also important to recognize good practice. If you hear voices, feel levitated, or see Buddha, this not good. This not right practice. This is spirits tricking you. This why important to have master guide you. You travel through Asia and find masters. Many masters no speak English. It problem for you. But you'll find. Certainly you will. This is important." He deliberates. "Maybe master at BaoVan Tu monastery in Vietnam good for you," he says. "No speak English but can find interpreter. He very high level master. Almost a Buddha! He meditate in forest for long time. No eat, no sleep. Can look at sky and see stars in daytime. Can even know what you thinking. Very accomplished master."

"Can you give me directions to get there?"

"Yes. Difficult to find. Far in jungle. Take buses and motorcycle. I give you directions in Vietnamese. People help you find."

We stand a moment overlooking the lake.

"One more thing, Mark. Meditation. Don't miss day. Very important. Miss one day make second day easier to miss." He shakes his head. "You can do?"

"I can. Thay Huyen Dieu said the same. I'll practice daily."

The two nuns who remained join us for lunch. SuBa sits next to me. Everyone is talking in Vietnamese but this time I feel left out. SuBa does most of the talking and again I notice the others listen intently, especially Yen who has her hands clasped. While talking, SuBa occasionally lifts food from the main dish with her chopsticks and places it on my plate.

How kind! I figure she recognizes that I'm left out of the conversation. Occasionally, I return the gesture. This continues throughout our meal.

Afterward Yen approaches me. "Mark, you must realize that SuBa's a very high level master. She's in charge of hundreds of monks and nuns in the many temples under her direction. This is a special opportunity to interact with her."

"But I don't understand what she says. What does she talk about?"

"She's talking about dharma. I'll translate for you when I can. I apologize. It's difficult to listen and translate at the same time. Also, Mark, when she picks up food and puts it on your plate, this is a gesture of friendship. It's very special, not common. Seems she's taken a liking to you."

"I wish we could talk."

At dinner, Minh Do and SuBa join us without eating. As SuBa speaks, Yen does her best to inject translations. SuBa and I again put food onto each other's plate. SuBa asks me, through Yen, about my background and the goals for my trip.

"Come to Ho Chi Minh City and stay at my temple, Mark," SuBa says. "I'll show you many temples in Vietnam. You can stay at one for as long as you want to practice."

This is the opportunity I was hoping for. I've no connections in Vietnam except for that jungle monastery Minh Do mentioned. I accept.

"How will I contact you when I arrive?" I ask.

"I'll have SuCo Huong Nhu arrange the connection. She speaks good English," SuBa says.

"SuCo" means 'Sister' in Vietnamese and Huong Nhu is her given Buddhist name. It's acceptable to call her SuCo. It's also acceptable to call her by her given Buddhist name, Huong Nhu.

Later, Yen says, "Mark, this is incredible! I told you SuBa is accomplished—she has the ability to transmit thoughts. She was here last year and wanted to talk to the Japanese monk and he just showed up. You must visit her in Vietnam. It's a good connection."

The next morning, I meet SuCo Huong Nhu and we make arrangements to meet in Vietnam. She's highly energetic and her eyes sparkle with joy. She has a strong command of English; she seems brilliant. I feel a connection to her, similar to when I first met Minh Do. Sadly, SuBa and SuCo leave that day.

I must leave Nepal in seven days, so I bike to the village after lunch to arrange transportation. Jupiter, a man in his twenties, a student of Thay Huyen Dieu, helps me.

"I can get tickets for you to travel on the eleventh," Jupiter says. "Come back tomorrow. But a Bandh has been declared as of noon today."

My last visit was complicated because of a Bandh— which is a transportation strike called by rebel groups. It's been called because the government is writing a new constitution that offends a local rebel group. I'm concerned.

"How long will it last?" I must leave Nepal before my visa expires.

"We never sure. Usually one or two days, sometimes three. You've seven days so don't worry."

I order the tickets and return to the temple. Thay Huyen Dieu is in the hallway with a new tour group. I approach him.

"Did you know that there is a Bandh in place?" I ask.

"Yes. We're discussing this. This group is stuck here now."

The visitors will miss a flight if delayed more than one day. If they risk traveling under the Bandh, their bus could be attacked, the windows broken, and tires cut.

One day turns into two and then into three. Jupiter is having difficulty getting my ticket. On the fourth day I go see him.

"Good news, Mark. I have your tickets."

"Great! Bandh is lifted?"

"No. Your tickets were delivered by bicycle." He looks worried. "It's very unusual for a Bandh to be this long. People in the village need supplies. Food stock is low. Businesses are struggling. Tempers are getting short. How can we go on with life like this?"

He seems at his wit's end. "Living in this country is difficult even without Bandh I tell you!"

"Hopefully, it will lift soon," I try to encourage him. "But what if there's a Bandh on my travel dates? How'll I get to the border?"

"Only bicycle rickshaws are allowed to travel. It's eighteen miles to the India border, that's several hours by rickshaw. It's a long trip but you can do it."

Food supplies at the monastery are shrinking. The tour group missed their flight. Thay Huyen Dieu is trying to get the group to a small airport nearby where they can charter small planes.

Since I'm leaving soon I decide to join the Japanese drummer who marches past in the pre-dawn darkness. I slip out the gate. There's barely a glow in the eastern sky as I follow the path through the unlit fields. I'm again carrying a brick through the dark wooded area, this time in fear of dogs rather than an imaginary attacker.

Finding my way to the main path, I hear the Japanese drummer approaching. I shiver slightly as I watch a light bob up and down, growing larger as the drumbeats get louder. I use my flashlight to avoid frightening the monk. Then I see there's not one but seven monks, plus two five-years-old boys in monk's robes trailing behind the single-file procession. Each monk wears white; they look like a karate outfit. They have clean shaven heads and each monk holds a small white drum inscribed in Japanese, which they beat in unison.

I gesture to the lead monk my intention to join and, seemingly pleased, he motions me into line. The last boy in line is terrified when I suddenly appear out of the darkness. He shrieks and scurries to an elder monk, fearfully clinging to his arms. The horrified child looks back at me and I clasp my hands and bow to him with a smile.

He quickly calms and falls back into position. Another minute passes and he hands me his drum. I smile again, amazed that within minutes, his perception of me changes from dangerous stranger to trustworthy friend.

The assembly marches for a mile, to the Buddha's birthplace, encircling the brick building. The eastern horizon now glows a warm yellow and birds have started their day-break serenade. We enter the well-lit building and march to the twenty-six-hundred-year-old birth site, sit on floor cushions, and chant from booklets. The chanting ceremony is followed by fifteen minutes of silent meditation.

As we casually walk back to our different monasteries, the younger monks ask to practice their English with me. The other monks quiz me about my practice and where I live. They explain that their practice is Nipponzon Myohoji, an order of the Nichiren Buddhists dedicated to promoting peace and nonviolence worldwide, in part by marching to a drumbeat while chanting a powerful mantra. Before parting, they invite me to join them tomorrow morning. I accept.

Back at the temple, breakfast is ending. Minh Do and Yen are still sitting at the table. They set aside food for me. They look concerned.

"Problem in village last night," Minh Do says. "Violence there. Three men killed in violence because Bandh."

Shocked and saddened, I might have guessed this could happen. Everyone has been so tense. It's been like a pot ready to boil over—and now it has—and it could get worse. My instincts tell me it's best to leave tomorrow. I tell Minh Do and Yen, who look disappointed; I'm disappointed too.

As I lie in my room, I ponder the situation. Three men lay dead nearby and their families and friends are grieving. It's a small community and grief will grow into anger and then into revenge. The police will get nervous. Armed reinforcements will arrive, and that's when further clashes could begin. The situation could quickly escalate. Tomorrow's not soon enough—I must leave now.

I knock on Minh Do's door. "Thay, I'm worried more killing may occur. I'm afraid that the army may come and the situation could grow out of control. My visa expires in a few days and the situation could trap me here. I'm sad to tell you—I must leave now."

"It okay. I understand." He looks hurt.

"I want to stay in touch. I have your phone number written down. Do you have that paper with my phone number and address?" He nods. "When you come to United States, please call. I've learned so much from you. Thank you." I pause. "I'll bid farewell to Thay Huyen Dieu and Yen as well."

He steps forward and gives me a hug, which is hopefully not good-bye but a 'see you later.'

Leaving the Lumbini preserve seems surreal as I mindfully place each footstep not only because I'm staying in self, but also to extend my time on this sacred soil. My seven weeks here have given me rich insights. My life has changed in no small way.

At the gate, I negotiate with several rickshaws and choose a needy looking driver. I swing my backpack into the bamboo basket behind the heavily worn leather seat and pull down the crude bamboo canopy so that I can take in my surroundings, but not stick.

Normally an eighteen-mile rickshaw ride through quiet rural villages, surrounded by rice fields would be a lovely experience. But it's eerie to see the normally active streets empty of only a few pedestrians. I feel sorry for these people whose lives are hard—even without these political problems.

Ahead, four policemen stand in the road with two bicyclists pulled aside. Two have rifles, two have bamboo poles. I avoid eye contact fearing they might stop us. But we coast right through the checkpoint.

Shortly after, as I feared, a large flatbed truck loaded with thirty military soldiers in full riot gear passes us, heading toward Lumbini, the small village I just left. My heart sinks.

PART THREE

Vietnam

Chapter 13

The Gift

Ho Chi Minh City, Vietnam

> You will see the Buddha nature is in you. This is the main thing.
> SuBa Hue Giac
> **Quan Am Monastery**

I've arrived on the corner of Bui Vien Street, a commercial area in Ho Chi Minh City with rows of guesthouses, shops, and artists' studios. I'm searching for a guesthouse and the street is hustling with motorbikes, rickshaws, and curbside vendors selling hand-picked fruit and today's fresh catch.

I've been traveling for days by rickshaw, bus, train, and a plane. Unfortunately, my mind is unsettled; travel does that to me. An example used at Kopan was of a clear glass of water with dirt shaken up, which then gradually settles. The dirt in my mind is stirred up right now.

Ho Chi Minh City is a pleasant compromise between a fully developed western lifestyle and the impoverished but simple third world lifestyles of Nepal and India. My room is air conditioned, roadside cafés are clean, and transportation is easy and fast. But I'm feeling panicky, engulfed as I am in endless sensory stimulation—neon lights, unfamiliar smells, and chaotic traffic. This is a hectic cityscape. I've accomplished much in calming my mind the last few months—and now I'm losing those gains.

In Lumbini, the stallion was in the pen, confined by the wooden fence of regular practice and surrounded by peace and quiet. Now the stallion is disquieted with nervous energy and I'm afraid he'll jump into the wild once again. As a fix, I alternate meditation every other hour with mindful walks through the city. This experiment helps yet I feel a depression creep over me like a storm in the night. I'm anxious and I miss my teacher, Minh Do.

I have to adjust quickly. I must visit SuBa, the master who was with Minh Do in Lumbini and invited me to her monastery on the outskirts of this city. I call SuCo Huong Nhu, SuBa's senior nun who speaks English.

"You stay at SuBa's monastery tonight Mark, right?" comes her cheerful invitation.

I breathe a sigh of relief. "Yes, thank you. I look forward to seeing you again, Huong Nhu." We arrange to meet and the next afternoon, Huong Nhu arrives at my guesthouse on the back seat of a motorbike driven by a young woman.

"It very good see you, Mark!" she calls out with the same vitality I noticed when we met in Lumbini. Huong Nhu's wearing light blue robes without a headdress; her head is shaven. She's petite, with thick, dark eyebrows, bright sparkling eyes, and a vivacious smile. Her English is much better than Minh Do's.

We sit on a carved bench in the clean open-air lobby of a guesthouse.

"Mark, SuBa welcome you to her monastery. She arrange a car take us tomorrow to temples in coastal mountains. We have lunch and dinner at temples. SuBa say maybe one is good place for you practice. If you agree, she will arrange."

Huong Nhu and I sip tea as we arrange my travel to SuBa's monastery by motorcycle later this evening. With a bow, Huong Nhu returns to the motorbike and leaves.

That evening, I board the motorbike wearing my fifty-pound backpack. I stuff my duffle bag between me and the male driver and hold the seat. When the bike accelerates I roll backward and nearly fall off the back because of my backpack's weight. Only by quickly grabbing the driver's shirt—nearly ripping it—do I keep myself from falling upside down on this busy street.

The sun is setting as we weave through rush-hour traffic. The streets are flooded due to an earlier storm and traffic is backed up. Vehicles drive on the curb and sidewalk, but my driver takes us through deep water. Without a chance to object, my pant legs and calves are flushed with dirty, oily water. Fortunately my pants dry by the time we reach the university where Huong Nhu waits.

"Hurry, please" she calls, "I have taxi waiting take us to SuBa's monastery."

In the back of the taxi, Huong Nhu and I become engrossed in conversation as our route transitions from busy city to unmaintained rural roads. Huong Nhu teaches Buddhism at the Buddhist Academy a few days a week and helps SuBa the remaining days.

"We run many charity trips to villages to help poor people and blind people," she says. "SuBa get donations, and she instructs me buy food, books, and medicine. We drive hours to villages far away and hard get to. Very bad roads, you know. Still, I do. SuBa put much effort to help needy villagers."

I ask what tradition she practices.

"We practice Pure Land tradition," she says.

Pure Land Buddhism is practiced in much of eastern Asia. It focuses on Amitabha Buddha, the Buddha of infinite light and comprehensive love. Pure Land Buddhists often repeat the Buddha's name, recite scriptures about the pure land—a heaven of sorts—and visualize Amitabha Buddha.

"In Lumbini, Pure Land practitioners had many chanting sessions in the temple," I tell her.

"Yes, here we practice a combination between Buddhist meditation—purification—mysticism. Mind purification comes from chanting six sessions every day. Meditation not always at sitting posture, it can be standing, or walking with mindful chanting Buddha's Scriptures and Buddha's name. Chanting is done very fast. You listen to us?"

"I joined one session. Even with the printed words I couldn't follow. They're very fast."

"Yes. Chanting very fast holds the mind so it cannot jump to sensational feelings or thinking," she says. "Chanting is approachable to all people by simply memorizing Buddha's teaching. Reciting can purify body, speech, and thought and help us not say hurting things, telling lies, misguiding others. Also we offer dharmic sounds to all realms of existence, visible and invisible. Our collective therapeutic energy empowers existing lower realm let go on rebirth path. We practice giving care to lower realm existence as nurturing compassion," Huong Nhu explains.

Most Buddhist traditions include chanting to varying degrees. My core Zen-Shin practice at home is a unique combination of Japanese Soto Zen with Jodo Shinshu Pure Land traditions in which chanting plays a significant role. Though my sangha places greater focus on sitting meditation, I've experienced alert and calm states of mind during chanting, especially when the words are Japanese, which allows me to focus on sound and pronunciation instead of meaning. Zen Shin chants are slow and exacting, much different than the rapid chanting I observed in Lumbini. Yet, despite the focus on chanting, I hope they'll have a meditation room.

Huong Nhu continues to explain Pure Land practice. "Other practices also important. Prostrating, by touching four limbs and head to earth hundred times in session trains our body not involve in killing acts, harming acts, and gains merits for our ego training. Also we visualize Amitabha Buddha which help focus on virtues of Buddha's great vows and offers benefits to all sentient beings."

Turning off the dark road, we pass through a metal gate to the monastery. This older, well-established monastery rests under the watch of mature trees. Brightly colored shrines and sculptures nest in gardens. Prominent is a large white statue of the female deity, Quan Am, a central figure in this tradition, who personifies compassion. Pots of bonsai trees line the walkways. The grounds are clean and, aside from the elaborate statues, quite modest.

I ask how many live here.

"One hundred monks here. Over one hundred nuns, too," she tells me. "Monks stay one side, nuns on other." She points out the separated areas. There's no air conditioning and I'm sure the intense heat will challenge me. Perhaps the huge shade trees will provide relief.

It's a bit noisy though. The monastery is bounded on one side by a busy road and a rail line on the other. Many monasteries throughout Asia battle encroaching development and this one has not been spared. Built long ago on land of natural beauty and solitude, monasteries now find civilization wrapping around their quiet oases leaving them no choice but to adapt.

A young monk walks up and Huong Nhu introduces us. "Mark, this is Gia Dong," she says. "He assist you while here."

Gia Dong's in his late twenties, and has been handpicked for this role. He wears light blue robes and his head is recently shaved. He holds himself erect yet relaxed. I try to converse with him but his English is limited. Gia Dong leads me to an eight-person dorm room for visiting monks, but I've the room to myself. He hands me a light blue robe worn by other monks. It's meant to go over my clothes. I unroll my sleeping bag onto a bare wooden bench and drape a mosquito net from the ceiling. The room is dimly lit. The soft sounds of a recorded Vietnamese chant filter in from an adjacent room. Boxes of books, robes, and miscellaneous monastic articles are stored against the walls. Gia Dong hands me a printed schedule, pointing to the chanting practice at 3:00AM. With a bow, he exits. He radiates balance and composure that I now recognize as characteristic of a strong practitioner. I'm immediately drawn to him.

I've come to realize that I can recognize meditators—yogis—no matter what tradition, by their composure, by their balanced presence. They project a keen awareness that is a direct result of their practice. This characteristic can be felt, influencing others in a calming way. I've met people who think meditation practice is self-serving, that instead of helping others, people who meditate only try to improve themselves. I disagree. The principle is to improve our minds so that we can better help others. Meditation develops this clarity and awareness that shows itself in qualities of wisdom and compassion. It empowers us to respond compassionately in difficult situations. Instead of reacting out of anger, for example, we respond out of peace, which can only help. That's my goal: to meditate not only to deeply understand *self*, but to learn to handle life's difficulties with compassionate composure, thus making life better for everyone.

It's late and I push through one half-hour of unsettled meditation before switching off the lights, and falling asleep to the recorded chant.

I wake at 3:00AM to join the two-hour chanting session. Later I join the shorter 7:00AM session as well. Forty monks pack into a rather small temple and sit on the cold marble floor as they recite memorized sutras. It's a beautiful practice that I'm sure yields clarity of mind, but I long to meditate.

The lavatory has those dreaded squat toilets. The showering system is different, too. A concrete cistern, the size of a refrigerator, holds cold, unfiltered water. To bathe one scoops the cold water with a plastic bucket and pours it on oneself while standing. Sharing the bath water makes me uncomfortable, but . . . *When in Vietnam . . .*

After breakfast. Gia Dong brings me a more formal robe. Holding it out to me, he says, "Must wear. See SuBa."

I don the full length garment over my clothes and he guides me to the nuns' dining area where Huong Nhu is waiting, looking bright and happy.

"Morning, Mark," she says. "We greet SuBa first and go travel after."

I've mixed feelings about this trip. After spending almost two months in a meditation retreat, the past week has been the commotion of traveling through large cities. I'm thirsty for solitude and meditation. But SuBa and Huong Nhu have exerted effort to arrange this trip. They're generously exposing me to alternative Buddhist practices—which has been one of the goals of my trip. So I take this trip as a learning opportunity.

A few minutes later SuBa rounds the corner. She wears the same type of attire she wore in Lumbini, and holds the same wooden staff. She looks directly at me as she speaks in Vietnamese to Huong Nhu who translates.

"Mark, I very pleased you come," SuBa says. "Since Lumbini, I often thought of you hoping you'll visit."

I'm caught off guard with the feeling of being honored.

"Today you go with Huong Nhu and others for visit some temples," SuBa continues. "More than one hundred fifty temples connected to this monastery. You see some today. I want you meet abbots, prostrate at very important Buddha shrines, and be present in holy place in mountain."

I nod, still wondering why I deserve this.

SuBa's not finished. "Mark," she looks at me intently, "I know you searching within. I know you diligent seeker. You find place that right for practice, I arrange. It important to me help you with this meaningful discovery."

I barely know her, yet she looks at me with a caring gaze, almost that of motherly love. I thank her and bow.

"Now you go," she says. "Car waiting."

Huong Nhu, three other nuns, and I take seats in a newer SUV with a hired driver. We follow the coastline watching the Pacific Ocean jump in and out from behind hills of rice paddies and rolling sand dunes. The dry ground surrounding farm houses is often topped with harvested grain drying in the intense heat.

Two hours pass before we turn onto a dirt road, squeezing past tiny village houses and entering lush jungle with sweeping, broad-leafed tropical

Master Suba Hue Giac (standing) and Suco Huong Nhu
Ho Chi Minh City, Vietnam

trees. Excited children run from their huts waving. The road climbs, and our vehicle leaves a trailing cloud of dust. Rounding another bend, we roll to a halt.

"Now we walk up mountain to temple, Mark!" Huong Nhu says springing out and fastening on a traditional conical bamboo sun hat. It's a brilliant, cloudless day and colorful birds glide through the green overhead playground. We climb for an hour, passing several smaller temples while monkeys frolic overhead.

Our destination is just short of the mountain peak and the residences and worship buildings are enveloped by jungle foliage. Huong Nhu introduces me to Linh Mai, the nun who's lived here more than forty-five years. During the Vietnam War, Linh Mai left to live with SuBa because the Viet Cong occupied this temple, which was then destroyed by bombing. After the war, she returned with several monks and rebuilt it.

Linh Mai is a slender woman, short, and only slightly younger than SuBa. She gazes at me in a tender way as Huong Nhu tells me the story. I feel an affinity toward her that I cannot explain. It's not romantic in any way and I'm at a loss to understand it. I regret we can't converse but I acknowledge her with a bow. As we step away to tour the premises, I look back to see Linh Mai still looking my way and I feel like I'm breaking a connection.

The main temple has a traditional red-tiled roof with corners sweeping upward and outward. Each corner is guarded by carved gold dragons. The massive entrance doors are exquisite.

"Close door quickly and be careful," Huong Nhu says. "Monkeys very smart, can open. Monkey come in and take fruit from altar, then leave happy." Aside each altar, plates are stacked with oranges, grapefruit, and bananas. I can certainly understand the monkeys' interest.

We pause for reflection, bow, and leave. A few steps out the door, two large monkeys spring from the bush, scoot to the door, grab the large brass handles and viciously tug in a brazen attempt to enter. We chuckle at their ambition.

Up the path, a glass-enclosed temple is perched well above the others.

Steps take us to a path that encircles the temple. A small altar is visible inside.

Huong Nhu explains that the glass vials in the window have sacred 'relics' from Vietnamese masters and saints. When an accomplished master is cremated, these 'relics' are found in the ashes and are signs proving the master's accomplishments. Relics take the form of pearls, multicolored gems, or delicate hair-like structures. Kopan monastery displayed some 'relics' from a highly regarded rinpoche. I can't help but wonder that they form in the same way glass beads are fused of silica. But Huong Nhu heads off any such discussion. These "holy signs," she says, are only found in the remains of very high level masters.

She directs us in silent walking meditation three times around the temple.

I feel calm and a clearness of mind. The power of the practice is refreshing. We conclude with a respectful bow to each other and quietly walk to a patio where Linh Mai has spread out a vegetarian lunch.

Throughout the meal Linh Mai and I exchange a few glances. After lunch, Huong Nhu says, "We go now, many more temples to see."

She turns to Linh Mai and they speak in Vietnamese. Then Huong Nhu turns to me.

"Mark, Linh Mai say that you are good man. She know you dedicated to meditation practice. Linh Mai say she will take care of you here so you can continue your practice to enlightenment. You understand her?"

I don't know what to say. Her invitation seems in earnest. I came here to admire a temple and end up with an invitation for a long-term stay. But there's no meditation hall here. It just doesn't feel right.

"I'm grateful for your offer but I cannot accept," I say with a bow. "Hopefully we can meet again in the future. May I visit again?"

Huong Nhu translates and Linh Mai nods. We bid farewell and hike to the car.

Hours later we visit a jungle monastery where children are educated to be monks, then to a small temple run by Huong Nhu's elder sister who's also a nun. Lastly, we visit a recently renovated temple in the city. We visit a total of five temples. At each stop, we see Buddhist concepts expressed through architecture, design, and paintings. I carefully consider SuBa's encouragement to spend time in meditative practice at the temple of my choice, but I've yet to see a single meditation room, a single cushion. The hospitality is overwhelming but my pursuit is sitting meditation and I'm feeling out of place.

Our SUV finally lumbers into Quan Am monastery's front gate, and I'm back "home." I thank Huong Nhu and the others for their time and effort. I head to my room to rest. Gia Dong appears to help me settle and arrange dinner.

Alone on my bunk after dinner, I try to meditate. But the noise from monastery activity and the relentless recorded chant combined with the stifling heat have my monkey mind swinging to and fro. I persist but it's fruitless. Frustrated, I open my eyes to catch two young monks peering into my open window. Having caught my attention, they quickly scuttle away. I suppose they want to catch a glimpse of the western meditator and that's understandable. But I feel like I'm on display; I'm self-conscious now. My practice becomes even more difficult and, even though Venerable Bhaddamanika predicted periods of poor concentration, I'm ill at ease with this situation.

I have to face a truth: Quan Am is not for me. This tradition of chanting doesn't feel right, at least not now. Certainly Pure Land Buddhism is effective, and wholesome. But it's not for me. I'm missing the practice of sitting in quiet, uninterrupted meditation where I intimately access my mind. In Lumbini, I was progressively accessing deeper levels of *self*. Without daily practice, I'm losing ground.

One of my goals is to establish a firm meditation practice that I can carry back home. I continue to debate if this is a reasonable goal. Should not the seven weeks in Lumbini have been enough to embed such a practice? After only a few days in Ho Chi Minh City and my short time here, I feel the hard-earned, clear, and exact awareness I gained giving way to mental agitation. Now I'm worried more than ever about how I'll be able to maintain strong mindfulness in the midst of my busy life back home.

I feel an urgent pull to that isolated hut deep in the jungle at Bao Van Tu monastery—the one Minh Do told me about. He spoke highly of the master and seemed certain it would be good for me. I trust his judgment. I'll leave Quan Am tomorrow.

It's nearly 9:00PM, and that means lights out, but I must let Huong Nhu know that I'll leave tomorrow. We meet at an outdoor bench near the dining hall, conversing in whispers because of the hour.

"Huong Nhu, I feel it's urgent for me to resume sitting meditation and I find it difficult to practice here. I need to practice intensively as I did in Lumbini. There's a monastery a few hours from here where I can do that. I must leave tomorrow."

Huong Nhu listens attentively. "I don't want SuBa to misunderstand," I continue. "She's treated me with such care as have you. I'm impressed by SuBa's temples and the work she does. I don't want to hurt her feelings. Everyone has been so kind."

"Don't worry, Mark," Huong Nhu says. "SuBa will understand. You can meet her after breakfast tomorrow. Say goodbye then. It no problem."

I head back to my room, feeling sad about leaving after having been treated with extraordinary hospitality.

I'm in a deep sleep when the lights go on. I immediately assume it's for the 3:00AM monastery routine and I listen for the gong to sound—but it doesn't. I look up to see Gia Dong standing at the light switch in my room in his composed manner, with my robes draped over his forearm. My watch reads 2:00AM and I know something's up.

"Robes on please," Gia Dong says. "Must SuBa see you now."

As a master, SuBa sleeps very little. I've been told that advanced monks sleep three hours while those younger discipline themselves to five. I heard that a rinpoche at Kopan monastery often sleeps just one hour sitting up at his desk. Two in the morning is prime time for SuBa and she wants to chat about my departure.

I dress and Gia Dong escorts me to a small chapel. Only the amber glow of altar candles lights the room. Sticks of incense release slender streams of grey smoke. Gia Dong motions for me to sit on the marble floor then stands to the side. It's now 2:30AM and a gong begins to ring in a slow cadence from a distant building.

Moments later a solemn looking Huong Nhu wearing formal yellow dress robes enters carrying a silver platter with three small, wooden boxes. The box tops have ornate, hand-printed Oriental designs. SuBa follows gripping her wood staff. She stands by the altar with what I think of as humble authority. Huong Nhu places the silver tray on the marble altar. Huong Nhu, Gia Dong, and I respectfully bow three times to SuBa, then sit together on the marble floor. With surprising agility, SuBa slides onto the hip-high altar and assumes a full lotus position facing us. I'm keenly alert.

SuBa speaks Vietnamese for a couple of minutes, her voice echoing off the temple walls. She pauses so Huong Nhu can translate.

"Mark, SuBa know you are serious seeker and wish you find good meditation place." Huong Nhu pauses to absorb what SuBa says. "There are many types of practice. They are different, Mark," Huong Nhu continues as SuBa speaks. "But they are same thing. Result is same. Yours is right practice. You must find good place to meditate."

Then Huong Nhu looks at me. "SuBa recognize you. SuBa say she know you very well from previous lifetime."

I'm shocked and must have shown it. I've heard that accomplished masters can perceive previous lifetimes.

"SuBa say you met her even in many past lives, not just this life," Huong Nhu says. "That is why in this life you meet again. Because it not easy to meet her since you living in foreign country. You meet her because of causality, in many past lives you had connected with her." Maybe this explains SuBa's kindred-soul attention.

SuBa turns to the silver tray as she continues talking. "Mark, these boxes hold very ancient artifacts from Buddha's time," Huong Nhu says as SuBa opens each and places the lids aside, leaving the open boxes on the tray. Then SuBa picks up a simple magnifying glass—missing the handle—and passes it to me.

"Please look at these," Huong Nhu gestures as SuBa finishes speaking. I understand that I'm being instructed to view treasured heirlooms. I step to the altar with the magnifying glass. In each fine box, nested in neatly tucked puffs of white cotton are small stone carvings. Each carving is about the size of my thumb, from the knuckle up. They're very intricate representations of Buddha in a cross-legged position with one hand extended straight out resting on his knee and the other hand bent at the elbow with palm upright. There's a flat, square base on each. They're made from differing shades of white marble.

I notice subtle differences in hand positions, robe style, head details but for the most part they're similar. I see sharp tool markings making it likely these were hand-carved. All edges are worn smooth, as if from years of handling, and my impression is that they're authentic and ancient. There's a missing finger tip on one carving and another has a significant crack in the shoulder but remains intact. I'm touched that SuBa is letting me view these. Huong Nhu and Gia Dong also take time examining them.

SuBa resumes. "Mark, these carvings were made in time of Sakyamuni Buddha after he achieved Nirvana twenty-five hundred years ago. They were made and passed to disciples. Not many exist. They've been passed as heirloom from master to student over the millennia. Not in museums. They protected by serious practitioners."

The echo from our soft conversation, the ringing of the gong, the smell of incense, and the candles' glow accentuate what's being shared. Huong Nhu continues. "SuBa very well known in Vietnam and respected by many nuns and monks. She's been entrusted with these carvings and other antiquities."

SuBa's fully engaged, speaking rapidly and with increasing intensity while looking directly at me. Huong Nhu is having difficulty keeping up with the translation, and motions SuBa to give her time to catch up.

"Mark, SuBa want you to have this carving as inspiration as you practice and teach." With great care, SuBa holds out one of the carvings still nestled in the box, and Huong Nhu rises and carries it to me. Their faces tell me this is an important gesture.

I'm taken aback. SuBa is giving me one of her most treasured gifts, an ancient artifact. To Buddhists, this carving is a sacred symbol of Buddha's teaching, an artifact preserved over millennia, deserving deep reverence. It carries immense archaeological and spiritual value. I shudder at the responsibility.

I glance at Huong Nhu. She nods with joy in her eyes.

For the next half-hour, SuBa gives me the guidance a master relays to a serious disciple. I give full attention, drawing in each word. As she speaks, I indelibly inscribe her heartfelt message into my soul.

"This is a gift for you," she continues referring to the carving. "You bring it to your country with you."

"Mark," Huong Nhu translates, "You can go many places, practice many traditions, can find many masters. Finally coming back your country and you see your heart, you see your mind, you check your heart, you check your mind. You observe what you think. You'll recognize the Buddha nature is in you. This is the main thing and this is the reason why you meet SuBa now. She like to make you know one very important thing: '*Buddha nature inside! Don't search outside. In yourself!*'"

Huong Nhu looks at SuBa who looks at me. "If you can examine your mind, if you can clearly observe your mind, then this means you have good practice. If you master your mind this is the truth. If from another person, if from another tradition, if from read books, this is only outside, not inside. You can hear yourself, you can see what you are thinking, observe what you are doing. You just observe your mind every day. From inside, Mark."

"Nirvana means quietness, it means calmness," SuBa continues. "When you get pure calmness and quietness in your mind it means Nirvana. It does not mean you die. Pure calmness! Practicing meditation, chanting the sutra and mantra purifies the mind. If you practice every day you'll find Buddha nature inside."

Then the punch line: "Mark, SuBa says that in the USA you will become monk. Maybe not now, maybe not in a year, maybe even five years, you will become monk."

I swallow hard, keeping my mind open. "When being monk, you will teach and lead people. You will benefit many others. Many students will follow you. SuBa envisions that in your future." Huong Nhu smiles, getting caught up with excitement at what SuBa is telling me. Her posture becomes more erect and attentive.

"SuBa knows it important you teach in United States," she continues. "It's about Buddha in the West."

A twinge of discomfort jabs my gut. I'm glad there's no opportunity to respond.

"SuBa give you this noble gift, and wish this inspire you diligently practice meditation so you become Buddhist monk in the future to benefit human beings. Because following the Buddhist way is very difficult. That why the teacher SuBa expect you become a Buddhist monk for helping human beings."

SuBa pauses, allowing what she said to sink in.

I feel like a bomb has been dropped. I don't know what to say. The conventional practice is to follow a master's direction, regardless of the difficulty. I'm not there . . .yet.

"No need to say anything," Huong Nhu says quietly. "Only listening is good enough."

I'm grateful for the reprieve. During this trip, I've experienced an inner nudge to become a monk. It has a certain appeal as I've observed the disciplined lives of masters such as Vivekananda, Minh Do, and now SuBa. It's not an easy life, but the simplicity and solitude of a committed contemplative life are enticing. The subject surfaces occasionally in my heart and mind, and my response varies between fondness and flat-out rejection.

But I've never had the unblemished faith needed to vulnerably place my life at the direction of a single person, a master. Yet, here I am and SuBa has placed such a choice in my lap. The weight of it makes me squirm. *What would Jayne say about this?* I'm a husband and a father. Just the thought of leaving family and friends to live a monastic life is weighty.

SuBa unfolds her legs and rises from her lotus position. She approaches me and motions me to stand and extend my hands. She places my hands within hers, palm to palm and presses her thumb in the middle of each palm. She closes her eyes and tilts her head upward, holding that pose as if she's sensing, apprehending, and absorbing energy. She then places her palm on my temple, and then on the back of my neck and on my chest, using first her right hand and then her left. Love and peace emanate from this master as she reads my body and spirit.

"SuBa can understand you and understand all her disciples," Huong Nhu says. "She reads what you thinking. She know you have many disturbance in your mind. Sometimes you get sick but it is not your health, it your mind. SuBa knows you work very hard. But working to attain is defilement of mind. Desire and attachment to result from work cause many problems in mind. Sometime you get headache because you think a lot from the defilement of attainment."

She has me pegged! I habitually work full throttle. Sometimes I overwork with such fervor that I collapse in bed for a day. And the headache thing? I always thought that came with the engineering trade.

Huong Nhu and I catch eyes. She's happy to be part of this. I feel a connection with her as much as with SuBa. We communicate through frequent glances. There's a sublime kinship.

I glance at Gia Dong sitting cross legged on the floor. He acknowledges me with a slight smile as if to say, "congratulations."

"Next time when you have opportunity," Huong Nhu translates, "come to Vietnam and visit. You meet SuBa today; you can meet in the future. But meeting in the mind is more important. Not by the physical body important but in the mind you can receive her spirituality again."

It is said that great masters can communicate over distances through the mind and I wonder if this is what she means. As Huong Nhu translates, SuBa speaks. "Mark, SuBa ask if you have Buddhist name?"

It's a common Buddhist tradition for a serious student to adopt a name that has special significance to his or her practice. Usually a master gives the student a Buddhist name. Lay people rarely use their Buddhist name in daily life, they use it in the sangha of practitioners.

"No, I haven't. Can SuBa give me one?"

SuBa reflects for a long pause as she looks at the Buddha statue. She utters my new name. "Your name is Phuoc Tan," Huong Nhu says with a gleam in her eye. 'Phuoc Tan' means 'diligent merit.' You like it?

"Of course. Thank you, SuBa!"

"Now we bow," Huong Nhu says as she, Gia Dong, and I rise and prostrate three times.

SuBa says one last thing through Huong Nhu. "Remember Mark, Buddha nature is inside!" SuBa then turns and walks away, staff in hand.

Chapter 14

A Hidden Hut

Vietnam

Temptation breeds greed and desire. You must learn to subdue all desires.
—Thich Giac Lam
Bao Van Tu Monastery

My motorbike driver navigates the wildly changing river of motorbikes, buses, and trucks on roads where lane markings are totally disregarded. He's taking me to a bus station on my way to Bao Van Tu monastery—the monastery Minh Do suggested I visit. Traffic grinds to a halt, and the driver jumps a curb and onto a dirt sidewalk. Squeezed on the stubby seat, my knees are spread wide and I quiver, fearing a cartilage-tearing snag as the, driver squeezes between vehicles.

I've devised a new form of meditation: "motorbike meditation." I focus my mind on absorbing the Asian countryside as I hold my mind inside and in the moment. Minh Do's advice, "Stick and see one thing, no stick and see all" seems clearer every day, and I use the mantra frequently. As wind whistles in my ears, I experience the green pastures, the mountains bulging from the horizon, thick bamboo forests, and rivers dotted with white cranes. It's exhilarating to see the whole picture and become part of it as well.

At the village bus station, I can't figure out which bus to take. I hand Minh Do's note, written in Vietnamese, to someone who points it out. I board and claim a back window seat. The more remote I get, the more difficult communication becomes. Bao VanTu monastery, on the edge of the Cambodian border, should prove challenging.

Passengers notice me, turning around to look at perhaps the only westerner to ever sit on their village bus. I like to mesh with the locals because it always brings rewarding cultural experiences. This time is no different. The packed bus stops for a man who drags on an eight-foot tall tree with a grocery bag haphazardly wrapped around the root ball. Later, a woman boards with two panicked chickens fluttering in a wire cage.

The bus driver kindly waves in his mirror to signal my upcoming stop. I nod thanks and jump off with the bus still rolling. The spot is sequestered. Only a few small buildings are in sight. I hand Minh Do's note to a man resting on a bench. He motions that he's willing to drive me to the monastery—on his motorbike, of course.

The rural, paved road turns onto a dirt path and then to a hiking trail bordered by dense vegetation and huge tropical trees. I'm in a jungle. He drops me in a clearing by a wrought iron gate. I make out small bamboo huts farther on in the jungle, just as Minh Do described. It's quiet. The only sound is the shrill song of tropical birds.

Entering the grounds, I nose through the jungle to a central bamboo hut. Dense groves of bamboo are interspersed with palm and banana trees. Long, curved vines dangle from towering deciduous trees. A flat stone path, lined with red bricks, weaves between bamboo huts and the huge trees.

A tiny, grey-haired woman wearing a light blue top, black pants, and worn flip-flops, approaches. Her name is Co Anh, the masters' sister. "Co" is the prefix for "woman teacher." I introduce myself but she speaks no English. Co Anh walks away and returns with "Dr. Thom," a Vietnamese-American medical doctor with moderate English skills. He's one of the master's students.

Dr. Thom and I stroll to a bamboo table in the shade of a straw hut. He begins by declaring his admiration for the master—eighty-four-year old Thich Giac Lam—who has meditated in this jungle since youth, developing his own Vipassana-style meditation approach based on exacting study of Buddha's scriptures. He'd meditate for days on a rock, much as Buddha did, his sister bringing food and water, which he'd often forego. Thich Giac Lam has reportedly achieved extraordinary mind control. Dr. Thom explains that he has extreme sensory skills. "Master can tell the color of student's shirt when talking on phone," Dr. Thom says. I recall Minh Do saying "He can see the stars in the sky on a bright sunny day."

Like any left-brained engineer, I'm a bit skeptical. But Minh Do and Dr. Thom's depictions of the master agree, so I'll try to stay open-minded. Such feats don't influence my goals, however. I don't seek special powers, experiences of bliss or even enlightenment. I only want to nurture a "clear, exact, aware" mind through meditation.

These isolated huts remind me of Panditarama. Intensive meditation in this jungle could be an extension of that unfinished work. Even without Thich Giac Lam's guidance, I can practice Vivekananda's techniques right here.

I turn to Dr. Thom. "Can I ask the master some questions?"

"Sure, first we assign hut for tonight" he says.

My hut is deep in the jungle, a comfortable distance from others. The entire grounds are sand with no grass and only light ground growth. Through thick jungle trees I can see perhaps forty other huts; many are brick with corrugated steel roofs, while others are bamboo and straw.

"More than one hundred seventy huts. Nearly all have student," Dr. Thom says. "men and women huts separated," he says, pointing. "Also there section for advanced students where master stay. I there," he says.

Inside my brick hut, Co Anh opens a panel that covers an unscreened window. The concrete floor is elevated two feet above the ground to discourage crawling creatures. The room has a miniscule bathroom, with, thankfully, a western toilet. However, instead of a shower head, there's a spigot, a bucket, and that darn plastic scooper—more bucket showers! Co Anh hands me bedding, including a bamboo mat to lay down on the wood frame.

"I arrange meeting with master tomorrow," says the doctor. "Meanwhile settle and practice."

"What time are meals?" I ask.

He pauses, hesitant to give the bad news, which I already know.

"Mealtime 10:00 AM. Master directs students eat one meal. Body needs one healthy meal, says Master. Eat for body nourishment not pleasure. Better for concentration. Big meal okay. Take much rice for energy. At ten, meal on outside table near kitchen hut."

I had adapted well to Panditarama's vegetarian diet of only two meals, but my concentration suffered in the evening and before breakfast. I understand the intent of eating less, but I'm skeptical of the benefits. Yet, I'm here to learn and must be open-minded. Thich Giac Lam is recognized as an accomplished master with hundreds of students. Surely something's right here.

At night, the jungle is quiet of human noise yet teeming with natural sounds. Crickets, locusts, night owls, and the occasional cry of some unknown creature make for my bedtime lullaby.

I feel at home here. My concentration is strong during evening and morning meditations. A cushion in the center of the room becomes my spot to travel inward. I wake early, but not at the 3:00 AM Quan Am time. I alternate between sitting and walking meditation, and reading a book Minh Do gifted me. Gone is the panic I'd been feeling in the city.

The comfortable day-break temperature transforms to sweltering heat by midmorning. My body overheats, and my clothes stick. I take refuge in the small washroom for a cool bucket shower. Bothered by spider webs near the toilet, I bucket wash the walls and floor. A load of water directed behind the toilet flushes out a squirming, slurping, foot-long lizard. I'm startled! The slimy brown creature with bright orange dots, stubby legs, an oversize head, and bulging eyes sloshes through the water in a frantic attempt to return 'home'—the backside of the toilet. Determined to give it a new home, I throw another bucket of water sweeping the reptile across the floor and over the edge to the outside. A third bucket ensures it won't return.

I inspect the rest of the washroom. Lifting the toilet seat, I'm terrified by a hairy brown spider, the size of my hand, with long, furry legs. It zips down the toilet, between my feet and under the bamboo wall. I re-gain my composure and again use my trusty bucket to discourage its return. I put a sticky note in my memory bank: *This is real jungle—inspect the toilet before each use.*

It's time to meet the master. Dr. Thom escorts me to an open-air hut with a palm-leaf roof. Twenty chairs face a wooden desk and the elevated tile floor shines.

"Master give daily talks, but only in Vietnamese. Only you no speak Vietnamese," he explains.

The master is a short and slender man, barely one hundred pounds. He wears large, dark, thick-framed glasses, a brown robe with bright yellow pants and his head is shaved. His movements are slow and precise. Dr. Thom and I stand with hands clasped as he passes. He sits and we bow three times in respect.

Dr. Thom acts as a translator and introduces me to the master who asks questions of me; how long I've been practicing Buddhism, and of what tradition. He speaks softly, slowly, often looking down.

"What is it you wish to ask?" he says.

I tell him about my journey and goals. As I speak, I can't help but notice his pin-pointed focus on me.

"However," I say in closing, "after months of effort I still find it easy to lose mindful awareness in a busy environment. Do you believe it's possible to maintain mindful awareness in a busy life?"

They spend several minutes speaking Vietnamese. I wonder, as I often do when speaking through an interpreter, if the true meaning will be communicated.

Dr. Thom responds for the master. "Mark, what you seek not easy. However, it possible. I develop technique that'll work and be sustainable. It difficult and take steadfast effort. I teach you directly but take two to four months, you stay in advance student section."

My mind races, calculating the logistics. My remaining itinerary includes a Zen monastery in the neighboring mountains as well as two Korean Zen centers. Although missing home, I'm committed to traveling until my goals are reached. Another two to four months is a big commitment. But according to Dr. Thom and Minh Do, this master could have a meaningful impact on my life. If it'll take extra time to solidify my practice, it'll be worth it.

"Can you tell more about your technique?" I ask.

"Mark," the master begins "as layman you surrounded with temptations; temptations for money, of fame and pride, of food, the pleasures of touch and so forth. Temptation breeds greed and desire. You must learn subdue all desires. To do that you must learn total command your body actions. All actions, motions, and thoughts must be intentional. The techniques will train you control body and breath. I'll train you control what and when you eat and how much you sleep. We eat only once a day to cultivate self-control and concentration. Gradually you take control of your sleep and reduce to four hours. Your last meditation session will end at 10:00PM and you'll eventually wake 2:00AM. Mark, this the start. This technique give control of your life and death."

He studies my face; I suppose he's assessing my level of commitment. "This isolation retreat, Mark," he continues. "For your benefit, must not contact your family."

I understand. Over the past few months I've come to recognize how I'm driven by desires. My mind is frequently occupied with wanting or avoiding. This was obvious as I walked the streets of Ho Chi Minh City. It makes sense that one can learn bodily control through continuous awareness. That was the basis of Panditarama's methods as well.

But I'm concerned about how well I can apply myself here—there are several serious challenges. Communication will be difficult; I'm liable to get weak from a single daily meal; I'm likely to become lethargic from reduced sleep. Then there's the overbearing heat. I'm afraid to admit it because it seems 'weak,' but I know I lose drive in such sweltering heat. And the isolation is no small thing, I relish the occasional internet chats Jayne and I've had from internet cafés. That's a fairly decent list of challenges. Then I remember the lizard and the spider in my hut—wildlife hurdles, too.

On the other hand, I've recently endured more than I ever thought possible; the bitter cold in the Himalayan Mountains, noisy environments and long sitting times.

I turn to Dr. Thom. "Do you realize that the master's offer makes me dependent on you to translate? That's not a fair burden."

"Not worry Mark. My practice good. We learn together. I happy help."

It's more than that though. Dr. Thom's English skills are moderate at best, and I worry that he cannot communicate my thoughts and feelings. I don't share my concerns; I know he'll do his best.

"Master, I accept your offer. Thank you. First, I must go to town to notify my family." The master nods his head, "We move you advanced student section. We start when you return."

Walking to my hut, I admire several life-size pure-white stone carvings along the jungle path. One is a carving of Siddhartha Gautama, the original Buddha, cutting his long hair as a symbol of renunciation. An engraved plaque reads:

> "To keep one's mind
> Is to put faith in the Dharma.
> However, do not let religion
> Guide one's mind"

The absence of any religious aspect is as refreshing here as it was at Panditarama. There's no ornate temples, golden statues, or chanting rituals. This is purely a meditation center. Religious 'faith' is not required, only disciplined inquisitiveness into the mind. Here, diligent mental work produces a self-controlled and wholesome mind. The scientist within feels at home with this approach.

Co Anh and two other people await at my hut.

"Mark there problem with police!" Co Anh says excitedly as Dr. Thom translates. "Local police know you here. They say you must get special approval. You first westerner stay at monastery. Dr. Thom is Vietnamese-American; ok for him. Police say you must travel to Religious Council in Ho Chi Minh City get approval for stay."

"Okay, Co Anh," I assure her, "no problem. I need to go there tomorrow anyway to call my family."

"No Mark, go now," she says. "Not stay tonight. Police say 'no.'" She's clearly uncomfortable dealing with the officials.

One thing I've learned about travel is to be flexible and accepting.

"Sure, Co Anh," I smile. "Let me collect a few things and I'll take a bus back."

"No bus, Mark, monastery arranged driver," she says. "We arrange place for stay and person guide to Religious Council."

"You're so kind, Co Anh." I bow, and a smile returns to her face.

I gather my essentials and Co Anh guides me through the jungle to the gate. It's midafternoon and brightly colored tropical birds glide through the branches. The buzz of crickets emanates from the undergrowth. I smile inwardly knowing that when formalities are resolved, I'll be immersed in this jungle setting to study my inner self.

I'm driven out of the jungle to Ho Chi Minh City to get approval from some unknown "council." What awaits me? Who'll I be with? Where will I stay? What's this approval process about?

Chapter 15

Communist Entanglement

Vietnam

I think of my life like a whisk broom. I live the day, I do actions and deeds, and when done I sweep it away and move on. Nothing remains.

—SuCo Quang Hue
Bao VanTu Monastery,

What I expect to be a quick-fix—a rubber-stamp formality— for permission to stay at Bao VanTu Monastery, is anything but.

Throughout the two-hour trip to Ho Chi Minh City, I concentrate on observing my mind, being aware of self. But in every direction, odd sights yank my mind from self awareness. A frightened piglet stares from a cage mounted on the back of a motorbike and my mind 'sticks' to the sight. Then my mind jumps to a woman laboriously pulling a rickshaw stacked high with slimy fish—some ready to slide overboard. Like a skipping stone, my mind jumps to this and that. I have to laugh—the stallion of mind has broken out of the corral—again.

The driver drops me at a chaotic three-way intersection in Ho Chi Minh City and points to a store with finished wooden furniture on display. As I walk in, three people rise. I introduce myself.

"Hello Mark, I'm SuCo Quang Hue," says a tall, slender nun wearing a full-length brown robe. Her head is tightly wrapped in a dark brown headdress that looks like a bandanna. "We've been expecting you." Her English is easy to understand. She introduces the shop owner, Mr. Giang, a grey-haired gentleman in his sixties. Mrs. Giang, his much younger wife, smiles.

"Each of us is student of Master Thich Giac Lam," SuCo Quang Hue explains. "We'll help you get the Religious Council approval to study at the monastery."

I bow. "You're very kind."

SuCo Quang Hue appears in charge. She projects confidence and purpose. "It's getting late," she says. "You'll stay at my friend's health spa business tonight. You can sleep on a massage bed there. Tomorrow morning, we'll meet the Religious Council chief," she says.

That's encouraging! If I get approved tomorrow morning, I can begin with the master in the afternoon.

With the sunrise glow on the horizon the next morning I head in search of an internet café. The streets are just coming to life as street vendors warm up woks. I pause to enjoy a cup of coffee, served by an elderly woman. The smell and taste of the thick black treat relaxes me. I ponder the day ahead.

At a computer, I call Jayne and explain my plan to enter this lengthy program. Even though I've been gone more than five months, she understands and approves.

"You really feel you need another disciplined retreat?" she asks.

"I do."

And that's it. She's there with me. She's amazing.

I return to find SuCo Quang Hue waiting with a hired motorcycle driver. It's inappropriate for a man to ride with a nun on a motorbike, so we follow her through the city's business section. I smile watching SuCo's robes and headdress flutter in the wind like flags. She drives assertively weaving through the sea of motorbikes, and my driver seems to enjoy the challenge of keeping up. I affectionately tag her "the flying nun."

We meet with the Religious Council's top Buddhist monk on the twelfth-floor of an air conditioned office building. We sit in thick cushioned chairs around a polished mahogany table. A distinguished looking monk in formal brown robes enters and introduces himself in Vietnamese. We smile and bow. SuCo Quang Hue explains our situation in Vietnamese. He seems confused, then rises, steps out of the room, then returns. He smiles at me, speaks to SuCo Quang Hue, and pleasantly shows us out.

"No need to come here," SuCo says. "This issue is for the *local* Religious Council, not this regional office. He called the local office and directed them to give approval. He says you'll have no problem. Let's have lunch before you return."

That's all!? I'm surprised it was that easy.

At a vegetarian restaurant, SuCo Quang Hue follows Master Giac Lam's program; she eats only a single meal.

"Order something special," I tell her. "I want to treat you in appreciation for your help."

"Thank you. All I need is steamed rice, vegetable soup, and Tofu please," she says. "I need little. We must control our desires you know. Food is like sex, money, and fancy clothing. The more we get, the more we want. Craving always results in more craving."

I mention my regret for the trouble that she, Mr. Giang and his wife have gone through.

"No trouble, Mark," she says. "This is what I do—help people. I've committed my life to helping people. I solve problems and then move on. No attachment to results. I think of my life like a whisk broom. I live the day, I do actions and deeds, and when done I sweep it away and move on. Nothing remains. There's no yesterday. Yesterday means nothing. There may not be a tomorrow. What I have is here and now. This situation right in front of me, it's all I have."

"When you say 'all that you have,' do you mean material things also?"

"Material things are not ours. They don't belong to us. When we die, we cannot take them, can we?" Her broad smile forms rosy balls on her cheeks.

"So you don't own many things?"

"I own nearly nothing. These robes and a couple of others are all I have. That motorbike is loaned from a friend. My flat is my sister's who lets me use it. Friends donate cash so I can do my work. I keep my life simple. I don't get involved with social gatherings. I don't even have my own temple, my flat is my temple. I've just a couple of friends I visit. I help remote village people and blind people when I find they need it."

"SuCo, how long have you been a nun?"

"I've been ordained six years. I left my boyfriend to become nun. I loved him very much. He loved me and wanted to get married. He did not understand why I want to become nun. It hard for him and he kept asking me to return. Finally he meet someone else. I happy for him and still care for him."

"How long have you been a student of the master?"

"I've been with Master Thich Giac Lam for two years. Before that I studied with great Master, Thich Nhat Hanh, in France. I've studied under other masters but only Thich Giac Lam has the skill to master his body and of life and death. The other masters are very skilled in living, but not in death."

That's a unique distinction. "What exactly do you mean?"

"Master Thich Giac Lam can control his breath. In deep meditation, he can stop breathing for long periods, many hours. This is how one enters Nirvana. Master can enter Nirvana by choosing to end his breath in deep meditation. This ability, this achievement, is why I choose to follow Master Thich Giac Lam and not others."

"SuCo, have you achieved this ability?"

"Not yet, but I practice diligently. If I don't achieve it in this lifetime, then perhaps the next. It's matter of commitment. Everyone can achieve this. I hope soon, Mark, you'll also achieve enlightenment. Of course, that's why you're here."

SuCo Quang Hue's a living example of how to weave Buddhist principles into life and she's given me new tools to help me do that. "We must move on," she says.

We make our way to Mr. Giang's store. With the council's approval assured and having my family's support, I'm ready to begin taking the master's direction.

Mr. Giang helps me navigate multiple bus connections back to Bao

VanTu. At the monastery, Dr. Thom, Co Anh and Mr. Giang combine efforts to gain the local Religious Council's approval. The four of us cram into a car that takes us to a small temple on an unkempt garden plot at the city's edge.

SuCo Quang Hue's left her mark on me. As I step out of the car, I'm inspired to release my worries with an inner whisk broom. I absorb the sight of palm trees and the sound of the branches waving in the warm breeze. I feel in the moment, aware of my breaths, in and out. I'm collected. That's how I enter the temple—in a calm state of mind.

A monk in yellow robes leads us to an outdoor table and bench. This tiny temple is simple, not ornate and has a single monk in residence. He's in his mid-fifties, relaxed and cordial. On his chin's right side grows a single curly hair, several inches long. I can't help but stare. I have a silly inclination to reach out and yank it and I have to chuckle inside. *Don't stick*, I kid myself.

Mr. Giang, Dr. Thom, and Co Anh chat with the monk. But their body language tells me things are not going well. What now? This was supposed to be simple.

Vietnam is a communist country that has battled the United States. Perhaps I'm entangled in political aftermath. After fifteen minutes, the conversation ends with tense, obligatory bows.

In the car, Dr. Thom says we must visit another Council member.

I'm starting to feel frustrated. "Why does the Religious Council need to approve my stay?" I ask.

"When Vietnam became communist," Dr. Thom starts, "not allowed to be Buddhist. No temples. But then, refugees were escaping country. Vietnamese boat people have many hardship at sea. Bad storms. Boats sinking. Some boats have Buddhist people that pray Quan Am, the Buddha of compassion. Miracles happen. People saved because of pray. Wives put pressure on leaders to allow Buddhism. First, no want. Reluctantly they allow. Now Communist allow some Buddhism, but make part of government. Religious Council controls Buddhists."

I'm still stumped. "Why control the temples? They're harmless. Can't the government see that the monastics help their country?"

"Vietnamese government afraid of Buddhist power," Dr. Thom says. "In Burma recently many Buddhists have street protest against government. Vietnam no want those problems! This why must control Buddhism."

By now, it's late afternoon and businesses are closing. I'm still not permitted to stay at the monastery.

Mr. Giang speaks to Dr. Thom who translates. "Mr. Giang owns small cottage in nearby farm fields. It simple place. Mr. Giang has room you sleep tonight."

Asians are aware that their often austere housing contrasts with the high living standards of westerners. Mr. Giang's invitation demonstrates trust and friendship.

Back at Bao Van Tu, I stuff my backpack, strap it on, and climb backside Mr. Giang's motorbike. A gravel jungle road narrows to a remote footpath and our elbows scrape the tropical foliage. It winds through an old cemetery, and beside rice paddies, chicken yards, and straw huts. A large, fierce-looking, dog—unleashed—lies in front of a hut, just aside the narrow path. Seeing us, the dog perks up and I worry about clamped teeth on my calf. He just stares meanly as we pass by. We stop at a crumbling, cast-iron gate that's secured with an ancient looking padlock.

Mr. Giang fumbles with his keys, unlocks it, and swings open the decrepit gate. Instantly, we're greeted by a collection of startled pets. A dozen chickens strut about and squawk nervously, three dogs in a cage yelp with excitement, and four large geese aggressively stalk us honking with alarm. Two geese charge me. Humored, I spread my arms, stomp my feet, and growl, which sends the geese waddling away but startles Mr. Giang as well! I bow an apology.

The concrete walls are weather stained, with crooked wooden bi-fold doors which Mr. Giang opens, and the interior of the cottage is unscreened. In the center of the room is a small altar with a Buddha statue and family pictures. Mr. Giang points to his parents, motions to the house, saying "This house, my father's, father's, father." He uses hand gestures to indicate that he's the fourth-generation heir.

"In war, house bombed . . . bad damage. I leave . . . go Ho Chi Minh City," Mr. Giang tells me. He motions me to the side of the house and points to a lovely pond where frogs are perched on lily pads; the pond is surrounded by an elevated dirt border. "From bomb during war," he says of the hole. "Very difficult time for me. No food. I eat like dog. Begging. Much begging. I eat street garbage. Very hard time. After war come back. House bombed. Rebuild with brother."

I try to ask how he feels about the United States' role in that war, but we have difficulty communicating. It makes us both quiet.

The gentle flitting of leaves from a soft breeze soothes my frustration about the approval process. As darkness settles, Mr. Giang strings hammocks between sturdy palm trees. We lie in silence watching brilliant stars emerge. I notice two lights moving in the jungle. Mr. Giang notices too. "Looking for snake," he says. "Look in tree branches. Find, catch, sell at market."

I fall asleep on an unfinished wood plank under a mosquito net thinking about this simple lifestyle. Life's hard here at times—sometimes very hard. But there's little of the underlying angst that characterizes western societies. Buddhists here seem content with what they have. "Enough" is plenty. Mr. Giang's hut could be cleaner, prettier, and more comfortable, but it's *enough*. There could be a bigger and tastier stock of food, but there's *enough*. Enough seems to be *enough*.

Over the next five days, we visit three other Religious Council members. We're also sent to three local police stations and a regional police station—each a part of the communist government. At each stop, we plead that I, a U.S. citizen, be permitted to study for months at Bao VanTu monastery. Some are sympathetic and encouraging, some congenial, others are cold and disagreeable. What each appears to be is fearful of making a decision to approve my stay. One elderly monk steers Mr. Giang to a donation box in his highly embellished temple—a clear bribe request. But a substantial contribution's not enough. We're all frustrated.

I'm concerned that I'm disrupting the monastery. Dr Thom, Co Anh, and Mr. Giang have their own matters to attend to as well. Perhaps I should leave for another monastery. But if I give up, I'll disappoint those helping me. I don't want their efforts to have been futile.

I stay with Mr. Giang for two days before he returns home. Then, I practice at the monastery during the day and return to a hotel evenings. In between, we visit officials.

I haven't seen another Caucasian since arriving. When in town, shoppers gawk, and teenage girls have approached me to practice English. Once, a boy of about six left his play group, ran up to me, touched my leg, then scooted back to his group proud to have shown his courage. Twice at the monastery visitors interrupted my practice asking for a picture with them. Being the center of attention can be annoying.

Despite my frustration, Dr. Thom, Mr. Giang, Co Anh, and I continue to seek approval. One morning as I meditate in my hut after returning from visits to two Religious Council officials and failing to win approval, I'm again interrupted.

"Mark, we make final trip," Dr. Thom says, excited. "Mr. Giang very angry with police. He influential in politics and brought local governor to help."

It's 11:00AM and the scorching heat has challenged me, so I welcome an escape.

As I walk with Dr. Thom to the gate, we pass many huts where practitioners are cultivating their minds. An analogy dawns on me that this monastery is a "mind farm" where minds come to grow. Here's where the seed for an enhanced consciousness is planted, cultivated, and watered with the teachings of Thich Giac Lam. As students leave, the fruit from this mind farm is distributed outside the monastery and benefits the entire world.

At the front gate is a new, metallic pearl, high-end SUV with leather seats and a full-option dashboard. This is a rare sight in Vietnam. Dr. Thom and I crawl into the air-conditioned interior which immediately chills my sweaty body. A tidily-dressed middle-aged man sits in the front passenger seat.

The distinguished politician is congenial, quiet, and appears sincere. After a twenty-minute ride, we come to our ninth temple seeking approval. This is home to a highly influential monk in the Religious Council—so I'm told.

A young assistant seats us at a richly finished table in a spacious room and begins a traditional tea pouring ritual, courteously dispensing us each a cup. The senior monk, dressed in formal yellow and orange robes enters and introductions are made. He passes a warm, down-to-earth smile my way.

The conversation seems cordial; the monk then steps out of the room. I glance around and note the absence of extravagant statues or paintings. Instead, there's an entire wall of shelved hardcover books and periodicals. This monk is learned and worldly.

He returns carrying a page-long, hand-written document. He pulls a signature stamp from a drawer and red-stamps it. I have approval. The ordeal is over. We express gratitude with bows and leave.

"Good news, Mark," Dr. Thom says in the car. "This is approval document. Copy go to police stations and other monks. You stay at monastery tonight and study master."

Yahoo! We're all smiling. Inside though, I have an uneasy feeling. "Forgive me for doubting, Dr. Thom, but I won't believe it's over until I've been studying here a few days."

"I understand," he says. "We frustrated, too. Think OK now."

It's good to be back at Bao VanTu Monastery and to know I can stay.

"Ready to start now, Mark," Dr. Thom says. "You in hut near master. You meet master at one o'clock."

Chapter 16

No Pain, No Gain

Vietnam

> You must learn to take control of your body and mind.
> Thich Giac Lam
> Bao VanTu Monastery

My hut sits within sight of Master Thich Giac Lam's. His is no different than a student's hut—only a desk and a wooden bench for sleeping. That he lives in such austere fashion at eighty-four-years old gives me confidence in his teachings.

The forty advanced student huts are in a clearing on the jungle's edge. My tiny single-room hut has brick walls, two screened windows, and a screened door. The painted interior is clean with a tiled floor and corrugated metal roof. The floor is elevated two feet off the ground with a narrow walkway around the periphery for walking meditation. Out back is a small washroom.

I'm buoyed by the opportunity to practice in this extraordinary environment, and with a great teacher. I toss my backpack into a corner and, without unpacking, sit in meditation. I feel relaxed. The jungle quiet is broken only by the peppy sounds of tropical birds. I'm surprised how quickly I return to a settled mind despite the days of tangled government interactions. My concentration is interrupted by the slap of a chubby gecko that lost its footing on the wall and belly-slammed onto the tiled floor. It quickly darts over the floor's edge and outside.

Just shy of one o'clock, Dr. Thom comes to take me for the master's first instructions. Thich Giac Lam sits cross-legged on a cushion as Dr. Thom and I face him.

The master begins as Dr. Thom translates: "You must learn take control of body and mind, Mark. What method use during meditation?"

His soft voice, fades to a whisper at times. His eyes are focused downward and he rarely looks at me. His facial expressions are few.

"I concentrate on my breath," I say. "I focus on air entering my nostrils, and feel it flow into my lungs. Likewise, I focus on warm air exiting my lungs and nostrils."

"This too passive," the master says. "We must take active role in controlling our body. We start with breath. Before taking breath, command yourself 'now I will inhale.' Then before you breathe out, you must command yourself 'now I will exhale.' This very important; it train the mind that you in control of breath. This the first and most important training exercise."

Minh Do also taught me this practice. Maybe he learned it here.

"I don't say this out loud, right? Just silently?" I ask.

"Yes. Give self permission to breathe then take breath. Do not inhale until you've permitted yourself. You in control; don't let body breathe on own. By practicing this technique, you take command of your breath and your body." The master looks down again. "Next, what you do when your mind wanders?" he asks.

"When I catch myself thinking, I refocus on my breath," I tell him. "I've been taught to accept and tolerate my wandering mind and not become angry or frustrated."

The master leans forward and looks at me closely. "You must deliberately guide mind to stay focused. In many ways, the mind like child in need of training. When mind disobey your intention to focus, immediately stop. Get up and begin walking meditation. Walk for ten or fifteen minutes and then resume sitting. If mind wanders again, do walking meditation again. Must train the mind and body follow our commands."

"Should I rise even if I've only been sitting a short while?"

"Yes, this way we tell our mind we not tolerate lack of concentration. These two techniques are most important. They put you in control of mind and body. There is much more. But first spend one week practicing. We'll meet next week."

The master rises and exits.

"I been practicing these instructions, Mark," Dr. Thom says, as we stroll to my hut. "They powerful. Your concentration will improve dramatically. He'll next teach to control body's movements. He taught me take command of my body by imagining it as vehicle that follow operator's commands. Before each walking step I give command to step. Before turning I give command to turn. Before sitting I command myself. We teaching our mind to control body."

His teaching is similar to, yet more assertive, than Vivekananda's instructions to 'note' all movements. Like most everyone, many actions are unconscious and automatic. Vivekananda's noting practice was very helpful. I can see how these practices will help me attain greater mindfulness.

The heat of the day peaks as I practice the new instructions. The brick walls are hot to the touch. I feel like I'm being cooked in an oven. My light blue robes are sticking to my body, so I take a bucket bath in the lavatory. But the water is hot from the sun beating on the supply pipes! Worse yet, the lavatory walls are hot making the tiny room a steam sauna. Outside it's 95°F, but it feels cool compared to inside. Three months ago I was freezing in the mountains wishing for a hot shower; now, I'd love a cold one. Comfort is an elusive perception!

The sun sets beyond the trees and a pink hue crawls across the sky. Sitting on the tile floor, cross-legged, I practice as instructed. 'Now I inhale. Now I exhale.'

The benefit of the practice is immediately apparent. If I don't give a command to breathe, I don't. When my mind wanders, it's forced back when I become short of air. It's a self-monitoring tool. Thich Giac Lam's method converts ordinary breathing into an alarm system that puts monkey mind on a leash.

As darkness wraps the compound, greyish-blue lights dimly glow inside the huts to repel insects, but I leave mine off, finding simple darkness more effective. The cooling evening air draws my neighbors onto their outside walkway for sitting and walking meditation. From my hut, I watch my fellow meditators practice. One student abruptly rises from sitting to begin walking meditation and I know his mind has wandered. It's comforting to see I'm not the only one with monkey mind.

At ten o'clock, the huts darken. I crawl onto my wooden sleep bench and listen to the jungle owls hoot, and the chirping of lonely insects. My neighbors will wake at 2:00AM, after only four hours of sleep. My agreement with the master is that I'll sleep six hours and gradually reduce to four. I'm nervous about that. Without enough sleep, I get shaky. Maybe I'll respond better here. Time will tell.

My alarm rings at 4:00AM—all too soon. I push myself through some yoga stretches before my first meditation. The sound of a gong from a distant temple penetrates the morning stillness. I've come to relish waking to a gong. I'll miss it someday. In the surrounding huts, my peers have been conditioning their minds for two hours. I admire their stamina. I wonder if I can generate similar self-discipline.

By 8:00AM, I'm physically weak from hunger, but I push on. *Only two more hours,* I tell myself. My stomach growls and my mental strength weakens, making it progressively harder to follow the instructions. I remember my mantra at Panditarama: "Determination, Persistence, and Effort." Mustering that DPE, I push through to mealtime.

My vegetarian meal instantly rejuvenates me. The home grown food is plentiful, flavorful, and nourishing. Freshly picked bananas accompany the serving. What a meal will do! Will I have this battle everyday nearing mealtime, or will my body adapt? Time will be the judge. I resume meditation with renewed concentration.

The heat intensifies and I hang a blanket in front of my door to block the scorching beams from baking my small room. The metal roof sometimes moans as in pain. After another bucket rinse, I exchange my robe for a cooler long-sleeved shirt and return to meditation. Despite these uncomfortable distractions, I practice as the master has instructed. I'm focused. Then I hear someone at the door. It's Dr. Thom.

"Mornin' Mark," he says cheerfully. "I bring special treat." He holds out a ripe mango. "It growing nearby and has your name on. Save for later when feeling weak. Don't let master see though!"

I thank him. I love mangos and it looks delectable. It seems wrong to shortcut the rules my first day, so I hide it in a corner—feeling a bit like Adam having been tempted. I sense Dr. Thom cheats with his eating and is looking for company.

He asks how meditation is going.

"Better now that I've eaten," I say, "and I'm benefitting from the master's techniques. However, the insects distract me so I hung my mosquito net from the roof eave this morning."

"Clever," he says.

"Don't the insects bother you?"

"I apply special balm" he replies. "But someday I not need. You see, the master not need insect repellent. Master has agreement with jungle insects and animals not disturb him. Many years ago, master heard two large snakes trapped deep in water well. He save them by put long bamboo pole into well for climb out. After, the snakes stay by his side. Protect him while he meditate. The master was grateful and tell snakes that Buddhists respect life. 'We not hurt you,' he tell them. 'We ask you not hurt Buddhists.' Now the master never has problem with animals or insects-not even mosquitoes."

Dr. Thom is a natural storyteller, and I enjoy listening to him.

"Is there anything you need, Mark?" he asks.

"I'm fine."

"One more thing, you must wear robe. The master not be happy if see you wearing shirt. You in war zone, man. Deep in the trenches. Soldier must wear uniform." His humor doesn't make him any less serious.

"What's the harm if I wear this shirt in my hut?"

"Mark, the master is quiet, but he very, very aware. Days ago, I need go Ho Chi Minh City, care for patient. When go to tell him, he start conversation by say okay go to city. He very aware. Just remember, he be watching you." Then, of all things, as he walks away, Dr. Thom sings lines from a song by Sting, *"Every move you make, every step you take, I'll be watching you."*

Dr. Thom's humor makes him easy to be with. There's one problem though: He doesn't hesitate to interrupt my meditation. He'll just walk up and start talking, and that troubles me.

I put on robes and resume meditating.

Heat aside, the jungle sounds inspire me. A few times each day the entire jungle, full of hidden locusts, breaks into a deafening buzz. The soothing melodies change by dawn, day, and dusk—as if organized by changing work shifts.

Days pass while I diligently practice. The unrelenting heat wilts me and my concentration. I resort to five or six bucket rinses a day to cope.

But it's not just the heat. The bugs are like an army on a mission to interrupt. Even draped under a mosquito net, a single infiltrator does as much damage to my practice as would a rock concert.

I'm sleeping about five hours a night now. I relish the tranquility of early morning hours, but I'm often groggy during daytime. Hours of shakiness and sluggishness precede my single meal. I know the body can adapt, and mine will too.

I'd like to read the master's teachings to glean more details of his methods but his writings are only in Vietnamese. Dr. Thom translates some, but he isn't an interpreter. He struggles to express the difficult teachings in English and I struggle to understand his choppy words. He also ad-libs, so I'm unclear which teachings are the master's and which Dr. Thom's contributions.

On my seventh day, after a full morning of meditation, I sit on the outside walkway with my mosquito net draped around me, watching the east sky brighten. A single, free-spirited locust begins to sing with all its might, inspiring others to join in and the whole jungle springs to life with a buzz. It's powerful music. Do these locusts wonder, looking at us humans, why we don't dance to their beautiful song? The roosters then make their announcements and several birds continue a melodic wake-up concert. A gecko scurries across the wall beside me searching for a mosquito breakfast.

I feel peaceful and tranquil even though I grapple with wandering mind. Part of my problem is that this is the second morning I've been seriously considering leaving Bao VanTu. I've questioned whether this is the right place for me. I'm stepping back to re-evaluate why I'm here.

The obstacles at Bao VanTu are many and they are draining me; my energy and will are both at low ebb. When I enrolled, I knew the challenges but assumed I'd adjust. Yet the heat, communication problems, meal and sleep schedules, interruptions, and pesky insects combine to feel like the gathering force of a tsunami. I'd hoped I could adjust—I planned to adjust and handle them all. Now, they're rolling over me like a storm rolls over a plain. They're taking a toll.

Nagging at me is a paragraph I read from Vivekananda's book, which said the environment must be appropriate for the yogi; the climate, food, and other factors need to be 'conducive to meditation' for a yogi to progress. I am meditating and I can spare comfort. But 'conducive' is lacking, missing. Yesterday I told Dr. Thom that I might have lost the battle, that I was thinking of leaving. He was not sympathetic.

"No pain, no gain Mark," he said. "Don't be a baby! Ignore the heat. Ignore your body's complaints. This is war, man!" He tried to be lighthearted, but it didn't help.

Do I let my willing feet take me elsewhere? I left Lawudo Gompa because of the biting cold and because I didn't have a master guiding me. I left Panditarama to spend time with Minh Do. I left Minh Do because my visa was to expire. Then I left Quan Am because I felt out of place—my meditation practice did not fit there. Here I'm weary from confronting a whole slew of obstacles. I sometimes feel like a coward.

Perhaps Thich Giac Lam's years of meditating on a jungle rock produced enlightenment and special powers. But I'm not seeking those. I understand that people seek such a path, and I admire them. But I'm after something else.

Then I realize I'm not willing to keep searching for something I already have—that I remember I already have! *"This is very important, Mark: The Buddha is within!"* That key teaching from SuBa has been going through my mind and I grasp it firmly. It's an antidote to my anxiety. I'm called to search within, to know that deepest part of myself, to intimately understand my mind.

I want to live in simplicity and practice austerity. I yearn to cultivate the goodness modeled in the teachers and masters whom I've met: Venerable Dondrub, Venerables Vivekananda and Bhaddamanika, Thay Minh Do, SuBa, SuCo Huong Nhu, SuCo Quang Hue, and Thich Giac Lam. SuBa's advice maps a path. I keep forgetting that what I'm seeking is within. *The Buddha is within.*

Buddha said, "Do not believe in anything merely on the authority of your teachers and elders. Do not believe in traditions because they have been handed down for many generations. But after observation and analysis, when you find anything that agrees with reason and is conducive to the good and benefit of one and all, then accept it and live up to it."

This I can believe. I've experienced SuBa's advice personally so I know it to be true. When I've gone alone into the wilderness, I've had experiences strikingly similar to those I've had in deep meditation. Though my meditation skills are immature, I've sometimes experienced the 'Buddha within.' I realize that I don't need to travel around the world to study my mind. I only need to latch onto the 'Buddha within' and live it out.

This doesn't mean my quest is complete. The stallion of mind is far from tamed and I've still no confidence that I can sustain mindful practice back home. But remembering to look within, I'll have a better handle on how to direct that effort.

Everything changes—that's for certain. And now my understanding has changed. Maybe the place that seemed to have the least to offer in terms of meditation practice—Quan Am Monastery—had the most to offer in wisdom: 'The Buddha is within!' SuBa has given me more than one precious gift in uttering those words.

The sun breaks past the treetops. I watch with reverence as my fellow meditators sweep leaves with a straw broom as a morning ritual of mindfulness. My heart bows to them. I bow to the stream of ants marching single file next to me in search of a gecko dropping for a morning meal. I bow to my wife, patiently waiting at home, ready to go to bed without a kiss. I bow to the universe.

My mind is clear. I'll leave Bao VanTu and move on, visit a few other monasteries to experience other traditions according to the goals I set. I must tell the master.

A bit later, I'm enjoying my daily meal, when I hear a loud conversation from the compound's center. It sounds all too familiar. Sure enough, Dr. Thom and Co Anh march over.

"Mark, immigration officers visit master this morning." Dr. Thom says anxiously. "They tell master want talk with you, me, and the other two Vietnamese-American ex-patriots here. Say routine questioning. Not take long."

"What about my approval?" I ask.

"They say approval for local police, not immigration. Not worry, though, say routine questions. Immigration meet us at local police station 1:30. Co Anh have van take us. Make sure bring passport."

I want no part of this. If I leave Bao VanTu immediately I may be able to spare myself and others the hassle of this 'routine questioning.'

I tell Dr. Thom about my decision to leave. "I should talk with the master now and leave right away to spare you and others this trouble," I say.

"It best for master if you go meeting, Mark. Monastery will look bad to officials if leave now," he says.

"You're right, I'll cooperate," I tell him. "But I must talk with the master after our meeting."

The van ride to the local police station is quiet and solemn. Unlike previous meetings for the religious council approval, other students have been pulled from their practice because of me, and a higher level of government is involved.

The van pulls onto a grassy lawn in front of a stark, single-story concrete building. It's unlike any police station I've seen. There's no marked cars, no receptionists, computers, or weapons of any sort and the interior is plain and poorly lit. There's only a few faded wooden tables and several heavily worn chairs.

Four officers in polished black boots, army-green uniforms with gold stars on their shoulders, and officer-style hats march forward. Their faces are stone cold. They look unhappy, and I feel sorry for them.

Dr. Thom, Co Anh, and the officers speak Vietnamese. Then an officer motions me to follow while others are paired with an officer and we're each escorted to separate rooms.

"Dr. Thom, can you accompany me to interpret?" I call out.

The officer assigned to me spins around. "No!" he forbids. "He go. English I speak." He glares at me. "You only. Come."

Dr. Thom is whisked away. This doesn't seem like "routine questioning." These are high-ranking officers and behind their hostile attitude, they seem nervous. They've separated us, without representation. This is anything but ordinary.

Yet, I'm surprisingly relaxed. I'm in a confrontation with a communist officer, yet I'm calm and present. In this testy predicament, I can see how my meditation efforts *have* borne fruit.

I'm directed into a small room with unpainted concrete walls, a single wooden table, and four wooden chairs. The floor's not been swept in weeks; the air is stale.

"Sit, sir," he sharply commands pointing to a chair. "We talk. I ask question. No good English speak. Must slowly talk."

He targets me with a series of demographic questions: "What you name? Where from? When come Vietnam?" He gradually ramps up his questions and they become more leading: "You have friends Vietnam? You have friends this province? How find out about Bao Van Tu? What do at monastery? Cell phone have?"

Each question is spit out sharply; he studies my face as I answer. When I respond that I do have a cell phone, he raises his eyebrows, again studies my face, and then holds out his hand. "Give now."

I hand over my phone, worried that it won't be returned. Instantly he toggles through the menu to the call history and begins writing down dialed numbers. He's very thorough, and returns it when finished.

No Pain, No Gain

He asks for my passport and pages through it studiously. After several minutes he states, "Mr. Mark, why at monastery?"

"I'm learning Buddhism."

"You are study?"

"Yes, I learn from the master. I cause no problems. Only learn."

"Mr. Mark, your visa is *tourist* visa. Not *study* visa. You say study. This mean not tourist. This violation of Vietnam law. This illegal." He pauses for a long moment to read my reaction and then leans forward.

"You break Vietnam law. Do you agree you break Vietnam law?"

What an incriminating question! If I agree, I give him a blank check to any action he chooses. I could be detained or deported.

"No, I do not agree!" I say. "I have approval to be at Bao Van Tu!"

He becomes irritated. "How say 'no agree'? I tell you illegal study with tourist visa!" he says. "You must agree break Vietnam law."

"I'm not aware of Vietnam law. How can I break a law I don't know?"

"No matter. Law you break. Do you agree that break law?"

It's time to redirect this conversation. "I need the U.S. Embassy phone number," I say.

"Not necessary!" he barks, as he leans forward. "Just answer."

I need support. I rise and briskly walk to the door. I don't leave the room, just call out to Co Anh who's standing in the hall.

"I need the phone number for the U.S. Embassy, Co Anh. Please, I must call them now!"

Co Anh looks confused and doesn't understand. I repeat my request, but the officer yells a stinging command in Vietnamese and she backs away like a kicked puppy.

We're at a standoff. I can either hold my ground and refuse discussions until I contact the Embassy, which will likely escalate tensions, or I can give vague and elusive answers that might temper the standoff. I choose the latter.

"I didn't break the law, sir," I tell him calmly. "I'm a tourist traveling to many places in Vietnam. Bao Van Tu is only one tourist stop."

"You say study master so need study visa." The stalemate continues. "You break law. Now *must* agree break law." He slams his hand on the table.

Eventually, the communist officer and I reach a compromise. I agree that he *told me* I broke the law, allowing him to save face with his commanding officer. He scribbles on a two-page form, has a heated discussion with his superior, then forcefully stamps the form with finality that expresses anger and authority. He hands me the form, snaps, "OK, go now."

I walk to the car with the others, happy the issue is resolved. I find that the others had similar drillings but, in the end, had their passports returned as well. On the way back, Co Anh reads the form. It demands I return in three days for 'further discussions.' The others have the same demand. I don't know about them, but I won't play that game again.

Back at my hut, I remind myself that this is an opportunity to practice putting mindfulness and kindness into a difficult situation. I resolve to remain calm and flexible.

I smile at how quickly things can change. Yesterday I planned to stay here for several months. This morning I decided to depart very soon. Tomorrow, I may be here at the monastery, en route to another monastery, deported from Vietnam, on a flight to Korea, or on my way back home. How interesting that life has such flux and fluidity! At Kopan Venerable Dondrub impressed this on all of us: "It is an illusion to think that life is ever stable and routine. In fact, our situation, and even our life itself, hangs by a mere thread that can snap and alter our entire existence at any moment."

I call the U.S. Embassy in the morning

"I understand your situation," says Mr. Biden, the U.S. Embassy official that I telephone the following morning. "Mark, government and religion are combined in Vietnam but mix like oil and water. You're remote, where local authorities wield much power. As a Caucasian, you draw a lot of attention. However, they're uncertain how to handle the situation. It seems that the monastery is on shaky terms with officials. Otherwise, they'd have avoided this. Local officials expect favor from the monastery and, if not given, conflict results. You're a pawn in that standoff."

"I don't want to get caught up in this," I tell Mr. Biden. "I was planning on leaving anyway. I'd rather leave now, but they demand another meeting."

"Here's my advice," he says. "If I were you, I'd just walk. Skip town. As I said, you're a Caucasian and to some degree that intimidates them. It'll be easier for them to let the problem fade. My bets are they'll not pursue if you up and leave. They've bigger fish to fry."

"Can I visit other cities?" I ask. "Vietnam requires registering my passport with the police at every destination, and I worry that local police will identify and detain me."

"You were at the police station. Did you see any computers?"

"No."

"FAX machine?"

"No, there was only one phone and it didn't get used."

"Exactly," he said. "They don't have a database at their fingertips. Don't get me wrong, if they wanted to, they can find someone with amazing speed and accuracy, but you're small potatoes, Mark. They'll get laughed at if they pursue this into other territories."

Then he throws the curve ball. "But no guarantees. There's risk in leaving. One never knows the outcome."

I'll take the risk. I thank Mr. Biden, return to the monastery, and ask for the master.

In the master's hut, I explain my decision. He listens with his characteristic presence and detachment. He kindly offers to guide my practice via mail. He also assures me that the situation will be remedied, and I can return in the future. I bow with appreciation and respect.

I bid farewell to Co Anh and Dr. Thom and head to Ho Chi Minh City. I depart with no way to study Thich Giac Lam's teachings. It seems unlikely I'll return.

Each monastery I depart, I carry new friends, a more refined value system, a deeper understanding of my mind, and perhaps even a more clear, exact, and aware mind. My time at Bao VanTu has brought me a significant step closer to achieving my goals—and to going home. But first, there are a few more monasteries to visit.

Chapter 17

Cool Zen

Dalat, Vietnam

> Meditation should be like jogger who jogs only because it's good for self. They know it's good for health and slowly good comes.
>
> Thay Duc
> Truc Lam Monastery

Truc Lam Zen monastery is tucked onto a mountainside in central Vietnam. Its elderly master, Thich Thanh Tu, has been influential in advancing Zen Buddhism in Vietnam.

Zen steers the practitioner to a direct experience of 'the true nature of self' through sitting meditation and a teacher's guidance. There's less scripture, ritual, and doctrine. As I've said, my practice at home is Japanese Zen.

"It good place for you, Mark," SuBa said when I phoned her from Ho Chi Minh City. "Much cooler. Mountains quiet. Very good meditation," she said. It felt good to have her support.

Curiosity about this well-known monastery has led me to risk being discovered again by Vietnamese immigration authorities after my problems at Bao VanTu. Truc Lam though is larger and in a touristy area. Local authorities are less likely to bother me—at least that's what the US

Embassy implied. I've only ten days left on my visa, so my stay will be short.

I travel by bus, watching from my window as the towering buildings of Ho Chi Minh City transition to mud-and-stick huts. We pass through arid dunes that morph into patchworks of green rice fields with water buffalo pulling single plow blades with farmers atop wielding a convincing whip. Everywhere women are spreading rice and grain on huge plastic tarps to bake in the sun. As we ascend camel-hump mountains, the bus engine growls on the steep hairpin curves surrounded by thick pine forests. I'm excited to be in the mountains again.

I arrive in Dalat, a mountain town near the monastery at 9:00PM, and book a guesthouse room. Although tired from the long ride, I sit in meditation for forty-five minutes. I want to master the stallion.

At 5:00AM, I awaken and do fifteen minutes of yoga before meditation. Out my third-story window, an elderly man moves down the dark street doing tai chi while the sounds of pots clanging and a man's soft song emerge from an open window. Distant mountains are just beginning to glow from the day's sunrise I can't yet see.

After breakfast, I stroll through this hilly city, reminiscent of San Francisco. The city has a French influence, complete with a large replica of the Eiffel Tower. The streets are wide and uncrowded; flower gardens border roadsides. Young Asian honeymooners stroll open-air markets holding hands.

An elderly Buddhist nun wearing weathered orange robes approaches extending a wooden bowl, hoping for an offering. Inside are beads and a few coins. I offer bananas and bread which she accepts with a smile.

Vietnam feels so different from India or Nepal in this respect: travelers are not besieged with beggars. It's a relief not to be subjected to overwhelming neediness.

My heart is calling me up the mountain to the monastery. I check out of the guesthouse, and hire a motorbike driver. At the monastery, tourists are roaming the grounds, yet, here again, I'm the only westerner among the crowd. I hope to convince the abbot to allow me to stay with the monks, separate from the tourist area.

The hilly grounds are populated with tall pine trees, and stone walkways wind deep into the forest. I startle an iguana sunning on a small patch of dirt sending it scurrying up a tree.

I see three monks, each wearing full-length goldenrod robes. They see me with a backpack and their attention shifts. One monk says something to the others, and walks away. I approach the two.

"Do you speak English?"

They shake their heads, *no*. "Here stay," says one monk tripping over the two English words.

I nod, understanding that I'm to wait for the other monk. A few minutes later a different monk, also wearing goldenrod robes, arrives. He's a slender man in his mid-sixties, with a shaved head, bushy eyebrows, and deep dark eyes.

"Me Khai Khen. How you I help?" He speaks with a gentle voice working hard at his English.

"I'm Mark. I'm a Buddhist student. I want to practice meditation here. Is it possible to stay here?" I speak slowly, clearly. He seems to understand.

"Please, join for tea. We sit. Talk."

He escorts me to an empty dining hall with bench tables for about thirty. We sit and he pours two cups of green tea.

"You meditate?" he asks, his voice echoing off the tiled walls.

I tell him about my Zen practice and my journey. "Now I study Buddhism in Vietnam," I tell him.

"Why here come?"

"This monastery is famous. I think it's a good place to study." His forehead wrinkles as he tries to understand my words. I try again "I want to practice with good teachers."

"Sorry, English not good. I try understand hard."

"I like to stay one week. Is it possible?"

He thinks for a long moment. "No. Not can sleep here. Can stay day but not sleep night."

It's unusual for an Asian monastery to turn away a devoted student. It's possible they've also had problems with the government or those difficult Religious Councils —and learned some lessons. Since I'm already a fugitive of sorts, I don't want to push the issue.

"Can stay and practice with us," he says, stepping over to a desk to sift through a stack of papers. He hands me a worn copy of a typewritten sheet; I'm surprised it's written in English. It has meditation instructions and the general schedule:

3:15 a.m.	awaken
3:30–5:30 a.m.	sitting meditation
6:00 a.m.	breakfast
11:30 a.m.	lunch
1:30–3:30 p.m.	sitting meditation
6:00 p.m.	repentance ceremony
7:30–9:30 p.m.	sitting meditation

"You stay Dalat hotel," Kai Khen says. "Come monastery 3:00AM. We send motorbike for you. Stay monastery all day. Go back on motorbike 9:30PM. Monastery arrange motorbike. Okay with you?"

He's trying to accommodate me. However guesthouses lock their doors every evening. Besides, I worry that traveling early will attract attention—and that could spell trouble for me. "Yes," I say. "But come 9:00AM. I have breakfast in Dalat."

He frowns. "No three AM? Why no? Meditation and breakfast at monastery."

"Three AM too early to travel. I sorry. Can only come at nine AM."

He nods, but I can tell he doesn't understand.

"Okay. 9:00AM motorbike from hotel." He looks pleased, we have an agreement. "Motorbike now take you, arrange hotel. Pick up tomorrow morning."

Khai Khen walks me to the parking lot and introduces the motorbike driver, Nam, a neatly dressed man in his late twenties. The spectacular thirty-minute ride to the hotel winds through secluded woodlands, occasionally breaking into upper elevation farm fields. The picturesque mountains are steep and craggy on the sides with tops that are rolling with the brilliant greenery of palm, bamboo, and evergreen trees. My trips back and forth will be treats.

When I register at the guesthouse, the owner requests my passport for police approval. This is standard procedure but my stomach tenses. If they find out about my illegal departure from Bao Van Tu Monastery, I'll be arrested and deported for sure. I surrender my passport and hope it'll slip through the system.

Nam departs and I head into town to grab dinner. I choose an empty café where I can read the pamphlet Khai Khen gave me. When I walk into the café, I startle a young man and woman lying on a wooden bench. They jump up and seat me. The café is drab and the paper menu is tattered with only a sketchy English selection. I order and they disappear into the kitchen.

Khai Khen's meditation instructions are preceded by short practice guidelines:

Practice

1. Know what you are thinking at all times. Be conscious of all thoughts and ideas but do not follow them.
2. Place no thoughtless mind in contact with the outside world.
3. Do not be stuck in the external . . . go beyond duality.
4. Always live with our real Buddha nature.

These are common Buddhist directives and remind me of Minh Do's teachings. Number three is my personal hurdle. Masters teach us to go beyond distinctions of black and white, hot and cold, high and low. They discourage labeling as a hindrance to accurately perceiving reality. I understand the non-duality concept intellectually. For example, a hot day for me may well be a cold day for a Vietnamese person. But I don't yet understand how non-duality applies to living my life as a Buddhist. I will seek further to find out.

The stages of meditation on Khai Ken's list are even more interesting:

Meditation Method

One begins meditation by concentrating on the breath and counting each breath. When inhaling say in your mind 'one'. When exhaling mentally say 'two'. When inhaling again say three. Do this until you get to ten and then start over.

Sitting sessions should be short at first and gradually increase.

As one advances, concentration improves. At some point one can stop the counting and simply pay attention to the breath.

As one advances even further, it is possible to then change your concentration from breathing to observing the mind itself.

This last step I haven't heard before. What does it mean to concentrate on 'observing the mind itself?' Minh Do taught me the advanced method of paying attention to everything around me. I've tried that a number of times and it has deepened my meditation experience—but it requires strong concentration.

I've practiced numerous meditation techniques over the years. Common to all is a chosen 'object' of concentration. That object may be the breath, a physical object like a statue, the sound of a voice chanting, or Minh Do's "everything around—but no stick" instructions. Breath as the object of concentration has worked well for me. Khai Khen's list asks the meditator to concentrate on the mind's activity or inactivity. Each technique steers the mind away from internal dialogue, which anchors the mind in the present and fosters keen awareness. These instructions suggest stepping beyond concentrating on objects, which 'anchor' the mind, in favor of concentrating on the mind itself. I'll have to experiment with this.

The next morning, Khai Khen sees me walking up the path and smiles. "Hotel okay? Sleep well?"

I nod.

"Ten AM we talk with midmaster. Very important. Approval for you practice here."

Here the term "master" is reserved for the aged Thich Thanh Tu, the founder of this tradition; so a midmaster is a high-level master below him. But just the word 'approval' makes me twitch.

Khai Khen describes the proper protocol: I must wear light blue, full length robes over my street clothes. I must be on time, bow when meeting, hold my hands in front and look downward when listening, talk very little, and bow at the end. Six times he instructs me to be on time. He appears apprehensive and I find that odd. But the Zen tradition has a reputation of strict and demanding masters. Perhaps this midmaster is that sort.

I've been shaving my head since Panditarama; it's maintenance free and helps me stay cool. Shaving my head, wearing robes, and using proper protocol makes me feel part of the monastic community. It somehow feels right.

Khai Khen and I meet the midmaster on a second floor outdoor walkway. The authoritative forty-year old master has thick, bushy eyebrows and seems curious about me. He questions my Buddhist experience, including why I'm here, how long I've been a Buddhist, the traditions I've practiced, and my future plans. Khai Khen translates with a hint of nervousness.

The midmaster utters some Vietnamese and a delicate smile crosses his face.

"We bow now," says Khai Khen.

Heading back to the main compound, Khai Khen says, "Very good meet." He smiles. "Midmaster happy you here. Says me give meditation instructions. Very special." Khai Khen then surprises me with a double thumbs up, and says, "Okay, cool man."

I chuckle out loud at the unexpected American gesture from this composed Buddhist monk. He smiles back.

He shows me the Ceremonial Hall, an elegant carpeted room fully furnished in mahogany. On the altar is a large sculpted figure of Bodhidarma, the master who brought Zen to China from India, and three smaller images of Buddha. "Repentance ceremony six o'clock tonight," Khai Khen says. "You join. Must wear robes."

The main Buddha Hall is a meditation hall with a large Buddha statue and flowers and fruit aside the altar. Outside is a gazebo with a double-tiered tiled roof, marble floor, and a prominent five-foot bronze bell. Thirty steps away is an identical gazebo with an enormous drum.

The complex is meticulously landscaped with potted flowers lining the walkways. This is a cool paradise.

Our last stop is the Meditation Hall, a humble building isolated behind a patch of pine trees. The carpeted meditation room is brightly lit with four rows of yellow cushions. He points to a cushion near the back.

"You here. Meditate. Sit and face wall."

I almost laugh at the size of the cushion he expects me to meditate on. It's about a foot high and a rigid eight inches across. It'll be like sitting on the tip of a narrow log. I doubt I can tolerate this for ten minutes, let alone two hours.

"Do you have bigger cushion?"

He points to a small cabinet and I dig through, finding a better choice.

He picks up a four-foot long bamboo stick. "Fall asleep," he says, then smacks his hand with a loud "whack."

Guess I'll avoid naps here.

"You read meditate instructions? Questions have?"

I want to ask about the 'observing the mind itself' instructions but our communication is nowhere near that level, so I shake my head *no*.

He leads me to the dining hall for lunch where the atmosphere is casual and numerous conversations are in progress. Noticing me, a younger monk stands beside me announcing something in Vietnamese that must surely be about our height difference. Laughter breaks out. I'm sure it's good-hearted fun and we smile at each other.

Meals here are formal and ritualized. The hall falls silent as the head monk enters. On his cue the group sings a chant. No one eats until everyone is served from the bowls of steaming rice and vegetables. I'm shown the proper way to hold the serving bowl, lift and touch it to my forehead before serving. We eat in silence and remain seated until the last person places his chopsticks down. No one leaves even a grain of uneaten food. Once finished, the master sings a chant and we then wash our plates outside under a garden hose.

"Rest now," Khai Khen says. "Come I show."

We walk to an extra residence room with two beds and a closet.

"Rest here anytime. I go now. Meditation one-thirty. You remember?"

"Yes" I point to my watch. I decide to walk the grounds instead of resting.

The monastery's public section covers acres of tall pine forests interlaced with stone walkways and flower gardens. Finding a secluded area, I take the opportunity for walking meditation. Concentrating on every step, I observe the feelings of my footsteps and follow my mind studiously. A light breeze swipes my cheek and plays with the wind chimes. The sun warms my side. Fragrant incense from the temple mingles with pine aroma. Pine needles crunch beneath my feet and a startled gecko darts by. I absorb the whole experience, aware, free of internal chatter.

I sit on a natural stone wall with a sweeping view of the surrounding mountain peaks. Below is a placid slate-blue lake, with a large island of green pine trees. The view is serene. I remember a teacher's advice from back home:

"It's easy to sit on the side of the mountain and meditate. But it's bringing this into the real world that's the challenge."

And that's exactly my challenge. Any hope I have of maintaining mindfulness back home depends on intimately experiencing it here so I can recall it when needed. Familiarity is key. It's like good friends who've spent many hours together and now they can rely on each other during hard times. Meditation is that kind of friend.

The twenty monks in the meditation hall are aware of my presence, and many are glancing my way when I take my place. The lead monk enters and we all sit. He rings a small brass bell three times and the hall falls silent.

A two-hour session is difficult for me. I've sat that long with Minh Do, but not without shifting position. This time is no different. I resort to occasional squirming on my cushion when knee and back pains surface.

The pleasantly cool climate, the quiet monastic environment, and my earlier walking meditation have settled my mind. But underneath, I'm concerned about the police reviewing my passport. The worry nibbles at my concentration. The odd-sized cushion is cutting off my circulation so I make an adjustment. It helps to think back to Bao VanTu Monastery, the sweat rolling down my face during meditation and the annoying insects. I appreciate this cool mountain environment.

Two hours end and each practitioner massages his face, arms, and legs to rejuvenate the body before standing and prostrating three times.

As I leave, Khai Khen approaches. "Meditation good?"

I nod.

"Six PM repentance ceremony. Meditation after. You come. Now you meet Canadian monk."

In the garden outside is a monk in his mid-thirties. "Hello. I Duc. I from Toronto on retreat." Duc speaks with a strong Vietnamese accent but his English is understandable. He wears typical robes and has a shaved head. He's big-framed and taller than the average Vietnamese.

I introduce myself and ask about Toronto.

"I have small temple," he says. "Originally from Vietnam. Move to Canada. I retreat here for one month."

I ask him how long he's been a monk.

"Five years been monk. Always been Buddhist, even in Vietnam. Not happy with lay life. Have many women, have many things, but never really happy. Not satisfied. Always want more. Finally say 'enough!' Not good. Then become monk. Now satisfied. Now very happy." He smiles contentedly. After chatting, he excuses himself and leaves.

"Free time now," Khai Khen says. "Rest or walk okay. Ceremony six PM. On time must. Wear robes important."

What to do for several hours? I return to the forest and enter my mind.

I later join monks at the repentance ceremony, which is intended to purify oneself, lead to freedom, and awaken the mind. It's a formal daily event.

Frogs croak in a nearby pond announcing the settling-in of darkness. Several monks huddle outside chatting, while others—including Duc—stand inside. Duc stands upright and still, hands folded in front, his eyes gazing downward in concentration. A young monk steps up to the gazebo and pounds the large drum in a fast ceremonial beat that echoes off the mountainside. As he does, all the monks find their places aside the altar, with junior monks and myself in back. The drummer moves to the other gazebo and sings over a loud-speaker system, occasionally striking the large bell. His voice is crisp and beautiful and the bell's vibrations reverberate in my body. I imagine all birds and animals on the mountainside also coming to attention.

After the song, the head monk leads chanting and prostrations. Everyone then exits and walks single file across the courtyard into the main Buddha Hall for more chants and prostrations. Every movement is performed with concentrated precision. This is as much a form of meditation as it is a ceremony.

A monk unexpectedly steps out of line and bends down to help a thumb-sized beetle on its back that's struggling to right itself. As if caring for a child, he carries the buzzing creature outside on the lawn and gently sets it down. What an act of compassion!

This is an all-male monastery. Nuns are on the other side of the mountain. The monastery becomes fully segregated once tourist visits end. With that, my tendency to impress females disappears. As a meditator, that's to my advantage. It's simply human nature, perhaps even my male flaw, but I find that without women around, my ability to concentrate is better.

The group moves silently to the Meditation Hall. The sun has set and a damp chill sets in. After an hour of meditation, discomfort again sets in. Yet, I settle into a deeper level of awareness. The cool and invigorating mountain setting and the monastic community's acceptance puts me at ease.

Khai Khen checks in with me frequently.

"How meditation tonight?"

"Very good. My mind was calm. I like it here."

"Good. Me happy. Come tomorrow, yes?"

I smile and nod.

"I think good practice for you here. Stay long as want. No problem." I'm touched by his invitation.

"Cool weather helps my meditation," I tell him. "Your kindness is helpful too. I'll stay several days longer. Thank you."

"Now we go motorbike. I arrange with Nam."

As Nam drives me back, I'm wishing I could communicate better with Khai Khen. I'd like to know him better. I wish I didn't have to leave the monastery every night. But now, I must check if the police returned my passport.

The ride through the meandering mountainside road to and from the monastery is a meditation in itself–a motorbike meditation. The sky is clear and a half moon illuminates the forest and farmland. The damp evening air has taken on a musky fragrance. Just a few farmhouse lights remain. I feel like I'm watching an entire mountain falling asleep.

Nam tilts his head back, keeping his eyes ahead. "You cold?" he asks.

"No. I'm from a cold city. This is comfortable."

We pass a huge patch of barren mountainside. It looks eerie in the moonlight. I ask Nam about it.

"Agent Orange," he says. "From war. No more grow."

It's another Vietnam War scar, like the bomb-made pond in Mr. Giac's backyard. I look for bitterness in Nam, but find none.

"Meditate?" he asks over his shoulder. "How long meditate?"

"Two hours evening and two hours afternoon," I say over the wind. "Do you meditate?"

"Sometimes. It's good for me."

We approach the outskirts of the city and Nam slows down, making it easier to talk.

I ask how long he's worked for the monastery.

"Work as helper two years. I monk before that. Studying. Then leave."

"Why?"

"Sacrifice not for me. My life is layperson. I like home. But also like monastery so I stay as worker. Now I meditate and practice dharma. Similar to monk but not sacrifice."

We arrive at the hotel.

"Okay hotel? Need help?" he asks.

I shake my head and bow to my good-natured motorbike driver.

As I walk into the hotel I've one thing on my mind; I go immediately to the front desk and ask the woman, "Has my passport been returned?"

"No sir, sorry. Police have. Maybe noontime tomorrow. No problem."

Easy for her to say 'no problem.' She doesn't know what happened at Bao VanTu. She can't guess why I look so worried. At other guesthouses, my passport was returned promptly. I accept what is.

The next morning, before going to the monastery, I check with a different desk attendant.

"No passport yet, sir. Noontime. No worry."

But I do worry and I don't want to worry all day.

When I arrive at the monastery, a dharma talk is in progress—in Vietnamese. I miss Minh Do's fabulous dharma talks. They're a short course on the principles I wish to live by. Dharma talks from Craig, my teacher in Cleveland, always inspired me, even when I'd heard the subject before.

I take to woodland meditation. Amidst the hush of the forest, I'm able to clearly observe my mind's mental play. Nature does this to me. I sit on the bench and pay attention only to my breath. Calm and peace arise, but so does an acute awareness of my surroundings. The sounds of birds and the wind whispering through the pines, the breeze brushing the hairs on my arm, the scent of pine, the view of the lake below, all rest in my mind as awareness rather than thought. It is a full and complete experience. Maybe this is what Venerable Dondrub meant when he talked about "clear, exact, awareness."

I hear the crunch of footsteps and turn to find Khai Khen seating himself next to me. "Good you come. Meditate here?"

"Yes. Awareness is strong here."

He smiles and nods but then looks away for a few moments.

"Sorry," he says looking back. "English not good. Understand very little."

I feel bad when others apologize for not knowing English. I don't know their native tongue; it is I who should apologize. "Sorry I don't speak Vietnamese," I say. I try to continue the conversation. "Where did you learn English?"

"During war," he says. "I airplane fly. Pilot. Talk with Americans. Learn then."

"How long have you been a monk?"

"Fifteen years. After war, started Buddhism. Learn more and more. Start meditate. Help very much. Finally become monk."

He's unpretentious and gentle, and I'm relaxed in his presence. We exchange only a handful of sentences in fifteen minutes together.

Just before lunch, Duc approaches me in the garden.

"I want to move to United States," he says. "Maybe next year but have problem with health care. Health care's expensive in the United States, isn't it?"

I explain what I know about the US health care system.

"Yes. Free in Canada. Good care in Canada." He looks to the distant mountains. "But it really not matter. So what? We all going die anyway. If mind is happy, free, and focused we move to better life when die. So, it not matter."

Duc is the only person here I can converse with at this level.

"You're a monk so your next life will be better, right?"

"Not just monk, if your mind is yellow then will get better life."

"What do you mean by 'yellow'?"

"Me a monk. I work on my mind and it get better. I can move on to better life. Some monks don't work on mind. No have yellow mind. You see?"

"Not really."

"You work on your mind in monastery. You meditate hard. You dedicated to meditate. Your mind is yellow, like monk. Maybe not wear yellow robes, but have yellow mind."

"Yellow means purity of mind?"

"Yes! You getting yellow mind. Yellow, like monks' robes. And when die will get better life. It like car. Car get old, turn it in, and get new one. Move on to better life if mind yellow. So health care really not so important."

Duc is at least ten years younger than I, yet so certain of rebirth that he can let go of this life, let go of the importance of having health care—without much thought! That's a strong combination of faith and courage.

After the midday meal, Khai Khen walks up, smiling. "Midmaster talk with me. He say okay you stay at monastery, you sleep here tonight."

I feel complimented! They trust me. But Khai Ken doesn't know how anxious I am about my passport. He doesn't know that if immigration found me, I'd be in serious trouble. I can't make the same mistake I made at Bao VanTu. Staying in a hotel, I blend into the tourist crowd and avoid visa problems.

Duc at Truc Lam monastery
Dalat, Vietnam

"Khai Khen, I'm sorry but I cannot stay," I tell him.

Disappointment and curiosity cross his face.

"I had problem in another monastery with immigration. Government didn't allow me to stay in monastery. I don't want a problem here." He seems to understand.

"I know. It okay." He forces a smile. "You second westerner here. One year last had westerner. Young man, very nice. Have problem too. But fix. Then okay, no problem. Stay one month, then go."

"I want to stay. Want to. But cannot. Okay?"

"Yes, understand." He bows and walks away.

But my worry doesn't go away. What'll I do if my passport isn't returned? I keep trying to accept my situation so I can free my mind to practice but the nasty worry keeps sticking its head up.

Most of my time is spent in the pine forest, the garden, and the meditation hall. I'm staying away from most people because I'm getting nervous about the attention I'm getting. It's feeling too much like Bao VanTu. Quite randomly, tourists, lay monastics, and even monks, approach and bow. Their intentions are good but I worry what could come of it. Just before the repentance ceremony one evening, a senior monk passes me from behind and pats me on the back, smiling affectionately as if to say "glad you are here." The monastic community warmly accepts me.

As I walk toward the meditation hall, two passing monks ask, "Hello, how are you? You hungry?"

"Yes I am," I respond. They must wonder how I'm adapting to no meal after lunch.

"No worry. After two or three weeks, you feel normal."

Incrementally, I'm learning endurance. I've always been focused on comforts; when thirsty I drink, when hungry I eat, when cold I turn up the thermostat. I've been a slave to cravings and I'm realizing they're never quenched. Venerable Dondrub gave a good example of craving: "It is like a child who's very content with his ice cream cone until his brother has one twice as big with sprinkles on top."

Monastic training has helped me control cravings through endurance, tolerance, and contentment. If I feel uncomfortable during meditation, I tolerate it and remain focused. If I don't feel like waking to the alarm, I accept that feeling, but wake anyway. In many ways it's freeing not to be a slave to my cravings.

My mind's growing calmer through practice here. I can hold my meditation posture longer with each session. I concentrate better in the absence of extreme cold, heat, insects, and noise—the things that hindered me in previous monasteries. This mountainous forest is helping me advance deeper into mind. It's unfortunate only a few days remain.

At the hotel I immediately approach the desk to ask about my passport. I've been rehearsing this in my mind all day. The same woman is on duty and looks up.

"Did you get my passport from the police today?" My heart beats fast.

She shuffles through her paperwork. "Don't know," she mumbles with concern as she digs her way ever deeper through the paper pile. "Oh yes! Here!" she finally says, smiling as she hands me the blue booklet. Two days of worry are over. She probably wonders why I look so relieved.

Even my daily morning walk in the city has become a more mindful one. My practice of going inside and knowing my mind leaves me joyful. Staying inside myself, observing my breath, and observing my mind's interaction with the buzz of the city makes everyday experiences more fulfilling. When I'm on a computer, updating friends and family I feel rich with peaceful awareness. More and more often I feel completely 'in the moment.' Perhaps I *can* carry this enhanced consciousness into my hectic home life.

The stallion isn't so antsy. He's relaxing and has stopped resisting my lead. He's letting me guide him as I walk at his side. Perhaps someday soon, I'll be able to climb on his back.

No doubt about it, this Zen monastery has caught my heart. The monastic community has taken me in. Every day before lunch, we laugh together. Several monks wrap their arms around my shoulders and speak Vietnamese that I can't understand. But it's all good-natured camaraderie.

Both Duc and Khai Khen regularly check on me to converse, or to just sit together in silence. One morning Duc inquires about my meditation.

"Not so good this morning," I reply.

"Physical or mental?" he asks.

"Mental. I'm frustrated when I cannot concentrate."

He thinks a moment. "Meditation like jogging," Duc says. "Some people jog for distance and want attain that distance. Some people jog for speed, run against clock and must achieve time. Meditation should be like jogger who jogs because they know it slowly good for health. Some days do five minute jog and some days one hour jog. Either time is good. No achievement. Just do what's right."

"I'm a jogger back home," I tell him. "I understand."

"Good, then you know five-minute day and one-hour day add up. Both good for health. No goal to attain."

Both Minh Do and SuBa had pointed this out —and I'd forgotten.

"I've a tendency to set goals and become frustrated when I don't attain them," I tell Duc.

"You recognize. Very good. Now, just let it be. Some days you tired, cannot jog well and only do short. Let it be. That's what meditation about."

It occurs to me that this trip has placed me in close contact with some of the most developed minds in the world and with that comes a natural absorption of sorts. Teachers like Vivekananda, Thay Minh Do, SuBa and now Duc and Khai Khen have provided nuggets of wisdom. They've shown me how to live a pure, disciplined, meaningful life. Another nugget has just been delivered to me.

As my meditation has become more concentrated—and therefore made me more peaceful—I've experimented with the curious instructions in Khai Khen's pamphlet: *"change your concentration from breathing to observing the mind itself."*

With the intensity of an engineer studying a technical problem, I carefully watch my mind and its inclinations. As I concentrate on my mind's activity, on what it's doing and where it's jumping, I expose subtle layers of urges, inclinations, and mental activity that I'd never noticed before. Tucked into the shadows of the mind's more apparent mental meanderings are little secrets not previously unveiled. Not only is thought evident, but the tendency that triggers it as well. You can expose it by studying the mind closely. I'm learning more of my mind's fundamental nature of constant motion, of its underlying workings. It's fascinating.

Every once in a while, for just the briefest moments, my mind rests. It rests quietly without thought. It rests in *no thought* and I become aware, without thinking. At those times, I see the mind as emptiness. I'm not yet able to stay very long in *no thought*, the state comes and goes quickly. But it's a tantalizing taste of pure awareness, an experience of clarity, a full nothingness.

Yes the stallion's in the corral and I'm leading it around. For brief moments, I'm able to get on his back and ride him. We're becoming familiar with each other.

My time in Vietnam ends, and I fly out of the country before my visa expires. I depart yet another monastery, yet another group of friends. But I don't leave empty handed. I leave with a wealth of wisdom passed on from great teachers.

PART FOUR

Korea

Chapter 18

West in the East

Daejeon, South Korea

The danger in the real world is desire and attachment. As soon as you want something, you enter a danger zone.
Bo Haeng Sunim
Musangsa Monastery

I'm heading west and getting closer to home. I've crossed the China Sea into the central mountain region of the South Korean peninsula. First, I'll spend a week or two here at Musangsa, a cozy monastery nested on the side of a gently sloped mountain. Then I'll spend a week at Hwagyesa Monastery on the edge of Seoul.

My journey is nearing its end. I'm content I've achieved my goals. Now I want to see what the Korean Zen tradition has to offer me. The inquiry driven practice here is referred to as the Kwan Um School of Zen. It also uses a metaphorical riddle called a Kong-an to stretch the mind's ability to grasp insights too obscure to convey through written or spoken teachings. It's rooted in the Rinzai Zen lineage. Sitting meditation is a key component.

Buddhism has a rich, well-preserved history in this cold, mountainous peninsula from which several legendary masters have flourished, most recently Master Seung Sahn who founded Musangsa before he died in 2004. Thousands of temples dot the Korean map.

From a cultural standpoint, I've made a significant stride toward home. Gone are hand-pulled rickshaws, bamboo huts, and the endless strings of street vendors. South Korea has modern and clean subways, buses, and high-speed trains. Streets are less crowded and people shop in upscale supermarkets and malls.

The bus's final stop has me standing in an isolated valley surrounded by rolling mountains about two miles from Musangsa Monastery. It's the rainy month of April, and it's chilly. Crouched under my umbrella, I trudge to a small shop in search of a taxi. Communication is surprisingly difficult in this modern country that sells millions of flashy cars to the West. The store owner struggles to understand my request for a taxi. Eventually, he makes a phone call and, on hanging up, bows slightly with a smile.

The taxi drops me off at the monastery, which I think of as my new classroom. Visible through the rain and hovering fog are three temples, each two stories high, in elegant dark red, slate blue, and yellow, a colorful contrast to the surrounding pines. The early spring rains have nursed this lush landscape of flowering red azaleas, evergreens, and budding birch trees. The premises have been meticulously cared for. It's beautiful.

Unlike other monastery visits arranged by a knock on the door, this one was prearranged. I submitted an online application that was approved by the abbot. I walk to the office, give my name, and the assistant pulls my paperwork from her neatly organized desk.

"Here you are," she says in excellent English. "How long will you be staying?"

I feel a bit like I'm checking into a hotel. "I'm a practicing Buddhist, not a tourist," I tell her. "I'd like to meditate for a week or two."

"The abbot approved your stay," she says. The abbot is the most senior monk responsible for all monastery affairs.

She points out the window to my second floor dorm in the community building. I'll be alone in the room, at least for now. She points out where the monks live, the meditation hall, and the main temple where I'll go for morning and evening chanting.

"Here's a schedule," she says as she hands me a paper. It's like other monastery schedules, rising at 3:00AM with morning and evening sitting and chanting meditations. They eat three meals here though and there's a daily work period, which I haven't had before.

"Please get settled and after dinner our head monk will meet you for meditation instructions," she says. "Before dinner, pick out a set of lay robes from the garment room."

My room is the largest I've had; fifteen people could fit comfortably. It's empty except for several clothing drawers, and a hibachi-style wood table for sharing tea. A modest altar is against one wall with a Buddha statue and incense sticks. There are no beds; thick quilts are laid on the heated floors as a mattress.

I browse the garment room for the thickest robes in my size. The grey pants are comfortably baggy, and the hip length robe is thickly quilted.

The dining hall is well lit, clean, and warm. Two monks and a nun prepare food while others arrange chopsticks and plates on hibachi tables. They place dishes of steaming hot vegetables on a wooden countertop. The aroma of sesame and spicy chilies hovers about; I'm hungry. A middle-aged monk greets me.

"Hello, I'm Bo Haeng Sunim," he says. "I'm the head monk. I'll be helping you settle." He's a white Caucasian, in his late forties. His English is perfect, with a slight Eastern European accent.

I introduce myself and ask the proper way to address him.

"Call me Bo Haeng Sunim. Just Sunim is okay, too." In Korean, "Sunim" means monk or nun. People are filtering into the room. Bo Haeng Sunim points out my cushion.

After the monks are seated and served, the lay practitioners serve themselves. It's now that I realize that the majority of monks and nuns are of western descent and fluent in English. I was told it's a good place for westerners, I see why: smack in the middle of eastern culture is an island of western Buddhists.

Mealtime is formal but friendly. A short chant precedes and friendly conversation follows. The group is neither hurried nor complacent. Afterward, everyone cleans their dishes and helps. I wash tables.

After dinner, Bo Haeng Sunim shows me the meditation hall. He leads me along a walkway to the adjacent building. It's gotten colder and windy and it's raining hard. Without my umbrella my left side is soaked. We enter the first floor of the monks' residence. I look down a long hallway that's softly lit and quiet.

The second floor meditation room has about twenty-five mats and cushions along the periphery. This is by far the best meditation hall I've been in! It's warm and bright, surrounded with tall windows, and has a soft yellow floor. A golden Buddha sits atop a wooden altar. Bo Haeng Sunim motions me onto a cushion and sits facing me.

"So, Mark, what type of meditation do you do?"

"Japanese Zen. I focus on breathing." He listens intently. "Recently in Vietnam," I continue, "I learned a technique concentrating on the mind's activity. I have been experimenting with this."

"Let's talk about the breath technique," he says. "What do you do when thought comes?"

"I simply let the thought go and return to breath. I refocus."

"That's a common approach," he says, his voice soft and calm. "But there is no force to it, Mark. It has no meat, no muscle."

As he says this, his fist is clenched and his voice climbs an octave.

"Instead," he says, "we ask forcefully, '*Who's having this thought?* We must ask, 'Whose thought is this?' and 'Where is this thought?'" His eyes are locked on mine as if there were nothing else in this world. "You must ask with energy and effort!" He acts as if he's telling me how to stay out of danger. "You must be in control!" He pounds both fists on the floor. I'm amazed.

At Bao VanTu, Thich Giac Lam instructed me to forcefully control my wandering mind by switching to walking meditation. Here, Bo Haeng Sunim instructs forceful inquiry.

I'm mesmerized as Bo Haeng continues his instructions in his utterly expressive and passionate way. He tells me where to sit, when to bow, and when to rise. His voice alternates between soft and strong. His movements are larger than life in a way. Like Vietnamese Zen, there's a number of exacting methods that must be learned, such as how to position my feet when I bow and where to place my hands.

Bo Haeng Sunim's expressiveness is extraordinary. His eyes are ablaze with intensity and energy. His hand gestures are as wild and uninhibited as his facial expressions. I can't help but believe him. I can't wait to practice.

He finishes my instructions just before the scheduled chanting session so we head to the main temple, which is carved into the side of the mountain above the other buildings. A half-dozen carvings of dragon heads hover above the entrance.

A monk, sitting cross-legged on a floor cushion, sings a melodious chant as he strikes the three-foot bell at exacting intervals. A double row of cushions extends over the carpeted floor with senior monks up front. There's a broad altar in the center and smaller altars on either side; above each hangs a huge painting. The ceiling has intricate blues and reds. The ambiance is glorious. Handmade, lotus lanterns with yellow petals and green pods hang from the ceiling in preparation for the Buddha's upcoming birthday celebration.

The monk sings a chant as the community filters in. Resident monks wear grey ceremonial robes with brown trim; an ochre shawl is wrapped over one shoulder and diagonally across the front to the waist. When the abbot enters, the forty-minute ceremony begins with bows, prostrations, and chants. The abbot plays a central role, at times chanting solo.

Chanting is synchronized by the striking of a moktak, otherwise known as a wooden fish, a handheld hollow wood carving that emits a thick percussive knock when struck. When the final bell sounds, the group moves to the meditation hall, single file by rank. Halfway through the hour-long meditation, we rise for walking meditation. I feel a little weak—I suppose from travel and the chilling rain—but my mind remains focused. When thoughts from my travels predictably arise, I follow Bo Haeng's advice and inquire, "Who's having this thought?"

It feels awkward to inject a thought-provoking question into a 'no-thought' effort. It seems like an intellectual exercise. But it does lead to the source of thought—my mind. "Observe the mind itself" were the instructions at Truc Lam Monastery in Vietnam. When I do, I become closely attuned to my mind's activity as I search for the source of thought. Eventually I return to observing my breath until once again a thought infiltrates and I ask again, 'Who's having this thought?'

As the session ends, I feel drained and head straight to my dorm, unroll my sleeping bag, and go to sleep.

A singing monk who's tapping on a moktak draws me out of deep sleep. My clock says 3:00AM. The sound of the moktak is even more uplifting than the gong I've become accustomed to. I'd treasure that job—to strike a moktak as I sing in the mountains' morning solitude.

Despite an uninterrupted sleep, I'm foggy-headed, and I've a runny nose, sore throat, and feel feverish. I force myself to dress and make my way to the temple, hoping the symptoms will dissipate.

I'm the first person outdoors. I pause to take in the pre-dawn magic. The rain has stopped, leaving a biting clamminess and a milky, calf-high fog that crawls across the ground. A train in the valley appears as a tiny string of Christmas lights and the rumble of its wheels is a faint whisper. A single bird's monotone chant sounds like the squeak of a door opening. The sound of frogs in the lake below merges with the taps of dewdrops falling from tree leaves.

The moktak tempo picks up, meaning it's time to get to the meditation hall, where we perform 108 prostrations that encourage reflection and concentration. The number 108 shows up frequently in Buddhist traditions: it's the number of beads meditators finger during meditation to help them concentrate and the number of steps up to a temple. Intended as a mind exercise, my practical-mind sees it as physical exercise in an otherwise sedentary lifestyle. It invigorates the body for sitting meditation.

But I'm getting sicker. My heart palpitates and I'm sweating profusely. I lose pace with the group. Prostrations completed, we file to the temple for morning chanting. The only sound is the soft footsteps of twenty-five monks.

During chanting, I become feverish and shaky. I try to push through, but feel dizzy and faint. I leave the temple for my warm sleeping bag. Basically, I collapse. I sleep right through breakfast. I've a fuzzy recollection of a monk coming to check on me.

A monastery is a difficult place to be ill. There's no couch to prop oneself up in. For sitting up I've only a cold wall for a back rest. At lunchtime, Housemaster Dok Sang Sunim wakes me with a cup of tea.

"Is there anything else I can get you?" he asks.

"Yeah, a La-Z-boy recliner," I mumble, trying to force a smile.

"I'll look," he jokes.

At dinnertime, he puts a plate of food at my side but I can only nibble on rice. It's lunch the next day before I rejoin the monastery schedule.

Dok Sang Sunim joins me during dinner cleanup. "We were worried about you," he says. "We're glad you are feeling better. Will you join us for this evening's practice?"

"I'm still weak and shaky," I tell him. "I want to, but won't be able to concentrate. I think I'll wait."

"It's important to practice," he says, "even if you have no concentration you should do your best. Meditating with no concentration is better than none at all."

His advice seems a bit harsh, but I'm here to learn. I attend the meditation and although it takes all my willpower not to slouch, I think Dok Sang is right. It's better that I made the effort.

I wake the next morning fully recovered and excited to rejoin the community. The morning prostrations are invigorating, chanting is inspiring, and my meditation concentration is sharp and strong.

After breakfast I ask Bo Haeng Sunim if we can talk after the daily house meeting. I feel a connection to this passionate monk and want to ask about my practice back home.

After the meeting, Bo Haeng and I return to the meditation hall where we sit on cushions.

"Sunim," I begin, "I've been struggling with a question." I explain my goal of establishing a good practice, calming my mind, and learning about other traditions. I tell him about my busy life and ask him what I've asked others: Do you think it's possible to be consistently mindful in the hectic western culture?

"Yes! Of course!" he says instantly. "You can do that but you must continue the effort at home. The key is to integrate practice with your daily life, minute to minute and moment to moment."

I nod. He's so sure.

"The danger in the real world is desire and attachment," he says. "As soon as you want something, you enter a danger zone. People will say, 'I have something for you, or I can do this for you, or I can take care of this for you.' If you have desire then you follow and get lost in it. You don't stay in yourself. If you follow then you're out of yourself. Stay in yourself!" He raises his voice sharply. "You must not attach!" He waves his finger insistently in his theatrical but inspiring way.

"When problems come, let go of emotions, let go of attachment, and address each independently. Continuously re-evaluate as the situation changes. Practice compassion and eliminate desire and attachment." He pauses and stares into my eyes.

"That's where meditation helps," he says. Meditation is like a fuel tank that you fill every time you sit and then tap into to bring awareness of desire and attachment. You go into life, address problems, and then return to fill your tank. Then you're ready to go again." He studies my face to see if I understand.

"But it's very difficult," he admits. "It's more difficult to practice as a lay person than a monk. I couldn't do it, which is why I'm here. I didn't have that strength."

"That's discouraging," I say, distressed. "If you couldn't do it, how will I?"

"You *can* do it!" he says, pounding his fist on the floor. "I lived in a meditation center in New York City for a while. Those people live busy lives. Some would come dirty from work and stop for twenty minutes to meditate. When one young man was meditating, his wife would phone him, interrupting his meditation to ask him to bring something home. The key is to attend to those needs and be in that moment. It's not about escaping or needing to be left alone. It's about 'Yes, honey, what can I get for you?'"

He leans back in thought and I hang on his words.

"My master once advised a student who pressured his family to keep quiet during Sunday meditation. His wife and kids worried about interrupting. The master told him that was wrong. He told him to attend to his family's needs, be compassionate and sensitive, and create a situation where the family is comfortable. Then they'll want you to practice because it benefits *them*. If it's right practice, it rewards the family."

"So the key to living mindfully back home is simply regular practice—to fill my tank?"

"Regular meditation is essential but true practice is not separate from life," Bo Haeng Sunim says. "Practice *is* your life. If you leave your practice on the cushion, that's not right. Driving down the road you can practice and your mind is like a mirror clearly reflecting reality. When the light turns red, just stop; don't think or evaluate. If someone runs in front of you, you instantly stop. This 'no thinking' reaction can apply to your entire life. You put your full self into it. You don't think, 'Oh that stupid person.' If you leave thought and opinion out, then you act from your heart and your mind."

"Is it like using intuition?"

"Not exactly. With intuition you're putting yourself into it. Act without injecting thought and opinion. This is your true self, your true nature. When things come up quickly, which they do in life, you can react very quickly. If a problem arises, don't say to yourself 'I've got to think about it' because then another problem will jump up, and then another. You get overwhelmed with things to think about. No! Address the problem and react, address and react. Do it sequentially."

He leans forward. His hands are finally settled in his lap, but his dark eyes are locked on mine.

"It's very, very, important that you understand death. It's one thing to acknowledge death and say 'I'm going to die.' It's one thing to see death in family and friends. It's another thing to be ready to die right here, right now!" His hands and body are moving vigorously and he pokes the ground to accentuate his point.

"We do die right here and now." His voice softens again. "Every moment is a death. This moment dies, the next moment dies. We start fresh with each moment. It's truly a new life each moment and what you had is now dead." He's ablaze again with expression. "Every day that passes becomes a dead day. Every one percent of your life that passes is one percent more dead. You must recognize this! It's very important that you're comfortable with death when you die. But it's hard! If you contemplate death every day, you can do it. You can greet death face on."

I like Bo Haeng. He's down-to-earth, practical, and realistic. But it's his passionate expressiveness that pumps me up with enthusiasm and energizes my practice.

This is the advantage of a fluent, English-speaking teacher. I think of the communication troubles I've had with Thich Giac Lam, SuBa, and Thay Minh Do—they're all great masters. Yet, articulate communication with a master makes a huge difference.

Everyone has temple duties, and there's a daily group work session as well. It's a sunny day so we tend to the potato and carrot fields. A group of twenty monks and lay persons kneel along troughs of sprouted potatoes yanking out weeds. Dok Sang, the Housemaster, works next to me. "I heard that you had an interview with Bo Haeng," he says.

"Yes, he's very helpful." Dok Sang tells me that Bo Haeng is Lithuanian and served in the Russian army. Afterward, he became a street mime for several years—which explains his expressiveness.

"Have you been given a Kong-an yet?" Dok Sang asks.

"No. I'm not certain what they are."

"If you stay, you'll be assigned one. It's a phrase or short story that poses a perplexing question. It stimulates deep thought that eventually leads to insight. The Kong-an is a key component of our Zen practice. The teacher assigns a Kong-an based on his evaluation of your practice. The student constantly meditates on the answer. The teacher has Kong-an interviews to test the student's progress and to guide him. Sometimes the answer comes quickly but sometimes it takes years. Some can be very esoteric."

"Is the Kong-an personal?" I ask.

"Yes, but the teacher does not make up the Kong-an. There are many Kong-ans, books of them. A good teacher has worked through many himself."

"So," I ask Dok Sang, "are you working on one?"

"Yes, but it's private."

"Can you give an example?"

Dok Sang quotes a famous Kong-an from Hakuin Ekaku: "Two hands clap and there is sound," he says. "'What is the sound of one hand clapping?' Of course, I cannot give you the answer." He grins.

I've heard little about Kong-ans until now, but reading Zen writings I find how arcane they can be. Sometimes I think Zen is like playing 'Where's Waldo?' You can spend a lot of time and effort looking for something that's literally right in front of you but you can't recognize it amidst distractions. I'm convinced that Zen, and Buddhism in general, offers the life-changing realizations if one is willing to exert effort.

That afternoon a young Korean man, about thirty years old, arrives and moves into my dorm, making a spot on the floor near me. His name is Wang San; he doesn't speak English. On first impression he seems uptight and nervous and spends a lot of time sitting in front of the altar in our room. When I enter, he springs up and faces me in a military manner. He must think I'm someone important and I do my best to help him relax. Before the evening ceremony, I take time to sit at the altar with him but, when I rise, he again stands excitedly to face me. I don't know how to help him be less anxious.

I stand outside the community building the next day to take in the natural beauty. Bo Haeng joins me.
"How's your stay going?"
"I'll be returning home in a few weeks and feel anxious about it. I understood your instructions, but I've been living pure simplicity for seven months and I know how easy it would be to get caught up in materialism and busyness. I've resolved to sell most of my belongings but your comments make me worry about remaining mindful."
"You're right to worry," he says. "Craving's a disease that grows. It's a hunger. In the West, there's no hunger of the body. We've plenty of food. But there's much hunger of the mind. It's so easy to let ourselves always want something. Want this, want that, want to go here, want to do that." He waves his hands wildly, shaking his head at the same time.

It's a perfect description of a busy mind.
"It's very dangerous." he continues. "It's what kills dharma and the

spirit. Better to be hungry of the stomach than hungry of the mind," he says, poking his abdomen.

That's what I've observed in India, Nepal, and Vietnam. Poor people live simpler lives with less food, yet their spirits often seem healthier. Richer cultures seem infected with craving—and their spirits seem poorer. Craving kills spirit. Maybe that's why I notice less personal warmth in developed cities.

"You can do it, Mark," Bo Haeng says. "You can overcome desire. You can do it in the West. You can do it right here and now . . . but don't think it'll be a breeze." He bows and departs. I'm left with fear and concern—and firm intention.

I think about my discussion with Bo Haeng. I hope some parts of the world remain poor—for their own sake—because their simple lifestyle is disconnected from materialism and its inevitable endless thirst to acquire. If you've never tasted lobster then you never crave it. In the West, we're incessantly teased with ads for things that'll make us 'happy.' That continual bombardment challenges the spiritual seeker who strives to eliminate desire.

I suppose that's one of the precious advantages of monastic life: a monastery offers isolation from material temptations and sensory stimulation. Monasticism boils life down to its essential needs. Living as a monk is becoming increasingly attractive.

One afternoon, I'm alone in the Meditation Hall. I sit for an hour, observing my mind's activity. I become aware that my perception is vivid and crisp. Not that it suddenly happened but rather I suddenly recognized it. I'm seeing, hearing, and smelling with a heightened intensity. This happened in Lumbini and at Truc Lam monastery as well. It's the "clear, exact and aware" state that Venerable Dondrub at Kopan described. I know, though, that this experience, while blissful, is temporary. I sit for some time, knowing that by gaining familiarity with the experience I can draw from that energy in the future. I'm 'filling my gas tank' as Bo Haeng says.

Maybe this stallion of mind *can* be tamed. I sometimes feel I'm riding on his back and it feels grand. It's not a stable ride by any stretch of the imagination; he still bucks and it wouldn't take much for him to throw me off and burst from the corral. There's much more work to do, but with sustained practice at home perhaps I can progress—and I will. And on that day I'll stand on a balcony looking at nature and profess, just as Minh Do did to me, that it's taken a long time but finally, every second, I'm able to 'stay in self,' that I know how to come home, that I've found that diamond—that Buddha within.

The next day after lunch, an ambulance pulls to the entrance. Wang San is loaded onto a stretcher. "What's wrong?" I ask Dok Sang Sunim.
"It's Wang San."
"He's my roommate!"
"He was found unconscious and we couldn't wake him. He woke briefly on the stretcher but passed out again."
After dinner, the abbot announces that Wang San is doing well. He's been diagnosed with a nervous breakdown.
Practicing Zen and having a nervous breakdown seem paradoxical. Sure Zen is mentally and physically challenging. But central to all Buddhist practice is accepting things as they are. Perhaps Wang San is learning Zen to help reduce anxiety. If he continues, I'd expect he'd be able to cure that problem . . . and many more.

The sun shines daily the remainder of my stay. My meditation is more tightly disciplined and I'm gaining control of wandering thoughts. I'm better at accepting the "fly around mind" as Bo Haeng calls it.
On my last evening before dinner, Bo Haeng is waiting outside and I take the opportunity to pose another question.
"Bo Haeng, I realize that concentration is something that must be developed. I know that I should expect to experience 'fly around mind.' But I believe my ability to concentrate is worse than average. In grade school, my teachers complained about my daydreaming in class. Even today I have the same challenge. I compensate for it by working harder. Do you have any advice on how to improve concentration?"

He thinks as he gazes at the mountain peak across the valley. "You told me you concentrate on breath during meditation," he finally begins.

"Yes."

"You might consider focusing on your body's emotional feeling center which is right here." He points below his navel. "Measure two finger thicknesses below your navel. This is a central energy point and I use it often."

"So I should concentrate only on that spot? That sounds difficult. It's static. There's no movement."

"There's a technique I use to help. I sit facing the wall and take a stick and prop it between the wall at one end and on my energy point on the other. I push hard against the stick to concentrate on only that point. I cannot help but concentrate there. It's very effective. I've talked with the abbot about this and he likes the method."

I'm interested but not convinced.

"One year ago there was a man here who had emotional problems," Sunim says. "He could barely concentrate. I used this technique to help. We sat facing each other and put the stick between us with each end in our energy points. We interlocked hands and pulled so the stick pressed in, forcing concentration. It's very good, very powerful. It's too late in your stay for us to work on this together but you can try it at home."

As the time draws near for my departure, I reflect back to Bo Haeng's advice about avoiding attachment and desire. "You can do it in the here and now . . . but don't think it is a breeze." He dotted every *i* and crossed the *t*'s. By applying practice to daily life, I can avoid the arising of desire that undercuts mindful living. Desire is not my friend. I know I'll be put to the test.

On my final morning, I lie in bed listening to the solitary monk drumming on the moktak and singing a chant. I lie there for several minutes. It won't be long before my routine changes from being awakened by gongs, bells, or a moktak to being awakened by a buzzing alarm clock. I choke up. A lump forms in my throat and I feel like crying. I'll sorely miss this.

I've been surrounded by a rich culture, eloquent rituals, and beautiful temples. Moving as all that is, what I'll miss most is the discipline, devotion, and virtue of the monastic aspirants.

At this moment, I hear a strong voice inside. It's an urgent voice: *Come here. Be that person beating the moktak. Be a monk.*

Chapter 19

Fitting Finale

Seoul, South Korea

This is a different style of teaching, Mark. This is mind to mind transmission.
The master is leading you to Buddha's mind.

Pohwa Sunim
Hwagyesa Monastery

I was first exposed to Korean Zen during a three-day visit to Hwagyesa Monastery two years ago, which ignited a simmering fire within me that eventually boiled over into this sojourn. The fire lit a passion to advance my practice, to explore my mind in a monastic setting, and to reset my hectic lifestyle. It's only fitting to end my journey at Hwagyesa, where the fire was lit. I feel like I'm rekindling a first love.

Comfortably nested in a secluded valley of nationally preserved mountains, Hwagyesa Monastery has lured international and Korean Buddhists alike. Its convenience, natural beauty, and seclusion make it a destination for Buddhists seeking spiritual rejuvenation. A crystal clear, cascading brook, famous for its healing qualities, runs alongside the temple. The Zen Jogye tradition is also practiced here as it was at Musangsa monastery.

My heart and soul are telling me it's time to end my seven-month journey. My flight home leaves in eight days. I've mixed feelings. I wonder how I'll adapt back home, and how I'll integrate these many teachings

Hwagyesa Temple
Seoul, South Korea

into my life. I often think of Jayne, I'm eager to see her again. Then comes the scariest thought: Am I called to become a monk in Asia? That inner question just won't go away.

It's early afternoon and a dozen cars are parked next to Hwagyesa's mammoth, four story main building. The complex has ten buildings, including two residences, one office, and four smaller temples. The monastery was established in AD 1522. It's good to see the grand structure again. A monk is chanting over a loudspeaker, a typical practice throughout the day.

Jina, a friendly Korean office worker, helps me settle in. The posted schedule is nearly identical to Musangsa's. But the lay robes she hands me are different: a pair of dark brown pants with a brown vest to wear over my own light shirt. She escorts me to a second-floor private room, a nine-foot square oasis, barren of furniture, wall decorations, or windows. Perfect.

"Must be quietly here," Jina says. "Monks and nuns live at end hall. Pohwa Sunim also around corner."

"Who is Pohwa Sunim?"

"He monk in charge. Come, I show you where to wash."

I tell Jina that I've been here before and remember where to wash.

"Yes, but new instructions since then. Me new also. I must show."

She leads me into a quaint tea room and points to a small lavatory to the side. It's not the same place I washed before.

"Okay wash here," Jina says. "Also okay have tea." She points out the hot water pot and an inviting selection of specialty teas.

"Come downstairs. Show you eating room," Jina says.

The ground-level cafeteria has seating for about one hundred. A small side room for the monastics has two separate tables, each sits ten people. A group of women are busy in the kitchen where the pungent fragrance of spicy Kim Chi—a Korean staple food consisting of pickled cabbage and red pepper—makes my nose tingle.

"Monks only at that table," Jina says pointing. "Separate places for food also; monk food there and you food here." She points out separate countertops. "Come upstairs."

On the third floor, she cracks open wooden sliding doors that reveal the enormous main temple. A service is in progress. The main temple can hold about two hundred, but now only thirty are kneeling on cushions, part of the local practice, and a monk stands at the long altar, chanting through a microphone in a deep, resonant voice while he strikes a moktak.

"This temple for chanting," Jina says. "But only morning and evening for you. Many local Buddhist practice here during day. Especially now, pray to Buddha for birthday. You know?"

I knew. Everywhere I look there's small, multi-colored Chinese lanterns dangling across walkways—hundreds of them.

"Big celebration," Jina smiles excitedly. "Many people visit, give offering and chanting. Sometimes chanting all night. Saturday night special parade in Seoul. Very big! Hwagyesa have float in parade. Monks and lay people in parade. You too join I think. I ask Pohwa Sunim about you. Okay?"

Jina's in her mid-twenties; she's very sweet and genuinely wants to help.

"I'd like that," I tell her. I leave the next day, so the timing's perfect. I hope Powha Sunim agrees.

"Go upstairs now," she says.

On the fourth floor a smaller sliding door opens into the meditation room that is very special to me from my previous visit. It looks much the same. The room's ceiling is sloped and tall windows flood the room with sunlight. A dozen cushions lay on either side of the oblong room; there's a modest wooden altar with a glass-enclosed sculpture of Buddha.

"Morning time wake with moktak," Jina explains. "Must be on time at 3:25AM for 108 bows. Come late, then must no enter. Also can come here any time, no problem. Now I go back but if you need, just ask. No question?" Before I can respond she adds, "Also can meditate in courtyard temples. Koreans use for praying but okay you sit there."

In my room, I put on the garments before walking the grounds, which I'm eager to see again. Next to the main temple is a cobblestone courtyard with several small, one-room temples. Each temple has an unevenly fitted wood plank floor that can accommodate just a few people. Incense burns on the altar, rows of candles are lit and offerings of rice and fruit rest to the side. One altar is sloped steeply upward with thirty long and narrow shelves each lined with a multitude of tiny stone Buddha carvings. They appear similar to the carving SuBa gave me at Quan Am, but definitely from a different time period. Hundreds of them are arranged and I feel like I'm facing an arena of Buddhas.

The monk's chant echoes from the loudspeaker blending with the sound of the waterfall that runs beside the monastery. There's an ambience to this preserved nook that's hidden at the edge of one of the largest cities in the world—something deep and spiritual.

Entering the meditation hall, I find a Korean man in a fisherman's cap meditating, facing the wall. I claim a cushion and try to ignore the chant from the temple below. Gradually, my mind settles—until a young monk enters the hall noisily, shuffles over, and loudly plops onto his cushion. I'm annoyed! I resume sitting. My mind grows calm. There's something about this place that energizes my practice. I sit for one hour. When I leave, the man in the fishing cap still sits motionless.

I enter the shower room off the tearoom that Jina showed me to wash up before dinner. Before closing the door, a Caucasian nun interrupts. She's perhaps thirty years old and wears traditional grey robes with brown trim.

"What're you doing here?" she says sharply, her cheeks flushed.

I'm taken off guard. "I was going to take a shower," I say.

"No, you're not!" she says harshly. "This showers for monks and nuns. You must use the downstairs shower." Her English is clear; her accent sounds eastern European.

"I was told I can shower here," I explain.

"I don't care what you were told. This is not your shower room. You must go downstairs."

I feel awkward; I bow and leave.

I'm familiar with the ground-level showers I used on my previous visit, so I clean up there. Returning to my room, I encounter the same nun coming down the stairs. She looks even more perturbed.

"Your alarm clock in your room has been ringing for fifteen minutes. Please fix it." Her tone is steely.

Strike two. I must've bumped the alarm clock switch while unpacking. Darn! Now she thinks I'm an "insensitive" traveler. This is an international temple where foreign visitors frequently arrive and depart; surely some are callous. But this temple, after all, is her home.

"I'm sorry, it won't happen again," I tell her, bowing. I return to my room. I feel a need to repair the relationship once things cool down.

The dining ambience is different here. A dozen or so resident visitors like me and the Korean lay workers sit separate from the monks. There's no interaction between the groups and it feels impersonal. It was this way on my last visit too. In other monasteries, it's been a learning opportunity to blend with the monks during meals.

Two other visitors—both westerners I believe—have just seated themselves. I fill my plate with brown rice and stewed vegetables. I'll miss these healthy vegetarian meals.

A monk in maroon Tibetan robes enters the dining hall and serves himself. He's a slender westerner with a grey goatee, probably in his mid-sixties. His robes are slightly tattered but he moves with distinctive fluidity—a characteristic of a strong meditator. He seats himself next to me.

"I'm Mitra," he says in a soft voice. His English is excellent. "Are you staying here?"

I introduce myself and tell him of my journey. But I notice that we're the only ones speaking. I try to shorten our conversation, but Mitra keeps talking. He's from Mexico, he tells me, and he travels from temple to temple across Asia—"wherever life takes me"—he says. "I'll stay here for another week before going on a retreat at another temple." He's peaceful but his chattiness disturbs me. I finish dinner and excuse myself.

The encounter with the nun is bothering me; I need to clear the air. She was not at dinner but I know which room is hers. The door opens quickly after I knock.

"Sunim," I begin, addressing her in traditional manner. "I want to apologize for causing problems. I realize this is your home and I don't want to be disruptive. I visit only to practice so I'll do my best not to disturb you."

"Thank you. I appreciate that," she says. We bow to each other and I return to my room down the hall. Five minutes later, I answer a knock on my door.

"I must also apologize," she says. "I was very harsh to you. I realize it was not your fault. I let Jina know which shower is for visitors. She's new here. Please join me for tea, won't you?"

In the tearoom, she pours fresh green tea and sits cross-legged on the floor.

"I'm embarrassed," she says. "People here can be insensitive and I reacted angrily from past experiences."

"No need to explain." I pause. "My name is Mark."

"Oh, I'm sorry. My name is Myong Dok Sunim. I'm staying here until I transfer to a different monastery."

She's from the Czech Republic. "I've been a nun for three years but don't have a home temple. I'm searching for that."

"So how does a woman . . ."

". . . from Czech Republic become a Korean Zen nun?" she interrupts.

"I'm sorry. You must get that question often," I say.

She smiles. "Back home I'm a famous poet doing recitals across the country. But I wanted more impact in the world. I stumbled upon a Zen center, met some people, and decided to travel. I left my boyfriend and family to come here. That was hard, but they supported my decision."

"Why this temple, Sunim?"

"I come here because my Korean is not good yet and it's easier to be here quite honestly. But it's also because this is a hub for westerners. You know Mark, more westerners are coming looking for Buddhism. This temple has international recognition and many people visit. Because of that, the culture is changing rapidly and Koreans struggle in dealing with that. You saw the main temple—what did you notice?"

"Only Koreans were there. Most of them were middle age."

"And was anything different about the way they practice?"

"They chant continuously. I haven't yet seen walking or sitting meditation."

"Right! Westerners tend to focus on meditation as the central part of their practice. They spend most of their time in the meditation hall. They're inquisitive and questioning. The Koreans, however, come to the main temple to pray, chant, and give for charity. All those bags of rice, flowers, and fruit on the altar are offerings from locals. They pray to Buddha for family health and children's success. Those are very different types of practice you see. Here, there are two different Buddhist practices on different floors by different cultures. It's hard to combine both in that way but it's done well."

She sips her tea. "Korean Zen is transmitted linearly," she continues. "Traditionally, it's passed verbally from male to male. The master passes his knowledge through spoken instructions and mind challenging exercises. Now, with all the westerners coming and going, and with attitude changes in younger Koreans, the transmission of Korean Zen is also changing."

As she talks, the deep pulse of a drumbeat begins and Sunim's eyes widen. "Oh, they're starting! I must go ring the tower bell." As she rises she nearly falls to one side. "My leg is asleep and I must move quickly. That's a bad combination," she chuckles.

I offer to help but she manages so I follow her. Outdoors, in a gazebo, a monk pounds a six-foot drum and intermittently strikes both a fish-shaped bell and a wooden percussion instrument shaped like a bird. The ritual symbolically awakens all beings in the ocean, on land, and in the air. It's not an awakening from sleep, but rather an awakening of all beings to pull themselves to a higher consciousness. Myong Dok Sunim swings a bulky log hung from two ropes into an eight-foot bell. The reverberations echo the valley.

Group chanting and sitting meditation follow in exactly the same format as they did at Musangsa. At nine, the entire complex shuts down for the evening and I lie in the darkness of my room concentrating on my breath and enjoying the stillness. I feel at peace and at home here—'here' being a monastic setting, Korea, and even Asia as a whole. At a deeper level, an uneasiness is building because I'm about to leave it all.

I awaken in darkness when I hear footsteps in the hall followed by knocking on a moktak. It's 3:00AM and I spring up for a quick wash before meditation and bowing. Halfway up the stairs to the Meditation Hall, I pause on the balcony to absorb the morning magic. The glow of a half moon peeks out from behind a dragon sculpture on the temple roof. The fragrance of burning incense flows down the stairway from the meditation hall.

Eight people sit on mats, five males on one side of the room and three females on the other. Three are monks, and a sizable bamboo stick sits beside the center monk, who I assume to be Pohwa Sunim, the head monk.

At exactly 3:30AM, Myong Dok Sunim slides the doors closed and Pohwa Sunim sharply smacks the bamboo staff on the floor three times initiating the session.

After morning practice, I approach Pohwa Sunim. "Thank you for letting me stay at your temple," I begin. "I've been here before but you were not here then. It's beautiful here."

"Jina tells me that you'll stay several days, right?"

His English is nearly perfect, embellished with a Korean accent. He's in his early forties, of average height like most Korean men, trim, and strongly built with tinted wire-framed glasses.

"I've been traveling for seven months; this is the end of a long journey. I depart for home soon."

"Then I have a special ending for you," Pohwa Sunim says. "Seoul has an annual parade for Buddha's birthday. It very big! It's an international event covered on television. We have a float and all monks and members will march alongside. I think it's good for you to join us, won't you?"

"Of course!" I say, and then change the subject. "Sunim, I have a question regarding my return home. I could use some guidance. Is it possible to talk sometime?"

"Certainly! But very busy today. Many preparations and ceremonies. Can we do tomorrow after breakfast?"

I have the day to myself. A steady rain holds the entire valley in a cold clammy embrace. Feeling reclusive, I spend time in meditation alternating between the hall and my windowless room.

In the meditation hall, I sit as raindrops tap the tile roof and a bird chirps outside. The soft breeze from the window seems to flow right through me.

Today, I'm able to hold extended periods of deep concentration. My mind is undisturbed like a beachfront that receives the lake's gentle ripples on a motionless morning. When it does wander to thought, I gently nudge it to the present. I can observe my mind resting.

Consciousness is peering at its own inner workings. I'm aware of my breathing, but not focused on it. My breath is slow, completely relaxed, and at times barely noticeable. It's like I'm breathing space and not air.

I'm aware of emptiness and fullness—both at the same time. I feel that the fullness of my true self, my true nature, is just *being*. There's an absence of the clutter of normal thought. It is like peacefully resting in a pristine vacuum. A smile cracks on the edges of my mouth because I've discovered a new window to peer through into untainted consciousness. I've come upon a deeper self.

I'm sitting atop the stallion, reigns in my hands. Then, a thought enters. Instead of simply letting it fade, I push it away. I cling to the peaceful state and try to force my mind to remain clear. That's a mistake. I'm grasping, and that leads to more thought, effort, and struggle. The peaceful state slips away. What happened? Desire happened. I remember Thay Minh Do telling me: "Wanting good meditation is desire. And desire to attain even good things is hindrance of mind. Just accept what is and observe the mind."

That's all I have to do—accept what is. I do it for the entire day, exploring my inclination to grasp and trading it for acceptance. At day's end, I know myself in a deeper way. I feel like I got a promotion in my meditation. What a reward after such hard work. I'm excited but I can't forget Venerable Vivekananda's instructions: "Don't be elated when things are good. Don't be depressed when things are not good. Equanimity is important."

A question remains: Is this sustainable?

I've been coming to understand meditation as an exercise regimen. In the same way that physical exercise strengthens the body and education strengthens the intellect, meditation strengthens and evolves consciousness. It's curious that the former two are encouraged in the West whereas meditation has been marginalized.

Pohwa Sunim pulls me aside after breakfast the next day. "The sun is shining and I think we both need time outdoors. How about we do mountain hiking meditation? We can talk at the top."

Putting on our hiking shoes we meet at the trailhead behind the Temple. It looks odd to see a monk in robes and hiking boots. "No different than walking meditation," he says. "Walk mindfully but no need to go slow. Just feel your feet on the ground and keep mind here. No need to strive for top or think about yesterday or tomorrow. Mind is here only."

The well-defined dirt trail is wide enough for two people but we keep within ourselves and walk at a casual pace. Forty minutes later we reach a breathtaking mountaintop view of Seoul. The city is abuzz like a beehive, street traffic flowing between skyscrapers like water between boulders in a river.

"We sit here," Pohwa Sunim says pointing to a level, sun-warmed boulder. "So, how may I help you?" he asks.

I tell him my story, my situation at home, and about my job. I tell him how much this journey has helped my practice. "Sunim, my key question is this: Is it possible to engage a busy western lifestyle and work to solve complex engineering problems while I keep my mind clear, aware and, fully mindful?"

He thinks for a while.

"There's always a challenge in society, so we need to be diligent. We must always be awakened and that's why you ask. Our life is like a grape tree. With a grape tree, we tend to focus on the grapes, not the branches or roots. Likewise, in our practice we tend to emphasize mindfulness and meditation. But if you want a healthy grape tree you must attend to the whole tree—branches, roots, and grape. How do we understand the whole tree? The whole tree is one. Branches are not separate from roots. Grapes are not separate from branches. The Kong-an helps us see the whole tree."

I remember Dok Sang Sunim explaining Kong-an riddles at Musangsa, but I didn't expect them to be the core of Pohwa Sunim's answer.

"It's a practice that shares the fruit of words," he says. "Focus is on words to comprehend meaning. Very hard to do at first. Trying to understand the total truth is not separate from the now moment." He pauses, and then continues "Buddha taught that there are eight levels of consciousness. Mostly we use only three or four levels and that's why we don't understand the whole truth. The eight levels are connected to enlightenment, meaning connected to the whole truth. But Kong-an can help us understand all levels even though it's very hard to express deeper levels. To understand the whole truth is much effort but Kong-an always leads to the whole truth."

I don't yet see the link between my question and his answer.

"But with meditation only, it's hard to see the whole tree. Even a small Kong-an, when meditating deeply can lead to understanding the whole tree. Over the centuries, masters have developed many Kong-an using simple words that lead to the whole tree. When you follow a Kong-an and understand its meaning your mind gets bigger and your heart warmer. Then you can use the whole tree for good. That means to help people see whole tree."

He looks at me to see if I'm following. I understand him but I'm not convinced his advice will help. He continues.

"You can do Kong-an at any time. Many times you cannot meditate, or cannot go to temple, but can always ponder the Kong-an. Then every moment becomes an expression of the whole truth."

I look over the vista. "So you're saying it's possible to live a mindful busy life if you live it with the whole truth by practicing a Kong-an?"

"Yes!" he says. "You make every moment an expression of the whole truth. People have done this. Jesus got it. Buddha got it. When sitting, chanting, or praying you can really feel it—it's not far away. But you must cultivate the whole picture in your life by making your work, intention, and concentration good."

He leans forward. "This is a different style of teaching, Mark. This is mind to mind transmission. The master is leading you to Buddha's mind." He's speaking of the Asian practice of following a 'master' who guides the practitioner on a personal, one-on-one basis. "You cannot read it in a book. I cannot tell you how to see the whole picture. But I can lead you there through a Kong-an. It is my mind guiding your mind to see the whole picture."

"I understand. You're telling me that I'm missing an important part of my practice, the Kong-an. Can you give me a Kong-an to work on?"

"Yes. I tell you now and give you written so you can remember."

He looks out at the vista. "A monk once asked Master Yunmen a question: 'When not producing a single thought is there any fault or not?' To this Master Yunmen said, 'Mount Sumeru.'"

He turns to me. "What is the meaning of Master Yunmen's response?" He pauses. "You must meditate on this. Live this Kong-an. When you have ideas you can e-mail me and we can discuss that way. We can also Skype chat. How does that sound?"

I have to be honest. "It sounds like a puzzle, and I've never liked puzzles. But if it'll help my practice, I'll try."

"Whole tree, Mark."

Pohwa Sunim's an example of how Zen changes perception and evolves consciousness—not through ritual, dogma, or scriptural study, but experientially, through a master giving a student clues that point toward an experience of truth. It's like I'm in an unlit room and being given verbal instructions to find a hidden light switch. Instructions point the way but only determination, persistence, and effort will find the switch.

I've been handed many clues—whispered teachings and counsel from wise teachers. They'll all become part of my refined life style and value system and support my concerted efforts to live in a fully mindful way." Through a clear, exact, and aware mind I must break through misperception to see the true nature of things. I've a new tool to get me there, the Kong-an. But there's no guarantee that I can solve this puzzle. Yet, as vague and unpromising as I find this riddle, I'm compelled to accept the challenge.

I can't find my room key! When Jina gave it to me, she said to be careful because there's no duplicate. Did I leave it in my room or drop it on the mountain? Above the door there's a small ventilation window and I think I can squeeze through. As I look for a step stool, Pohwa Sunim walks by. I explain my predicament.

"No problem," he says.

Before I can say anything, he springs up, grips the eight-foot high sill, pulls himself upward, swings his feet into the narrow opening, and wriggles into the room with one smooth motion. The door swings open and the Zen master hands me the key I left inside.

"Sunim, I didn't mean for you to do that, I'd have done it."

"No problem, Mark. I'm not only a monk, I'm monkey!" He gives me a big smile and walks on.

Mitra sits next to me again at lunch. He suggests a walk afterward. As we stroll, I mention my concerns about practicing mindfulness back home.

"You've been at it only seven months, Mark. It's all very fresh. It'll take some time to stabilize."

Only seven months? I think. It's been an effortful seven months. That's in addition to eight years of casual home practice!

"I've been practicing for twenty-two years," Mitra says. "I've done many intensive retreats. A day never passes that I don't practice at least two hours, most more than that. My morning meditation is most important, I'm fresh then and can immediately clear my mind."

"Is there a place that's better for you to meditate than others?" I ask.

He smiles. "My best meditations were in prison. But don't let that bother you. I'm a good man. I have taken monks' vows and keep most all of them."

"You wear the maroon robes of a Tibetan monk. Is that your practice?"

"These robes were given to me. I only own two sets. I own very little, my suitcase is half the size of your backpack."

"What type is your practice? What tradition?"

"Theravada."

"That means you practice Buddha's teachings as described in ancient scriptures, right?"

"Yes, I find the practice most accurate," he says. "There's no flaws. The Mahayana practice has some fluff. With Theravada nothing's missing and nothing's too much. It's very scientific. We are scientists who study the inner self."

We pause for a moment next to a large sand-filled clay pot full of burning incense sticks.

"You've traveled a lot, Mitra. What temple did you like best?"

"I try not to focus on what's outside, rather on what's inside. There's many beauties outside but that's not proper focus. Outward beauty is superficial and fleeting."

"So if you saw a beautiful woman you wouldn't be attracted."

He laughs loudly.

"I've had relationships with many women, probably hundreds. But I've been celibate for twenty-two years. I'm celibate mentally as well. This clears the mind and allows me to focus on more important things."

We're standing on a hill overlooking the temple.

"I look back to when I was sexually involved," Mitra says, "and compare that to playing with toy cars as a child. Why would you waste time that way?" He throws his hands in the air. "Practicing dharma you become self-sufficient and happy because you're not depending on companionship to make you feel attractive and feed the ego!"

He's very excited.

"It's bad enough that I have to live with this monkey mind," he says, pointing to his temple "but in a relationship there are two monkey minds, and that causes all kinds of headaches."

"Watching my mind for seven months has made me aware of how often sexual desire occupies my mind," I tell him. "I know what you mean. I don't yet have your level of control, but I'm working on it."

Mitra is an independent type, similar to SuCo Quang Hue in Ho Chi Minh City. Because he's not tied to a temple, he travels broadly with the sole purpose of advancing his practice.

The lives of Mitra and SuCo Quang Hue highlight the difference between Theravada and Mahayana Buddhism. Mitra's Theravada practice aspires to personal achievement and Nirvana—and in the end, it benefits all humankind. SuCo Quang Hue's Mahayana tradition places the interest of serving others first. I've heard people judge Theravada practice as selfish but I remember Venerable Vivekananda addressing that argument: "If you were up to your waist in quicksand next to someone else who was also, it would be useless to try to help that person. We must focus on the urgent matter of liberating ourselves before we can help others."

In twenty-four hours I'll board a plane—but first the big parade. I've always found flamboyantly colored floats and proud politicians sitting atop a convertible boring. But this is different. A chartered bus takes the temple's monastic and lay members to the staging area. Hwagyesa's float is slotted to appear near the end of the parade and I'm torn between walking in the parade and watching from the roadside. I decide to compromise, watching from the midway point along the route and then jumping in when my friends pass. Myong Dok Sunim tells me that'll be fine.

I stand on the curb of a ten-lane city street beneath tall buildings and neon-lit billboards. A crowd four layers deep pack the curb. A grandstand sits on every corner where VIPs watch. Music blares from loudspeakers. A middle-aged policeman in white gloves dances joyously in the street twirling his orange-glow flashlight. The atmosphere buzzes with excitement.

For a couple of hours, one temple after another—more than fifty in all—parade their messages past an enthusiastic crowd. International exhibits representing Burma, China, and Thailand, to name a few, roll past displaying fifteen-foot tall Buddhas, legendary Buddhist Masters, Yin/Yang symbols, and more. A golden-hued dragon, sixty feet long with red fins across its back squirms, snake-like along the parade route, roaring loudly and exhaling huge bursts of real flames.

Monks and nuns march ahead of parishioners who play music, dance, or carry illuminated figures. Mothers push infants in carriages and the elderly roll by in wheelchairs, all holding some symbolic craft.

Lotus Lantern Parade
Seoul, South Korea

Hwagyesa Temple arrives and Myong Dok motions me in. She hands me a pole on which hangs a two-foot lighted drum with a lotus painted on its face. She'd been carrying it for me; we've become quite good friends over the last few days. Among the extravagant floats, Hwagyesa's stands out as the most simple and meaningful. It's a fifteen-foot tall, lighted question mark, with the words "Who am I?" It's the epitome of Zen: simple, direct, inquiring.

The crowd chants the names of the passing temples as if cheering a football team. Only a major sports event could generate this level of excitement back home. What is it in this culture that generates this kind of public fervor for a religious event?

As I march behind the monks, I intentionally observe the scene in a detached manner. I remember what SuBa said: "You're there and you understand but you are not attached." This is what I feel.

It's an enriching experience to be both engaged and detached. In the past, my mind would've been immersed in the experience, sucked right in. I understand now how that is, in a sublime but real way, loss of self.

So here I am, a western Buddhist aspirant who just spent seven months on a walkabout through Asia studying my mind and deepening my consciousness. Things have mysteriously fallen into place throughout this trip. I've been guided the entire way.

I'll leave to go home in a few hours. Yet now, I'm mindfully walking in a premier international Buddhist parade amidst a cheering crowd. Could there be a more fitting finale?

PART FIVE

Home

Epilogue

Cleveland, Ohio

Initially, it wasn't easy coming home.

During those first few weeks back in Cleveland, I kept *noting* as Vivekananda had taught me. I noted how much I had missed Jayne and was happy to see her, yet I noted the lump in my throat as I already missed the Asian culture. I noted many times that my stomach was in knots as if I were grieving for a long-term loving relationship that had ended. And it had. Truthfully, I am torn between two loves: I love Jayne and my family. And now I have fallen in love with the Asian culture and an inner-oriented monastic lifestyle. I want both—but can I have both?

I brought home the spiritual treasure SuBa gave me, the small ancient sculpture of Buddha. She wanted me to have and hold this source of inspiration to remind me to live the change I envisioned.

It was rewarding to recognize the difference between the mind I had departed with and the more "clear, exact, and aware" mind I returned with. Jayne noticed the change: "You're so relaxed and less edgy," she said. "And less fussy too! You don't insist on doing things your way like you used to. That's a nice change."

I began by tending to duties essential to functioning in America. I bought a car, secured license plates, title, and insurance. I subscribed to domestic phone service and purchased a computer. I contacted friends, looked for employment, finished unpacking. I fixed the window in the house Jayne bought before I left, and repaired the leaky toilet. I caught up on mail, bills, taxes, and banking. As the to-do list grew—and it did quickly—I noted that I was sliding back into the same old hectic lifestyle of striving to catch up and keep caught up. It became too much, too quick.

Just two weeks after returning home after seven months away, I was desperate for solitude and inner reflection. I have access to a quiet condominium in a rural township sixty miles away. I told Jayne that I was going there—that I had to go. Now.

She looked stunned.

"It feels important. It feels right," I told her.

"I'm concerned what this means for us," Jayne said.

"So am I," I said.

Once again Jayne understood, and accepted my plan.

In my silent retreat, without a to-do list, I go over what my journey to Asia taught me.

I discovered that Asia feels like home to me. I'm certain I'll return.

I learned an even deeper appreciation for simplicity, which nourishes spiritual growth.

I've peered into my consciousness at a very deep level and have redefined my core understanding of self.

I experienced, at a penetrating level, fundamental Buddhist concepts like impermanence and the interdependence of all things.

I've become vividly aware of how desire and aversion—innate human characteristics—are at the root of life's suffering, of my suffering.

I've strengthened my ability to endure discomfort.

I've cordially shook hands with—although not yet fully embraced—my own death.

I was exposed to many religions including Hinduism, Jainism, Islam and several diverse traditions of Buddhism. Each offers the seeker truth. Each teaches kindness, morality, and virtue.

I've been handed precious advice from several accomplished masters—words that I can rely on through the difficulties of daily life.

I've grown an even firmer conviction that Buddhism is right for me. Its science-based inquiry into the workings of the mind yields more accurate perception, which we don't realize is usually otherwise absent.

I've come to believe that everything is divine—every pebble, every blade of grass, every being.

I never expected to make such a journey and come back unchanged. Neither did Jayne. When one partner changes, the relationship must adapt or crumble. When I return home from my rural retreat, Jayne and I talk. We discuss how to find what a new 'us' could be.

I tell Jayne that I am drawn, increasingly, to the monastic lifestyle. I tell her that SuBa predicted that I would become a monk. I assure her that I have no resolute drive to become a monk—not now anyway. But there's a churning within, I say, trying to be honest.

"That scares me," she says.

"Yes," I say. "Rightfully so. Me too."

There's no solution. Not right now. There are only questions.

"The seed to become a monk is planted in me," I tell Jayne. "Let's see if it sprouts and grows."

Jayne and I talk about a simpler lifestyle, and my need for sangha. We talk about her need for partnership and personal ambitions that she puts time into. We agree that, in all probability we can find middle ground.

Jayne and I have a love that will scour all scenarios to find the one that fits us both, one that will bring mutual peace and happiness. To that we commit.

For myself, I commit to continue the inner journey that I've begun in Asia, right here in Ohio. Going inward is where true peace is birthed. It's the key, the only key I believe, by which I—by which all of us—may achieve true peace.

Acknowledgements

I was bike riding with my daughter through the park one day when she asked me how the book was coming along. When I responded, I uttered the words 'my book' and it felt wrong. The more I thought about it, the more I realized that there's nothing about this book that is 'mine'.

From the moment the idea was conceived, until the printed books reached my hands, all was dependent on others. Even the idea emerged as a rather urgent message from within, not from 'myself'. Every step of my journey mysteriously followed what seems a logically formed path—that is certainly not from me. The teachers and masters I met kindly shared jewels of wisdom that are sowed within these pages—those are not mine—and I express immense gratitude and the deepest respect to each master, teacher, and Sangha member I encountered. The kindness of so many along the way formed the core content. My wife Jayne Bartish-Kacik especially contributed by emotionally supporting me and helping steer this work to finality. My entire family and close friends did the same.

Engineers are notoriously bad writers and so the patience and expertise of professional editor Deborah Burke has impacted this work tremendously. She spent countless hours shaping the story and has provided spiritual insights along the way. The community at Turning Stone Press contributed a major role in bringing this to the readers' hands.

At risk of omitting key contributors, I name just a few. I thank Jetsunma Tenzin Palmo for her contribution of the foreword section her kind support, and her spiritual direction. Maria Kacik-Kula, Teresa Jenkins-Fowler, Adam Deitrich, author Yen Tran, and Sandie King contributed time reviewing and offering opinions. Nepalese artist Jyoti

Prakash Tsapa painted the book cover, Paul Tamulewicz contributed graphical design and Latvian photographer Artis Rams has kindly shared his professional photos of Kopan monastery.

This work combines contributions from countless people and it's impossible to thank each individually. Instead I humbly bow in gratitude to all beings.

About the Author

Photo by Maria Kacik-Kula

Mark S. Kacik is a spiritual seeker who has traveled the world studying local religious practices and customs. Although his practice is rooted in Japanese Zen, it is significantly influenced by Tibetan, Vipassana, Vietnamese, and Korean traditions as well.

An avid backpacker and backcountry adventurer, he has learned to thrive by living simply and seeing in nature an unfathomably complex expression of the Divine.

Kacik is a mechanical engineer with a keen interest in quantum physics. He lives in Cleveland, Ohio, with his wife, Jayne.

www.ingramcontent.com/pod-product-compliance
Lightning Source LLC
Chambersburg PA
CBHW022106150426
43195CB00008B/283